Yanmar

YANMAR MARINE DIESEL ENGINE MODEL YSM

Service Manual

Yanmar

YANMAR MARINE DIESEL ENGINE MODEL YSM

Service Manual

ISBN/EAN: 9783954273003
Erscheinungsjahr: 2013
Erscheinungsort: Bremen, Deutschland

© *maritimepress in Europäischer Hochschulverlag GmbH & Co. KG, Fahrenheitstr. 1, 28359 Bremen. Alle Rechte beim Verlag und bei den jeweiligen Lizenzgebern.*

www.maritimepress.de | office@maritimepress.de

Bei diesem Titel handelt es sich um den Nachdruck eines historischen, lange vergriffenen Buches. Da elektronische Druckvorlagen für diese Titel nicht existieren, musste auf alte Vorlagen zurückgegriffen werden. Hieraus zwangsläufig resultierende Qualitätsverluste bitten wir zu entschuldigen.

YANMAR
SERVICE MANUAL
MARINE DIESEL ENGINE

MODEL **YSM**

FOREWORD

This service manual has been compiled for engineers engaged in the sales, service, inspection and maintenance of the YSM marine diesel engines. Accordingly, descriptions of the construction and functions of the engine are emphasized in this manual while items which should already be common knowledge are omitted.

One characteristic of a marine diesel engine is that its performance in a vessel is governed by the applicability of the vessel's hull construction and its steering system.

Engine installation, fitting out and propeller selection have a substantial effect on the performance of the engine and the vessel. Moreover, when the engine runs unevenly or when trouble occurs, it is essential to check a wide range of operating conditions—such as installation to the hull and suitability of the ship's piping and propeller—and not just the engine itself. To get maximum performance from this engine, you should completely understand its functions, construction and capabilities, as well as proper use and servicing.

Use this manual as a handy reference in daily inspection and maintenance, and as a text for engineering guidance.

Model YSM

CHAPTER 1 GENERAL
1. Exterior Views 1-1
2. Specifications 1-2
3. Principal Construction 1-3
4. Performance Curves 1-4
5. Features 1-6
6. Engine Cross-Section 1-7
7. Exterior Views 1-8
8. System Diagrams 1-12
9. Accessories 1-19

CHAPTER 2 BASIC ENGINE
1. Cylinder Block 2-1
2. Cylinder Liner 2-3
3. Cylinder Head 2-6
4. Piston 2-17
5. Connecting Rod 2-22
6. Crankshaft 2-26
7. Camshaft 2-31
8. Timing Gear 2-34

CHAPTER 3 FUEL SYSTEM
1. Construction 3-1
2. Injection Pump 3-2
3. Injection Nozzle 3-15
4. Fuel Filter 3-20
5. Fuel Feed Pump 3-21
6. Fuel Tank 3-24

CHAPTER 4 GOVERNOR
1. Governor 4-1
2. Injection Limiter 4-4
3. Adjust the Governor Link 4-5
4. Adjusting the No-Load Speed 4-6
5. Engine Stop Lever 4-7

CHAPTER 5 INTAKE AND EXHAUST SYSTEM
1. Intake And Exhaust System 5-1
2. Intake Silencer 5-2
3. Exhaust System 5-3

CHAPTER 6 LUBRICATION SYSTEM
1. Lubrication System 6-1
2. Oil Pump 6-3
3. Oil Filter 6-6
4. Oil Pressure Regulator Valve 6-7

CHAPTER 7 COOLING SYSTEM
1. Cooling System 7-1
2. Water Pump 7-3
3. Thermostat 7-6
4. Anticorrosion Zinc 7-7
5. Scale Removing 7-8
6. Kingston Cock 7-9
7. Bilge Pump 7-10
8. Bilge Strainer 7-12

CHAPTER 8 STARTING SYSTEM
1. Starting System Construction 8-1
2. Electric Starting System 8-2
3. Overdrive Hand-Operated System 8-3
4. Chain-Overdrive Hand-Operated System 8-5

CHAPTER 9 REDUCTION AND REVERSING GEAR
1. Construction 9-1
2. Installation 9-6
3. Handling the Reduction and Reversing Gears 9-7
4. Inspection and Servicing 9-8
5. Disassembling the Reduction and Reversing Gears 9-14
6. Reassembling the Reduction and Reversing Gears 9-17

CHAPTER 10 REMOTE CONTROL SYSTEM
1. Composition 10-1
2. Construction 10-2

CHAPTER 11 ELECTRICAL SYSTEM
1. Composition 11-1
2. Battery 11-3
3. Starter Motor 11-6
4. Alternator 11-14
5. Alarm Circuit 11-22
6. Other Electric Equipment 11-25

CHAPTER 12 INSTALLATION AND FITTING
1. Propeller and Stern Arrangement 12-1
2. Engine Installation 12-2
3. Stern Equipment 12-10
4. Interior Piping and Wiring 12-14
5. Front Power Take-Off 12-19

CHAPTER 13 OPERATING INSTRUCTIONS
1. Fuel Oil and Lubricating Oil 13-1
2. Engine Operating Instructions 13-8
3. Troubleshooting and Repair 13-12

CHAPTER 14 DISASSEMBLY AND REASSEMBLY
1. Disassembly and Reassembly Precautions 14-1
2. Disassembly and Reassembly Tools 14-2
3. Other 14-11
4. Disassembly 14-12
5. Reassembly 14-16
6. Tightening Torque 14-21
7. Packing Supplement and Adhesives 14-22

CHAPTER 15 INSPECTION AND SERVICING
1. Periodic inspection and servicing 15-1

Printed in Jap
A0A1001 8311

CHAPTER 1
GENERAL

1. Exterior Views. 1-1
2. Specifications. 1-2
3. Principal Construction 1-3
4. Performance Curves 1-4
5. Features 1-6
6. Engine Cross-Section 1-7
7. Exterior Views 1-8
8. System Diagrams 1-12
9. Accessories 1-19

Chapter 1 General
1. Exterior Views ────────────────────────── SM/YSM

1. Exterior Views

1-1 Starboard

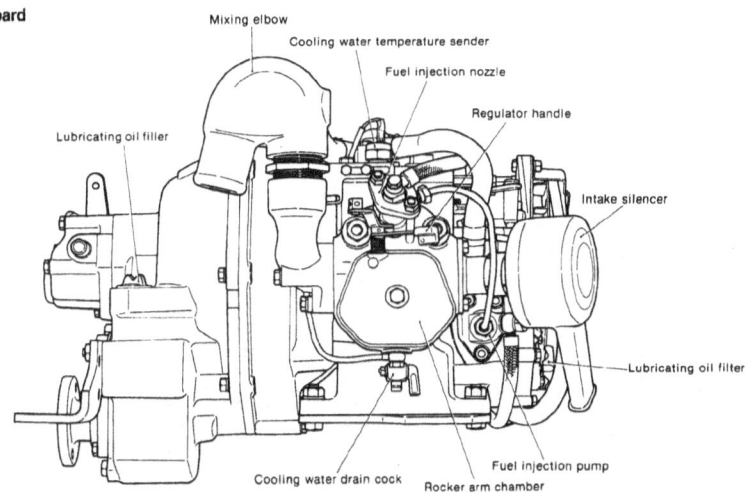

1-2 Port

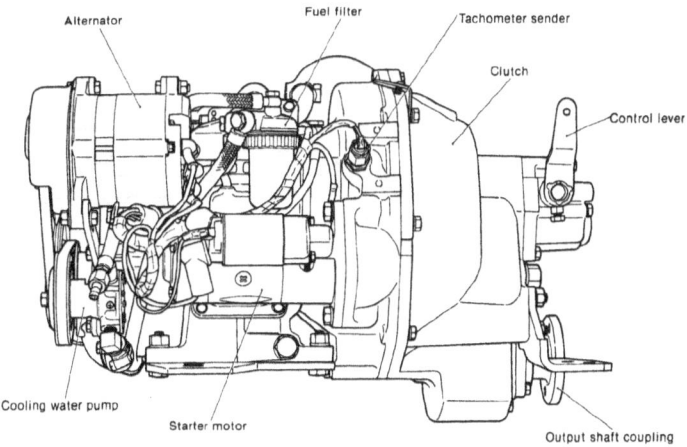

Chapter 1 General
2. Specifications

SM/YSM

2. Specifications

Model				YSM8-R		YSM8-Y		YSM12-R		YSM12-Y	
Type				Horizontal 4-cycle water-cooled diesel engine							
Combustion chamber				Precombustion type							
Number of cylinders				1							
Bore × stroke			mm	75 × 75				85 × 90			
Displacement			ℓ	0.331				0.510			
Continuous rated output (DIN 6270A)	Output/crankshaft speed		HP/rpm	7/3200				10/3000			
	Mean piston speed		m/s	8.0				9.0			
	Propeller speed		rpm	1639	1093	1639	1093	1518	980	1518	980
One hour rating (DIN 6270B)	Output/crankshaft speed		HP/rpm	8/3200				12/3000			
	Mean piston speed		m/s	8.0				9.0			
	Propeller speed		rpm	1639	1093	1639	1093	1518	980	1518	980
Compression ratio				23:1				21:1			
Fuel injection timing			deg	bTDC 25							
Fuel injection pressure			kg/cm²	160 ±10							
Engine weight (dry)			kg	102		92		130		120	
Power takeoff position				Flywheel side							
Direction of rotation	Crankshaft			Counterclockwise (viewed from clutch side)							
	Propeller shaft			Counterclockwise (viewed from clutch side)							
Cooling system				Sea water forced cooling (rubber impeller water pump)							
Lubrication system				Closed forced lubrication							
Starting system				Electric with manual		Manual		Electric with manual		Manual	
Reduction gear system				Spur gear constant-mesh system							
Clutch				Wet single-disc mechanical type							
Reduction ratio	Ahead			1.95	2.93	1.95	2.93	1.98	3.06	1.98	3.06
	Astern			1.95	2.93	1.95	2.93	1.98	3.06	1.98	3.06
Engine size	Overall length		mm	608		598		638		628	
	Overall width		mm	602		576		673		647	
	Overall height		mm	436		544		485		591	
Lubricating oil capacity (rake angle 8°)	Crankcase Total/Effective		ℓ	1.9/0.8				3.0/1.0			
	Clutch Total/Effective		ℓ	0.7/0.2				0.7/0.2			
No-load engine speed	Maximum		rpm	3400		3400		3150		3150	
	Minimum		rpm	650		600		650		600	

3. Principal Construction

Group	Part	Construction
Engine block	Cylinder block	Integrally-cast water jacket and crankcase
	Cylinder liner	Wet type coated with anticorrosion paint
	Main bearing	Metal housing type
Intake and exhaust systems and valve mechanism	Cylinder head	Gasket separate valve guide
	Intake and exhaust valves	Poppet type, seat angle 90°
	Intake pipe	Intake inertia type steel pipe
	Exhaust silencer	Water-cooled mixing elbow type (optional)
	Valve mechanism	Overhead valve push rod, rocker arm system
	Intake silencer	Round polyurethane sound absorbing type
Main moving elements	Crankshaft	Stamped forging
	Flywheel	Attached to crankshaft by tapered
	Piston	Oval type
	Piston pin	Floating type
	Piston rings	3 compression rings, 1 oil ring
Lubrication system	Oil pump	Trochoid pump
	Oil filter	Full-flow type, steel plate element
	Oil level gauge	Dipstick
Cooling system	Water pump	Rubber impeller type
	Thermostat	Wax pellet type
Bilge system	Bilge pump	Rubber impeller (tandem type) combined with C.W. pump (optional)
Fuel system	Fuel injection pump	Bosch PFR type
	Fuel injection valve	Semi-throttle valve
	Fuel strainer	Paper element
Governor	Governor	Centrifugal all-speed mechanical type
Starting system	Electric	Pinion ring gear type starter motor
	Manual	Over-driven chain starting
Electrical system	Charger	Alternator (with built-in IC regulator)
Reduction reversing	Reduction gear	Spur gear constant-mesh system
Clutch system	Clutch	Wet single disc mechanical type

4. Performance Curves

1. YSM8-R, YSM8-Y

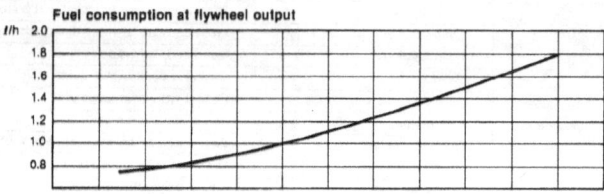

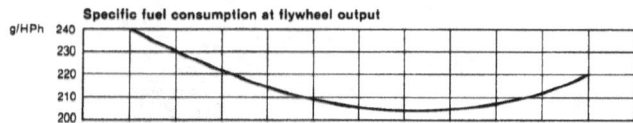

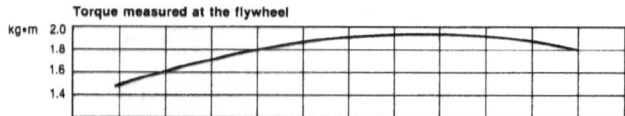

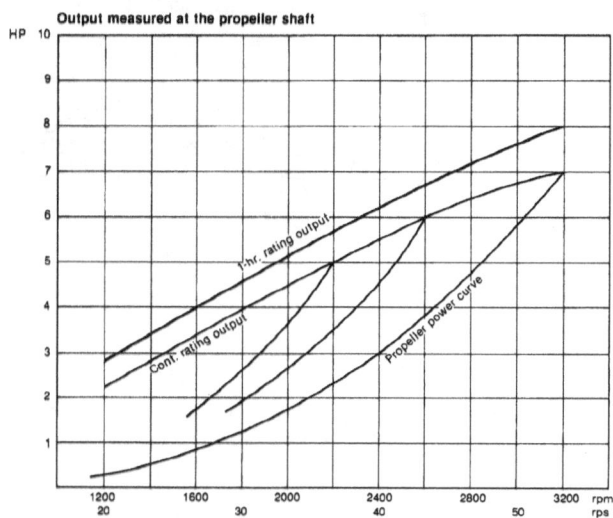

The Engine Flywheel Output is Approx. 5% Higher.
Note: These curves show the average performance of respective engines in test operation at our plant.

Chapter 1 General
4. Performance Curves ——————————————————————————————— SM/YSM

2. YSM12-R, YSM12-Y

Fuel consumption at flywheel output

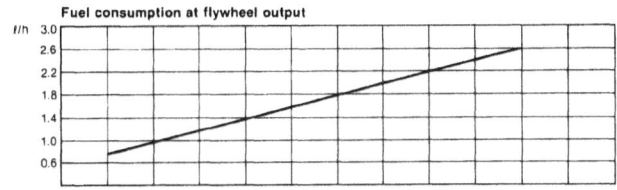

Specific fuel consumption at flywheel output

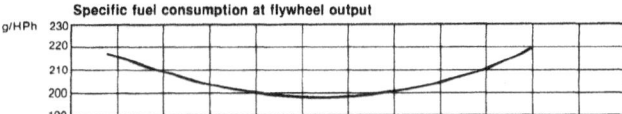

Torque measured at the flywheel

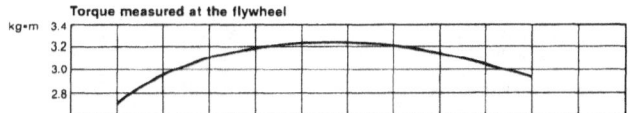

Output measured at the propeller shaft

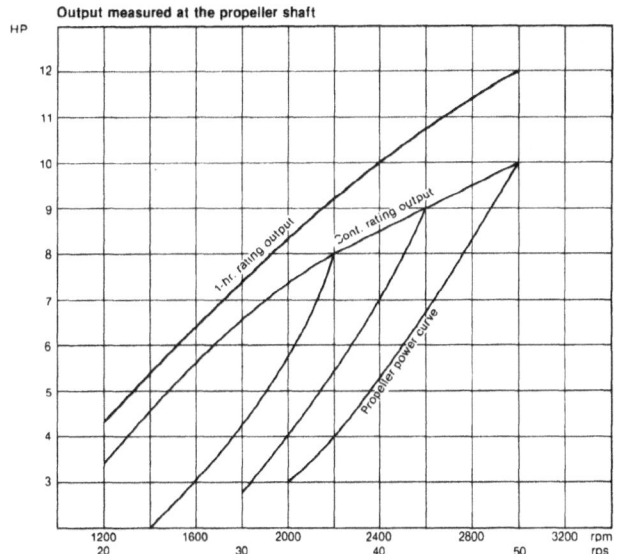

The Engine Flywheel Output is Approx. 5% Higher.
Note: These curves show the average performance of respective engines in test operation at our plant.

5. Features

1. Superior combustion performance
The unique Yanmar swirl precombustion chamber combustion system and new cooling system display superior combustion performance in all types of operation. Low-speed, low-load combustion performance, especially demanded for marine applications, is also superb, and stable performance is maintained over a wide range of speeds. Since starting characteristics are also excellent and warm-up is fast, full engine performance can be obtained within a short time.

2. Low operating costs
Excellent combustion and low friction reduce fuel costs, while the optimized piston shape and ring configuration and improved cooling system reduce oil consumption. Continuous operating time has been extended and operating costs reduced through improved durability.

3. Reduced weight and size
Reduction of the overall length and weight of the engine has been achieved by forging the clutch case and mounting of an aluminum alloy, and by adopting a new-type, small-size reduction and reversing gear, which is coupled direction to the flywheel. Moreover, since this is a horizontal type engine, its height has been significantly reduced, leaving much more space for cargo, etc.

4. Hundreds of hours of operation without an overhaul
The main moving parts, valve mechanism and combustion chamber have adopted designs and engineering materials which are ideally suited for high-speed engines. And since the cooling water is always kept at a constant high temperature by the thermostat, liner/ring wear is limited and the heat load around the combustion chamber is low, thereby ensuring lasting quality and increased durability.

5. Quiet operation
All the machine parts which produce reciprocating motions and are the source of vibrations in the engine, have been reduced in weight and perfectly balanced, cutting vibrations to a minimum. Also, because of the adoption of an intake silencer and mixing exhaust, noise has been greatly reduced without sacrificing engine speed.

6. Easy handling and simplified operation
(1) The slope of the breather has been increased to withstand violent rollings, even up to 30°, thereby eliminating lubricating oil worries.
(2) A bracket has been mounted on the clutch so that speed-clutch control can be performed with Morse remote control device.
(3) By taking account of cabin electric power consumption, the capacity of the alternator has been increased.
(4) Because of the adoption of alarm lamps which light up when there is a rise in the temperature of the cooling water or a drop in the pressure of the lubricating oil, engine troubles are prevented.

7. Easy installation
(1) The four-point support type engine installing leg has greatly facilitated engine installation.
(2) Since the instrument panel can be installed separately it can be placed anywhere on board for easy monitoring.
(3) Rubber hoses are employed for the easy installation of on-board piping.
(4) Electrical wiring can be connected quickly and easily with connectors.

Chapter 1 General
6. Sectional Views

6. Engine Cross-section

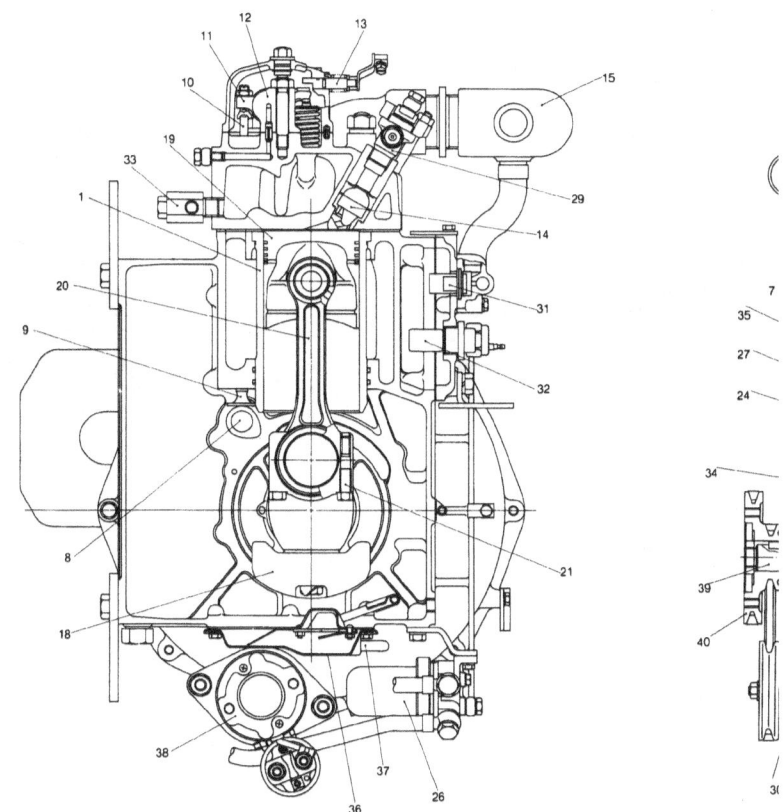

SM/YSM

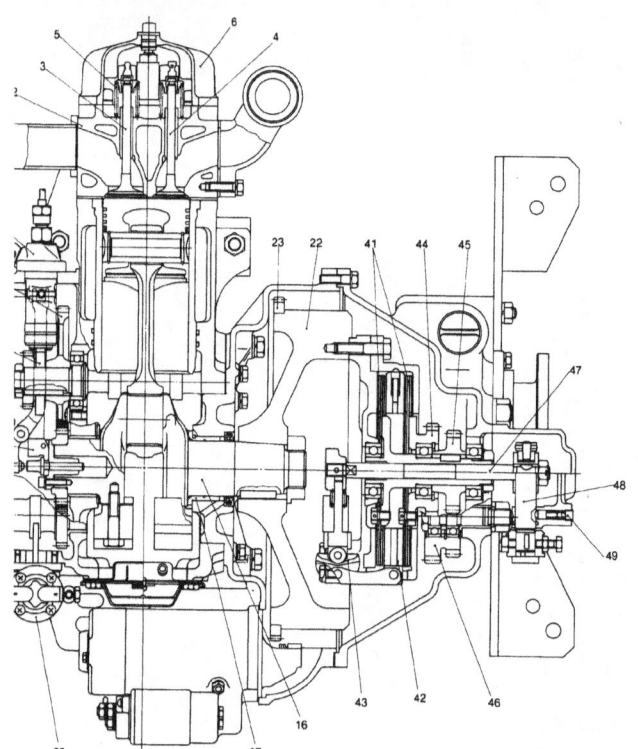

1 Cylinder liner
2 Cylinder head
3 Intake valve
4 Exhaust valve
5 Valve spring
6 Valve rocker arm chamber
7 Camshaft gear
8 Camshaft
9 Tappet
10 Push rod
11 Valve rocker arm
12 Valve rocker arm support
13 Decompression shaft
14 Precombustion chamber
15 Mixing elbow
16 Crankshaft
17 Main bearing
18 Balance weight
19 Piston
20 Connecting rod
21 Connecting rod bolt
22 Flywheel
23 Ring gear
24 Lubricating oil pump
25 Fuel feed pump
26 Fuel filter
27 Fuel cam
28 Fuel pump
29 Fuel injection nozzle
30 Cooling water pump
31 Thermostat
32 Anticorrosion zinc
33 Cooling water drain cock
34 Governor weight
35 Fuel injection limiter
36 Cylinder rear cover
37 Breather pipe
38 Starter motor
39 P.T.O. shaft
40 P.T.O. shaft pulley
41 Friction disc
42 Friction plate
43 V-lever
44 Reverse gear
45 Forward gear
46 Idle gear
47 Shifting shaft
48 Fork shaft
49 Neutral point set claw

7. Exterior Views

7-1 YSM8-R

mm (in.)

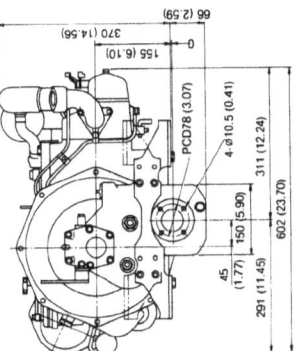

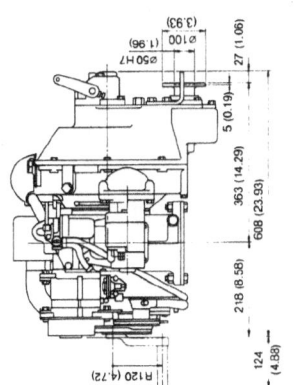
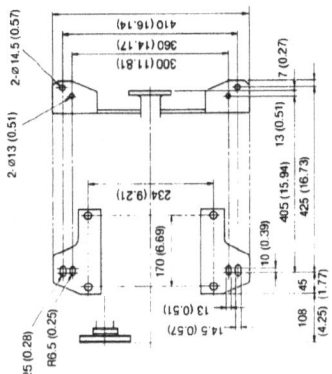

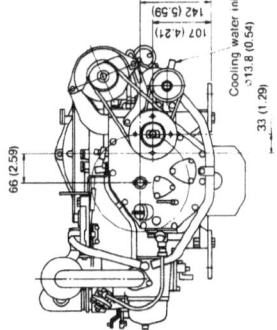

Chapter 1 General
7. Exterior Views ───────────────────────────── *SM/YSM*

7-2 YSM12-R

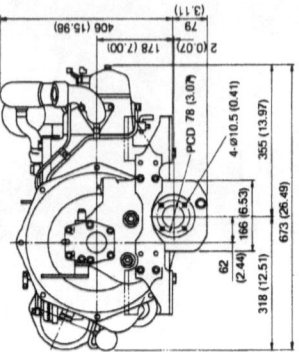

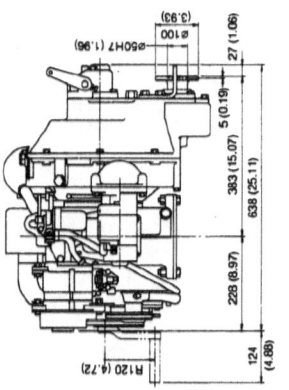

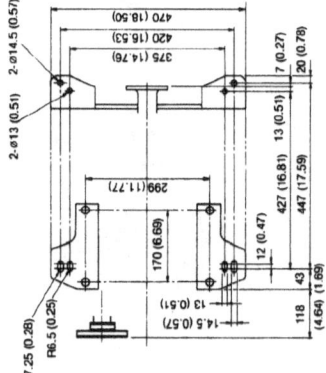

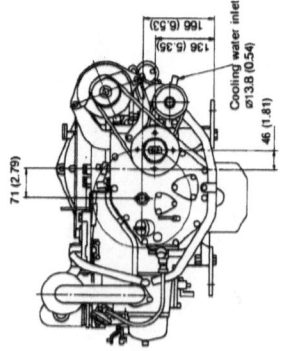

Chapter 1 General
7. Exterior Views

SM/YSM

7-3 YSM8-Y

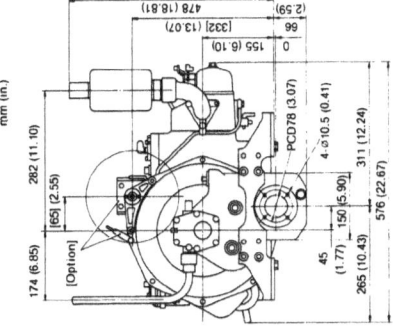

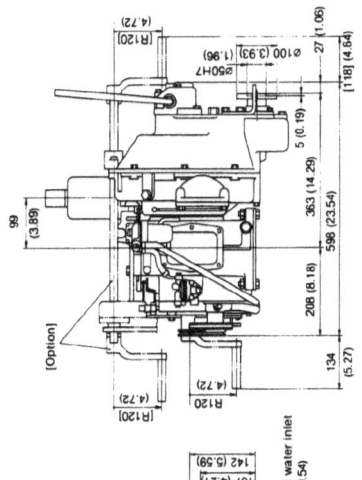

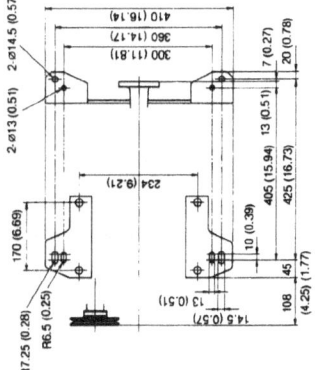

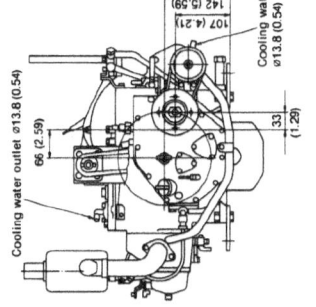

Chapter 1 General
7. Exterior Views

7-4 YSM12-Y

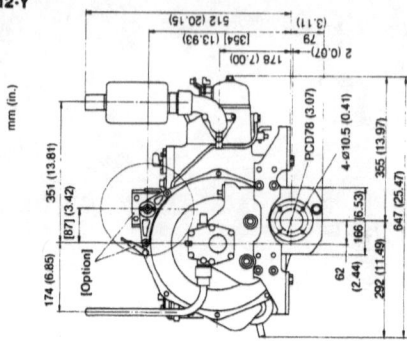

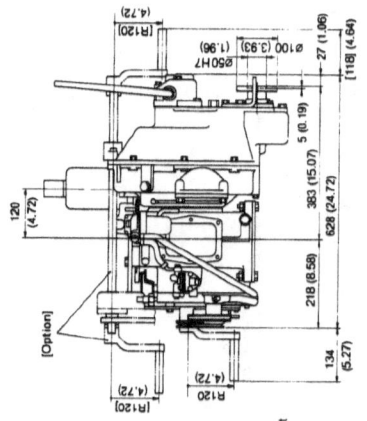

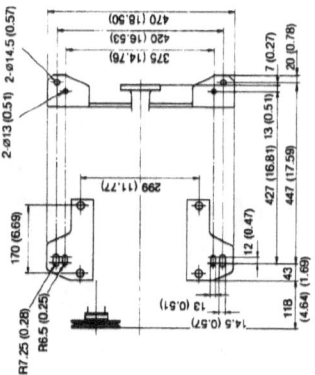

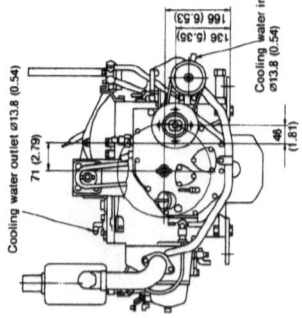

8. System Diagrams

8-1 Cooling system
8-1.1 YSM8-R, YSM12-R

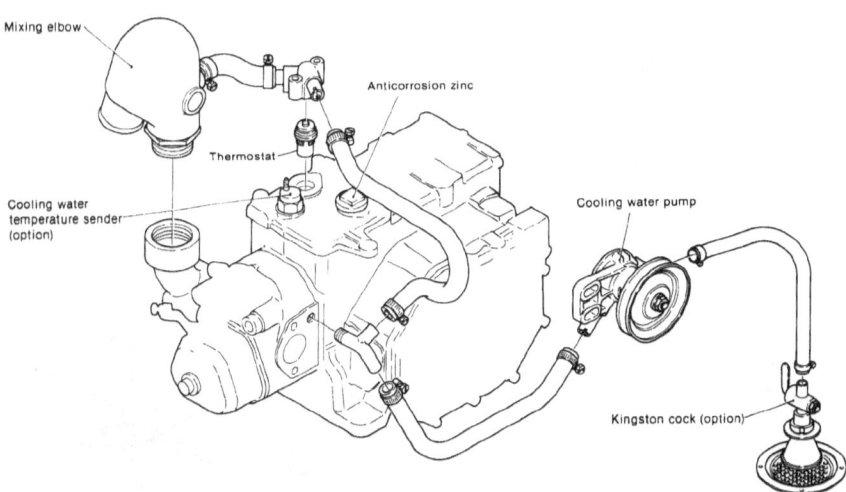

8-1.2 YSM8-Y, YSM12-Y

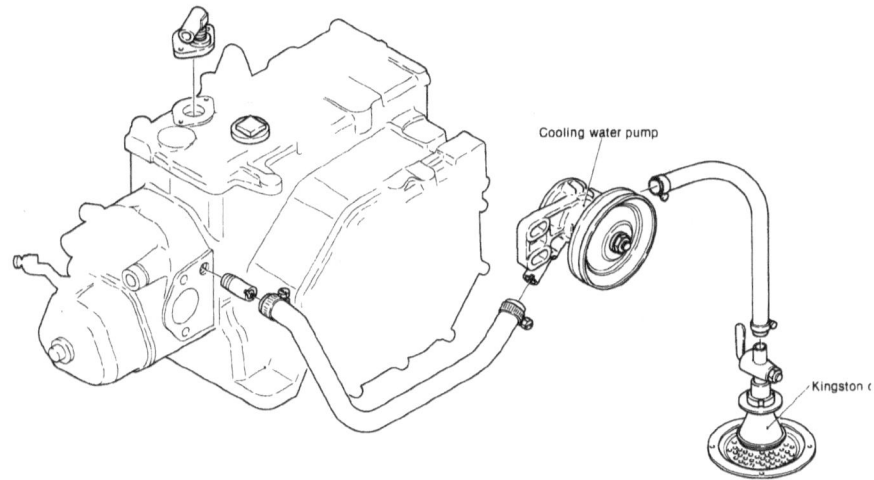

8-2 Lubrication system

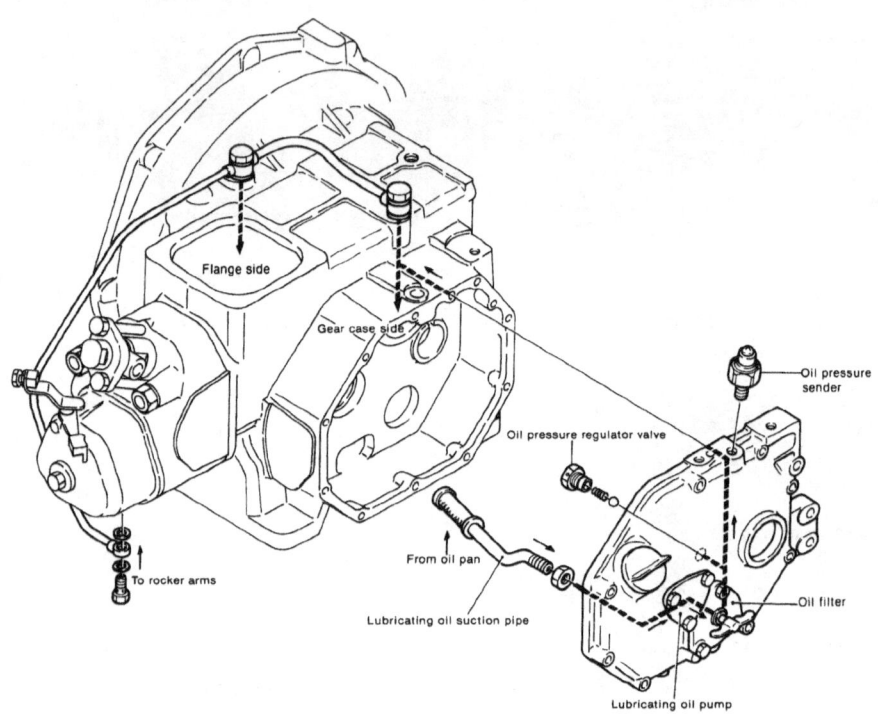

Chapter 1 General
8. System Diagrams ─────────────────────────────── *SM / YSM*

8-3 Fuel system

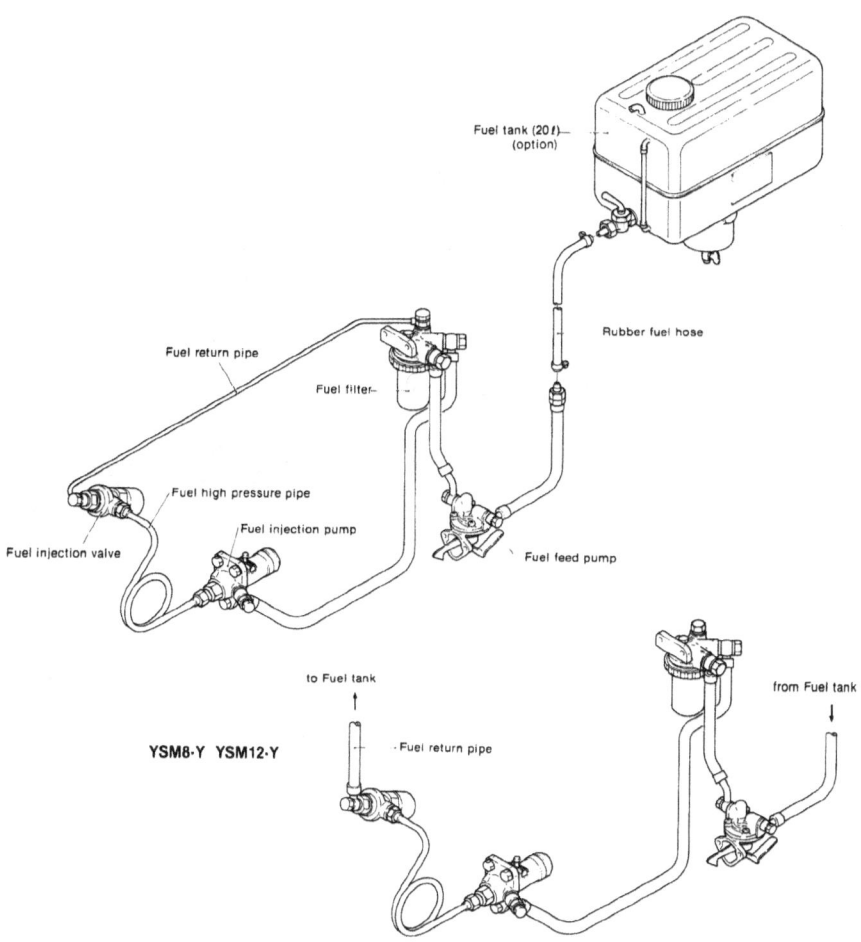

Chapter 1 General
8. System Diagrams

8-4 Electrical system

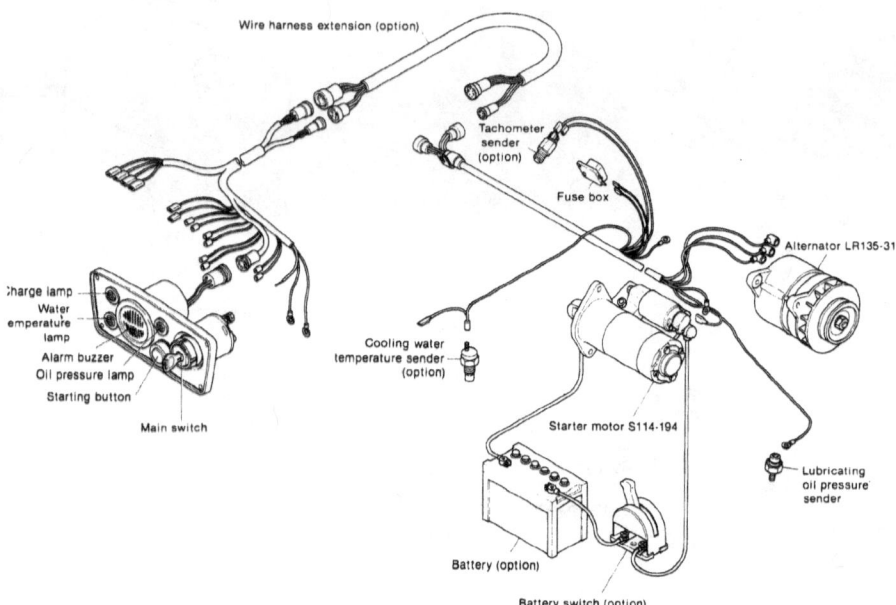

8-5 Timing gear train

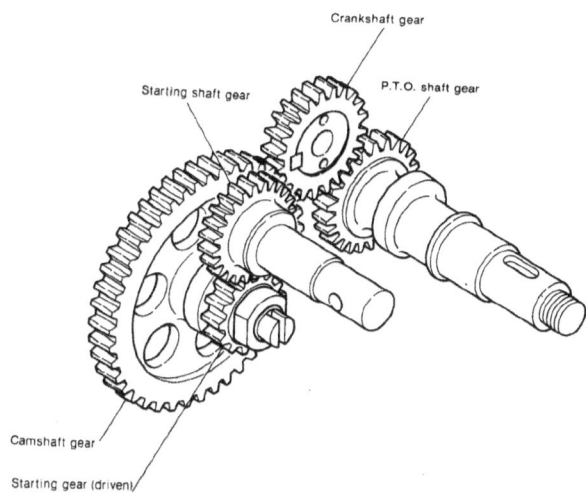

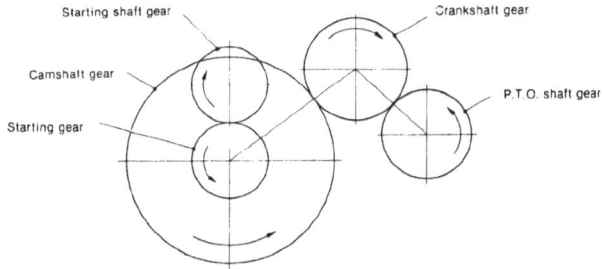

Chapter 1 General
8. System Diagrams

8-6 Reduction reversing power transmission system

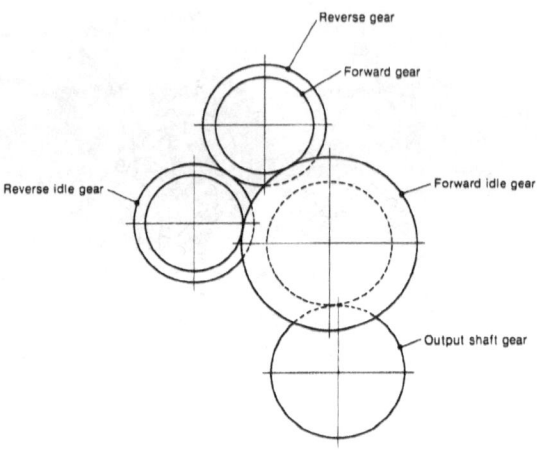

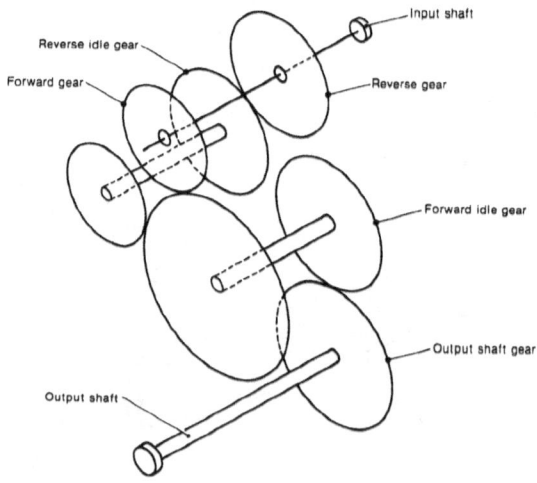

Chapter 1 General
8. System Diagrams
SM/YSM

8-7 Remote control system

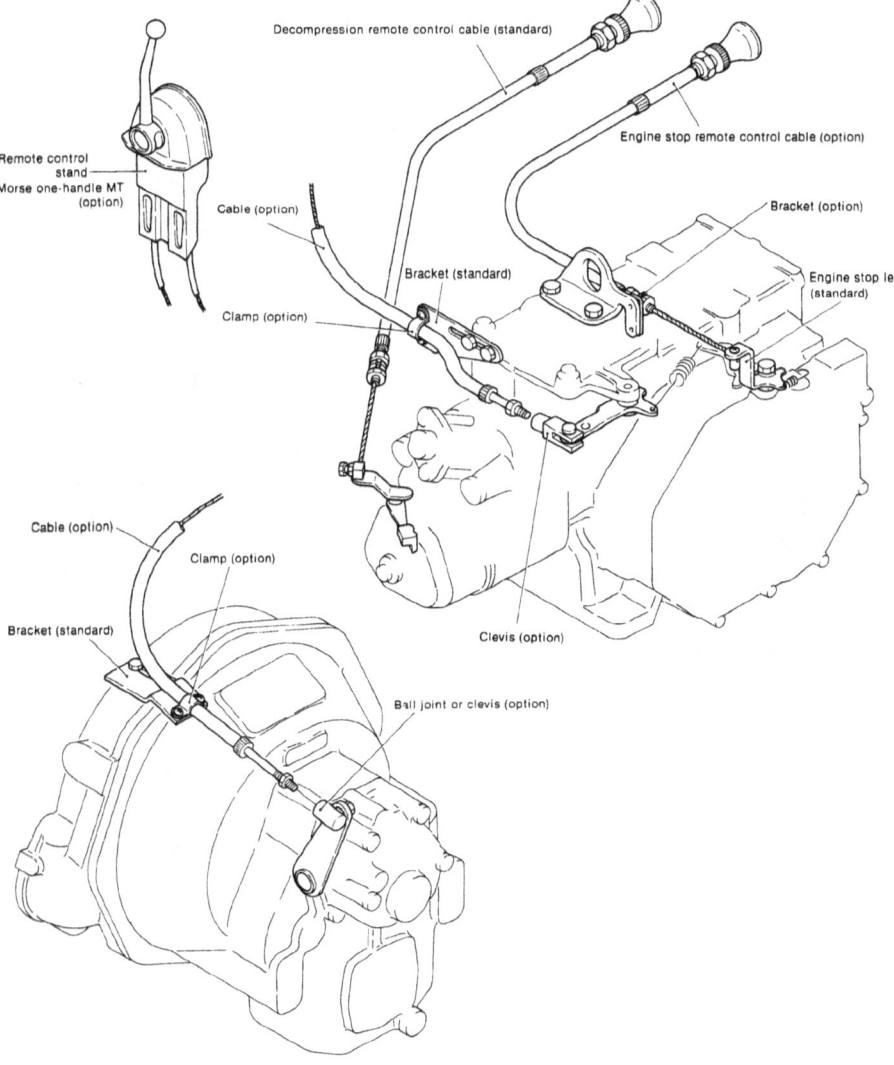

Chapter 1 General
9. Accessories
SM/YSM

9. Accessories

○ Standard accessories packed with engine
● Standard accessories mounted on engine
△ Optional accessories packed with engine
▲ Optional accessories mounted on engine

	Part name	R-type	Y-type	Remarks
1	Dry type exhaust silencer	—	○	
2	Exhaust pipe	—	○	
3	Water mixing elbow	●	—	U-type
4	Thermostat for cooling water	●	—	
5	Fuel oil tank with rubber hose	△	△	2-meter fuel hose
6	Fuel oil feed pump (mechanical type)	●	●	
7	Fuel oil strainer	●	●	
8	Chain starting device (stern side)	▲	▲	with stern side decomp. lever
9	Lube oil evacuation pump	△	△	
10	Bilge pump (mechanical type)	▲	▲	
11	Bilge hose and strainer	△	△	
12	Kingston cock with cooling water hose	△	○	
13	Remote control cable for decompression	○	—	3-meter
14	Cable for engine stop device	△	—	3-meter
15	Speed control lever with cable	—	●	1.5-meter
16	Single lever control (Morse MT-type)	△	—	with two 4-meter cables
17	Bracket for clutch remote control cable	●	—	
18	Bracket for speed remote control cable	●	—	
19	Flywheel ring gear	●	—	
20	Starting motor	●	—	
21	A.C. generator	●	—	
22	Wireharness	●	—	
23	Dash board (with 3-meter wireharness)	○	—	
24	Fuse box	●	—	
25	Lube oil pressure sender	●	—	
26	Lube oil indicator	—	●	
27	Cooling water temperature sender	●	—	
28	Battery switch	△	—	with screws
29	Tachometer sender	△	—	
30	Tachometer	△	—	
31	Flexible mountings (fixed type)	△	—	4pcs/unit
32	Flexible mountings (adjustable type)	△	—	4pcs/unit
33	Flexible coupling	△	—	with nuts
34	Exhaust flange and elbow	△	—	
35	Propeller shaft half coupling (solid, taper bored)	△	○	with bolts and nuts
36	Propeller shaft half coupling (slit type)	△	—	with bolts and nuts
37	Wireharness coupler for open board	△	—	
38	Foundation bolts	—	○	4pcs/unit
39	On board spare parts kit	△	○	
40	Packings kit	△	△	
41	Tools	○	○	
42	Special overhauling tools	△	△	
43	Starting handle	○	○	
44	Operation manual	○	○	
45	Wireharness extension	△	—	3-meter or 6-meter
46	Intake silencer	●	—	

CHAPTER 2
BASIC ENGINE

1. Cylinder Block. 2-1
2. Cylinder Liner 2-3
3. Cylinder Head 2-6
4. Piston 2-17
5. Connecting Rod 2-22
6. Crankshaft. 2-26
7. Camshaft. 2-31
8. Timing gear. 2-34

1. Cylinder Block

1-1 Construction of cylinder block

The cylinder, crank case and gear case are housed in a monoblock type cylinder block cast of high-grade cast iron. On the basis of stress analysis tests, the shape and thickness of each part have been optimized, and special ribs have been effectively arranged for increased rigidity and strength.

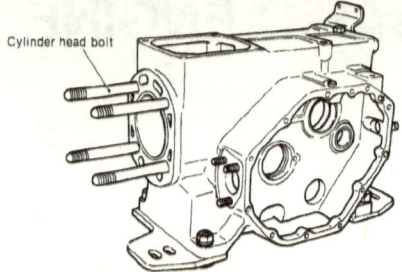

Cylinder head bolt

1-2 Cylinder block inspection

1-2.1 Inspecting each part for cracks

If the engine has been frozen or dropped, visually inspect it for cracks and other abnormalities before disassembling. If there are any abnormalities or the danger of any abnormalities occurring, make a color check.

1-2.2 Inspecting the water jacket of the cylinder for corrosion

Inspect the cooling water passages and cylinder liner contact parts for sea water corrosion, scale, and rust. Replace the cylinder body if corrosion, scale or rust is severe.
Cylinder body jacket corrosion depth limit: 1.5mm

1-2.3 Cylinder head bolts

Check for loose cylinder head bolts and for cracking caused by abnormal tightening, either by visual inspection or by a color check.
Replace the cylinder block if cracked.

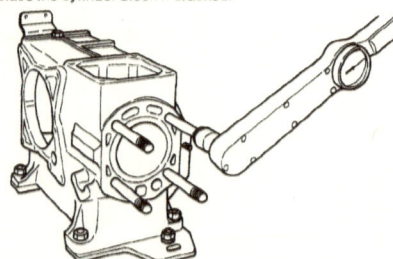

		kg·cm (ft-lb)
	YSM8	YSM12
Stud bolt tightening torque	450 (32.55)	450 (32.55)

1-2.4 Oil and water passages

Check the oil and water passages for clogging and build-up of foreign matter.

1-2.5 Cylinder bore and ledge

Perform a color check on the ledge at the top of the cylinder head bore, and replace the cylinder if any cracks are detected.

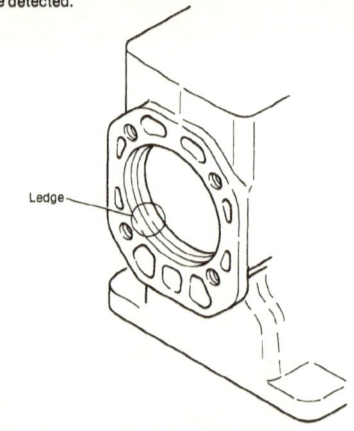

Ledge

1-2.6 Inspection of oil hole and cooling water hole

Check each oil hole and cooling water hole for continuity. When disassembling, also check each fitting surface for impressions, etc.

1-2.7 Color check flaw detection procedure

(1) Clean the inspection point thoroughly.
(2) Procure the dye penetration flaw detection agent. This agent comes in spray cans, and consists of a cleaner, penetrant, and developer in one set.

Chapter 2 Basic Engine
1. Cylinder Block

SM/YSM

(3) Pretreat the inspection surface with the cleaner. Spray the cleaner directly onto the inspection surface, or wipe the inspection surface with a cloth moistened with the cleaner.

(4) Spray the red penetration liquid onto the inspection surface. After cleaning the inspection surface, spray the red penetrant (dye penetration flaw detection agent) onto it and allow the liquid to penetrate for 5-10 minutes.
If the penetrant fails to penetrate the inspection surface because of the ambient temperature or other conditions, allow it to dry and respray the inspection surface.

(5) Spray the developer onto the inspection surface. After penetration processing, remove the residual penetrant from the inspection surface with the cleaner, and then spray the developer onto the inspection surface. If the inspection surface is flawed, red dots or lines will appear on the surface within several minutes. When spraying the developer onto the inspection surface, hold the can about 30—40cm from the surface and sweep the can slowly back and forth to obtain a uniform film.

(6) Reclean the inspection surface with the cleaner.

NOTE: Before using the dye penetration flaw detection agent, read its usage instructions thoroughly.

2. Cylinder Liner

2-1 Construction of cylinder liner

The cylinder liner is made of a special, highly wear-resistant cast iron. Its inner surfaces are finished by precision honing, thereby holding lubricating oil properly and greatly improving the wear-resistant properties of the piston rings and the cylinder liner itself. Two grooves for O-rings are cut into the outer surface of the cylinder liner. The two O-rings prevent the deformation and distortion of the cylinder liner, and at the same time, maintain maximum water tightness between the cylinder block and the cooling water jacket.

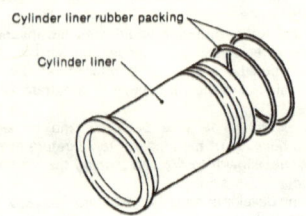

2-2 Inspection

Since the piston and piston rings constantly slide against the cylinder liner while the engine is in operation, and side pressure is applied to the cylinder liner by the movement of the crankshaft, eccentric wear occurs easily.
Moreover, if lubrication and cooling are insufficient, the inner surface will be damaged or rusted. Inspect the inner surface and replace the cylinder liner if the surface is noticeably damaged or rusted.

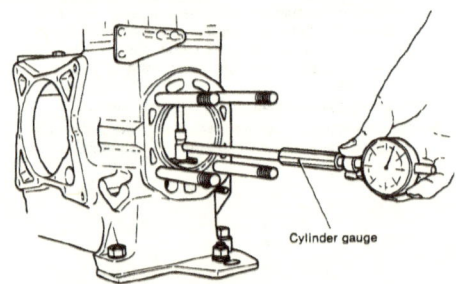

2-3 Cylinder liner bore diameter measurement

Measure the bore diameter of the cylinder liner with a cylinder gauge at the positions shown in the figure. Replace the cylinder liner when the measured value exceeds the wear limit.

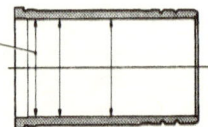

mm (in.)

		Maintenance standard	Maximum allowable clearance	Wear limit
YSM8	Cylinder liner diameter	$\varnothing 75 {}^{+0.03}_{0}$ $(2.9528 {}^{+0.00118}_{0})$	0.3 (0.0118)	$\varnothing 75.17$ (2.9594)
	Piston outside diameter	$\varnothing 75$ (2.9528)		
	Cylinder liner circularity	0.02 (0.0008)	—	0.1 (0.0039)
YSM12	Cylinder liner diameter	$\varnothing 85 {}^{+0.035}_{0}$ $(3.3465 {}^{+0.00137}_{0})$	0.3 (0.0118)	$\varnothing 85.19$ (3.3539)
	Piston outside diameter	$\varnothing 85$ (3.3465)		—
	Cylinder liner circularity	0.02 (0.0008)	—	0.1 (0.0039)

2-4 Cylinder liner replacement

(1) Pull the cylinder liner to the top of the cylinder block as shown in the figure, using the special cylinder liner puller tool.

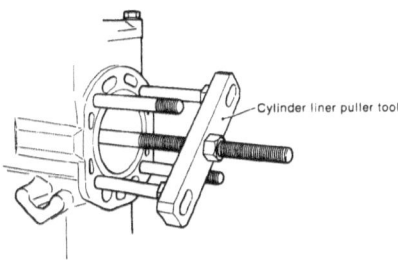
Cylinder liner puller tool

(2) Remove the rust from the area where the cylinder liner contacts the cylinder block.
(3) Install new O-rings in the two O-ring grooves of the cylinder liner.

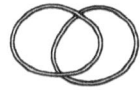

(4) Coat the outside of the cylinder liner with waterproof paint or grease.

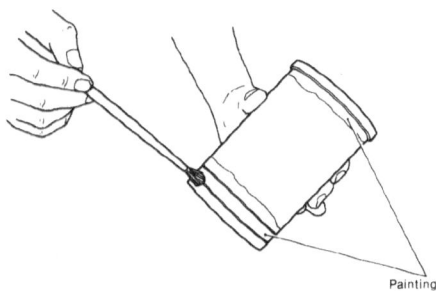
Painting

(5) Push the cylinder liner into the cylinder liner hole of the cylinder block.

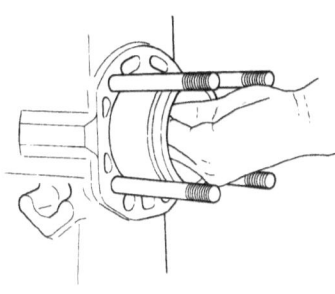

(6) After inserting the liner, measure its bore diameter.
(7) Measure the amount of liner projection.

Notes:
1. Determine whether or not the cylinder liner can be lightly inserted in the cylinder block in the absence of the rubber packing for cylinder liner.
2. Do not force the cylinder liner into the cylinder block. If there is some resistance when the liner is inserted, the cylinder block has not been derusted properly.
3. Always use a brand new rubber packing for the cylinder liner.

2-5 Measuring cylinder liner projection

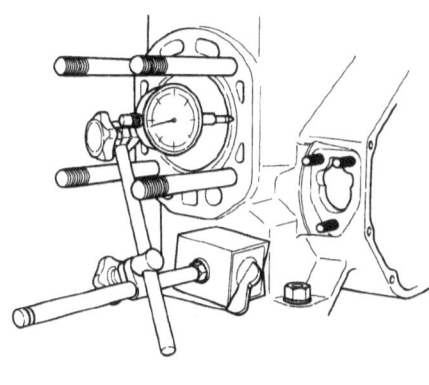

Chapter 2 Basic Engine
2. Cylinder Liner

If the cylinder liner projects too far from the block, the torque reactance will increase, causing the compression ratio to drop and the gasket packing to be damaged.
Excessive cylinder liner projection is frequently caused by incomplete removal of the rust at the ledge (part A of figure) of the cylinder block.

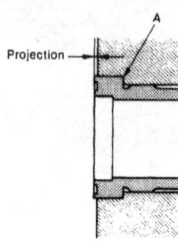

mm (in.)

Cylinder liner projection (YSM8/YSM12)	0.06 ~ 0.14 (0.0024 ~ 0.0055)

3. Cylinder Head

3-1 Construction

The cylinder head is of the gasket packing type and is independent of the valve guide. It is strong and rigid, and is fastened to the cylinder block with four bolts.

The unique Yanmar swirl type precombustion chamber is at an angle in the cylinder head, and form the combustion chamber, together with the intake and exhaust valves.

Large diameter intake valves and smoothly shaped intake and exhaust ports provide high intake efficiency and superior combustion performance.

Special consideration has also been given to the shape of the cooling water passages so that the combustion surface and precombustion chamber are uniformly cooled by an ample water flow.

In addition, lubrication of the exhaust and intake valves is done through the forced-circulation completely-sealed method.

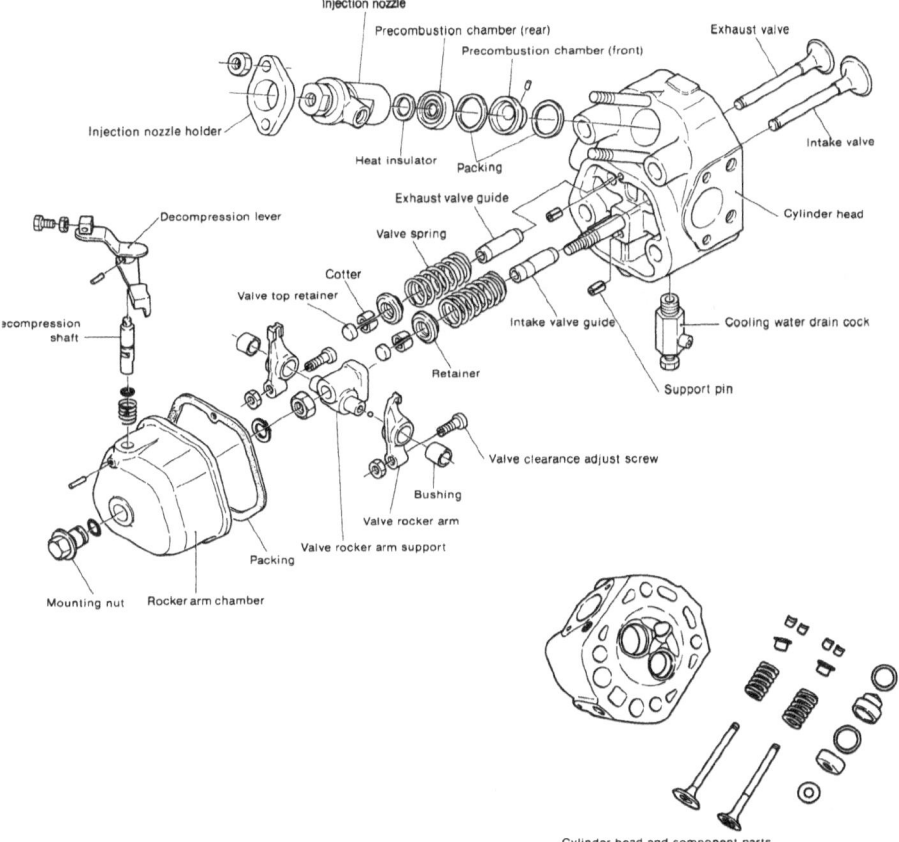

Cylinder head and component parts

Chapter 2 Basic Engine
3. Cylinder Head

— SM/YSM

3-2 Cylinder head inspection and measurement
3-2.1 Measurement of carbon build-up at combustion surface and intake and exhaust ports
Visually check for carbon build-up around the combustion surface and the port near the intake and exhaust valve seats, and remove any build-up.
When a large amount of carbon has been built up, check the top of the chamber combustion for oil flow at the intake and exhaust valve guides, and take suitable corrective action.

3-2.2 Deposit build-up at water passages
Check for build-up of deposit at the water passages, and remove any deposit with a deposit remover. When a large amount of deposit has been built up, check each part of the cooling system.

3-2.3 Inspection of corrosion at water passages
Inspect the state of corrosion of the water passages, and replace the cylinder head when corrosion is severe.
Corrosion pitting limit: 2mm (0.0787in.)

3-2.4 Cracking of combustion surface
The combustion surface is exposed to high temperature, high pressure gas and low pressure air, and is repeatedly flexed during operation. Moreover, it is used under extremely severe conditions, such as high temperature gradient of the combustion surface and cooling water passages.
Inspect the combustion surface for cracking by the color check, and replace the cylinder head if any cracking is detected. At the same time, check for signs of overloading and check the cooling water flow.

3-2.5 Cylinder head valve seat
The valve seats become wider with use. If the seats become wider than the maintenance standard, carbon build-up at the seats will cause compression leakage. On the other hand, if the seats are too narrow, they will wear quickly and heat transmission efficiency will deteriorate. Clean the carbon and other foreign matter from the valve seats, and check that the seats are not scored or dented.
Measure the seat width with a vernier calipers, and repair or replace the seat when the wear limit is exceeded.
When the valves have been lapped and/or ground, measure the amount of valve recess, and replace the valve when the wear limit is exceeded.

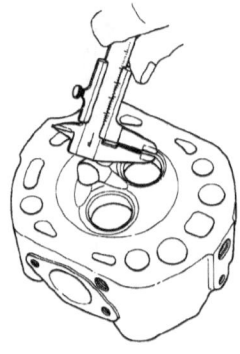

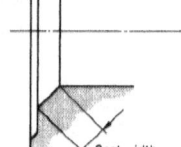
Seat width

mm (in.)

	YSM8		YSM12	
	Maintenance standard	Wear limit	Maintenance standard	Wear limit
Seat width	1.41 (0.0555)	2.1 (0.0827)	2.12 (0.0835)	2.5 (0.0984)
Seat angle	90°	—	90°	—

NOTE: Before adjusting the valve seat part be sure to check the intake and exhaust valve guides for wear; replace them if they are worn out.

Chapter 2 Basic Engine
3. Cylinder Head

(1) Lapping the valve seat.
When scoring and pitting of the valve seat is slight, coat the seat with valve compound mixed oil, and lap the seat with a lapping tool.
At this time, be sure that the compound does not flow to the valve stem and valve guide.

Lapping tool

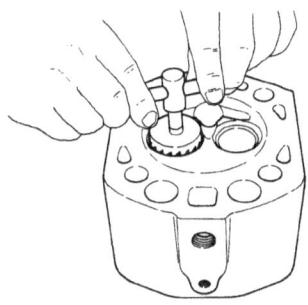

4) Mix the compound with oil, and lap the valve.
5) Finally, lap with oil.

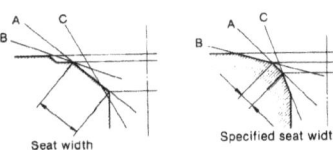

Seat width — Specified seat width
Before correction — After correction

(A) Grind with a 45° grinder
(B) Grind with a 15° grinder
(C) Grind with a 65° ~ 75° grinder

(2) Correcting valve seat width.
When the valve seat is heavily pitted and when the seat width must be corrected, repair with a seat grinder.

1) After correcting the contact area of the valve seat using a valve refacer, etc., note the spot where it comes into contact with the seat section for reference when applying seat cutters.
2) Apply the seat cutters according to the sequence shown in the diagram. First use a 45°-cutter, then a 15°-cutter; apply a 75°-cutter lightly to correct the contact surface.
3) The position at which the intake and exhaust valve comes into contact with the seat section should be at the center of the contact surface of the valve.
Therefore, when applying a 15°- or 75°-cutter, take carefully note the spot at which the valve comes into contact with the seat.

NOTE: (1) When the valve seat has been corrected with a seat grinder, insert an adjusting shim between the valve spring and cylinder head.
(2) When the lower part of the valve comes into contact with the seat, correct the contact position with a 45°- and 75°-cutter. When the upper part of the valve is in contact with the seat, correct the contact position using a 15°- and 45°-cutter.

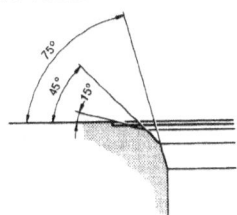

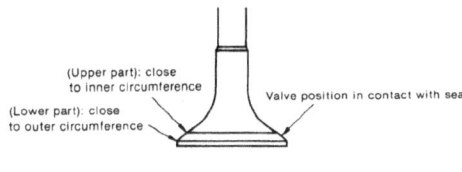

(Upper part): close to inner circumference
(Lower part): close to outer circumference
Valve position in contact with sea

Chapter 2 Basic Engine
3. Cylinder Head

3-2.6 Measuring valve recess
When the valve has been lapped many times, the valve will be recessed and will adversely affect the combustion performance. Therefore, measure the valve recess, and replace the valve and cylinder head when the wear limit is exceeded.

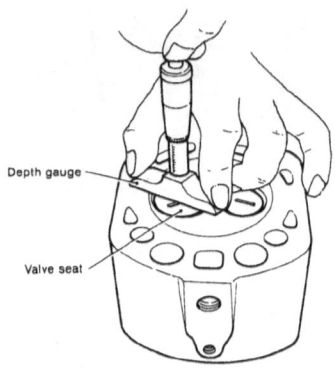

3-3.1 Cylinder head stud bolt assembly sequence
(1) Check for loose cylinder head stud bolts, and lock any loose bolts with two nuts and then tighten to the prescribed torque.
Cylinder head stud bolt tightening torque: 4.5kg·m (32.55ft·lb)

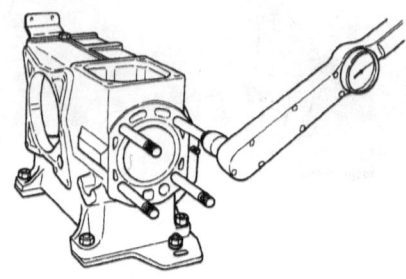

mm (in.)

	YSM8		YSM12	
	Maintenance standard	Wear limit	Maintenance standard	Wear limit
Valve recess	1.25 (0.0492)	1.55 (0.0610)	1.15 (0.0453)	1.45 (0.0570)

3-2.7 Other inspections
(1) Check the fitting hole of the precombustion chamber for corrosion, cracks, etc.
(2) Check the valve rocker arm fitting bolt, injection nozzle holder fitting bolt, and other bolts for bending, looseness, etc.
(3) Check the valve rocker arm chamber cover and valve rocker arm support pin for damage, etc.
(4) Check the cylinder head drain plug for water leakage, etc.

3-3 Dismounting and remounting the cylinder head
When dismounting and remounting the cylinder head, the mounting bolts must be removed and installed gradually and in the prescribed sequence to prevent damaging the gasket packing and to prevent distortion of the cylinder head. Since the tightening torque and tightening sequence of the mounting bolts when remounting the cylinder head are especially important from the standpoint of engine performance, the following items must be strictly observed.

(2) Checking the gasket packing mounting face.
Confirm correct alignment of the front and rear of the gasket packing, and install the packing by coating both sides with Three Bond 50.

(3) Installing the cylinder head ass'y.
Position the cylinder head ass'y parallel to the top of the cylinder block, and install the ass'y to the block, being careful that the cylinder head ass'y does not touch the threads of the cylinder head bolts.

3-3.2 Tightening the cylinder head tightening nuts
(1) Cylinder head nut tightening sequence   kg·m (ft·lb)

YSM8	YSM12
9.7 (70.16)	13.6 (98.37)

1) Coat the threads of the cylinder head bolts with lubricating oil, and screw the cylinder head nuts onto the bolts.

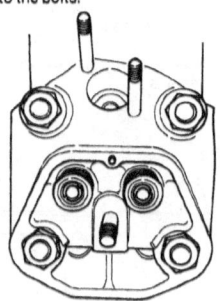

Chapter 2 Basic Engine
3. Cylinder Head

2) First, tighten the nuts sequentially to 1/3 of the prescribed torque.
3) Second, tighten the nuts sequentially to 2/3 of the prescribed torque.
4) Third, tighten the nuts to the prescribed torque.
5) Recheck that all the nuts have been properly tightened.

3-3.3 Cylinder head nut loosening sequence
When loosening the cylinder head nuts, reverse the tightening sequence.

3-4 Intake and exhaust valves, valve guide and valve spring

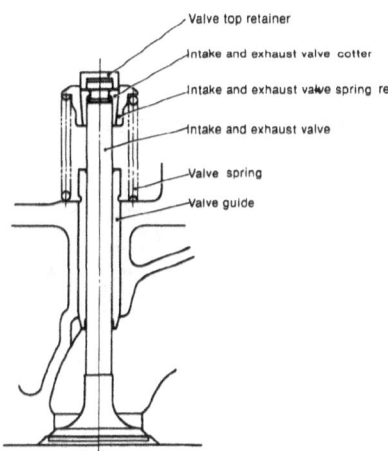

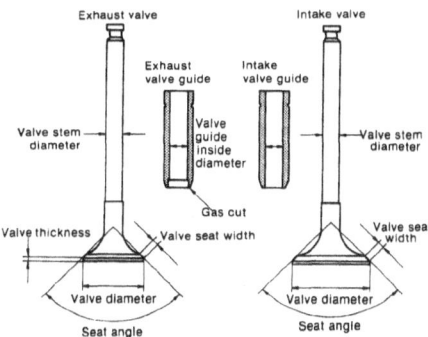

mm (in.)

	YSM8		YSM12	
	Maintenance standard	Wear limit	Maintenance standard	Wear limit
Valve seat width	2.8 (0.1102)	—	3.4 (0.1339)	—
Valve seat angle	90°	—	90°	—
Valve thickness	1.0 (0.0394)	0.5 (0.0197)	1.1 (0.0433)	0.5 (0.0197)

(2) Valve stem bending and wear.
Check for valve stem wear and staining, and repair when such damage is light. Measure the outside diameter and bend, and replace the valve when the wear limit is exceeded.

mm (in.)

	YSM8	YSM12
Valve stem bend limit	0.03 (0.00118)	0.03 (0.00118)

(3) Valve seat hairline cracks.
Inspect the valve seat by the color check, and replace the seat if cracked.

3-4.1 Inspecting and measuring the intake and exhaust valves

(1) Valve seat wear and contact width.
Inspect valve seats for carbon build-up and heavy wear.
Also check if each valve seat contact width is suitable. If the valve seat contact width is narrower than the valve seat width, the seat angle must be checked and corrected.

3-4.2 Inspecting and measuring valve guides

The valve guide is different for the intake valve and exhaust valve in that the inner face of the exhaust valve has a gas cut.
Be sure that the correct guide is used when replacing the guides.

(1) Floating of the intake and exhaust valve guides.
Check for intake and exhaust valve guide looseness and floating with a test hammer, and replace loose or floating guides with guides having an oversize outside diameter.

Chapter 2 Basic Engine
3. Cylinder Head

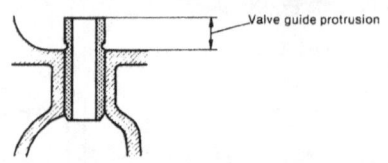

mm (in.)

	YSM8	YSM12
Valve guide protrusion	7 (0.2756)	10 (0.3937)

(2) Measuring the valve guide inside diameter.
   Measure the valve guide inside diameter and clearance, and replace the guide when wear exceeds the wear limit.

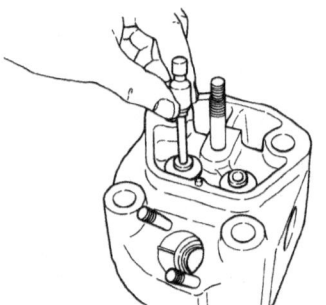
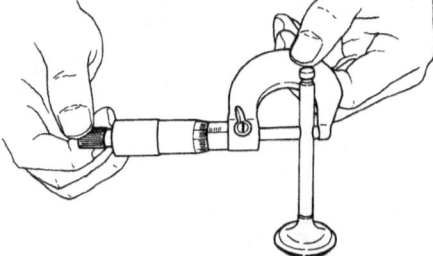
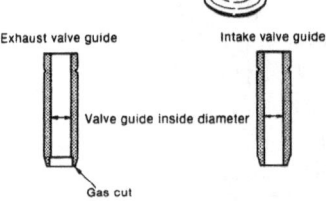

Exhaust valve guide   Intake valve guide

Valve guide inside diameter

Gas cut

mm (in.)

			Maintenance standard	Clearance at assembly	Maximum allowable clearance	Wear limit
YSM8	Intake	Valve guide inside diameter (after assembly)	⌀7 +0.015/0 (0.2756 ~ 0.2762)	0.040 ~ 0.065 (0.0016 ~ 0.0026)	0.15 (0.0059)	⌀7.08 (0.2787)
		Stem outside diameter	⌀7 -0.04/-0.05 (0.2736 ~ 0.2740)			⌀6.90 (0.2717)
	Exhaust	Valve guide inside diameter (after assembly)	⌀7 +0.02/+0.005 (0.2758 ~ 0.2764)	0.045 ~ 0.075 (0.0018 ~ 0.003)	0.15 (0.0059)	⌀7.08 (0.2787)
		Stem outside diameter	⌀7 -0.04/-0.05 (0.2736 ~ 0.2740)			⌀6.90 (0.2717)
YSM12	Intake	Valve guide inside diameter (after assembly)	⌀8 +0.025/+0.010 (0.3154 ~ 0.3159)	0.040 ~ 0.065 (0.0016 ~ 0.0026)	0.15 (0.0059)	⌀8.08 (0.3181)
		Stem outside diameter	⌀8 -0.03/-0.04 (0.3134 ~ 0.3138)			⌀7.90 (0.3110)
	Exhaust	Valve guide inside diameter (after assembly)	⌀8 +0.030/+0.015 (0.3156 ~ 0.3161)	0.045 ~ 0.070 (0.0018 ~ 0.0028)	0.15 (0.0059)	⌀8.08 (0.3181)
		Stem outside diameter	⌀8 -0.03/-0.04 (0.3134 ~ 0.3138)			⌀7.90 (0.3110)

Chapter 2 Basic Engine
3. Cylinder Head

SM/YSM

(3) Replacing the intake/exhaust valve guide
 (1) Using a special tool for extracting and inserting the valve guide, extract the valve guide.

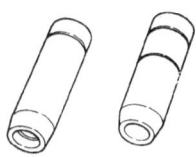

(2) Using the above tool, drive the valve guide into position by starting from the valve spring side and finish the inside diameter with a reamer.

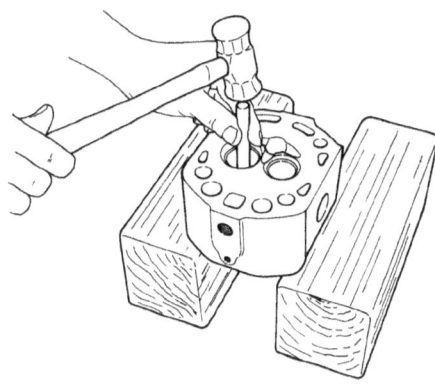

3-4.3 Valve spring
(1) Valve spring inclination.
Since inclination of the valve spring is a direct cause of eccentric contact of the valve stem, always check it at disassembly.
Stand the valve upright on a stool, and check if the entire spring contacts the gauge when a square gauge is placed against the outside diameter of the valve spring.
If there is a gap between the gauge and spring, measure the gap with a feeler gauge.
When the valve spring inclination exceeds the wear limit, replace the spring.

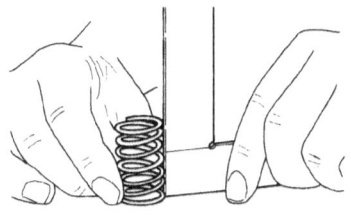

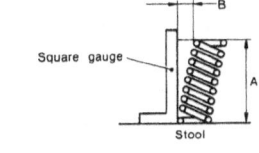

mm (in.)

Inclination limit (gap B)	1.4 (0.0551)

(2) Valve spring free length.
Measure the free length of the valve spring, and replace the spring when the wear limit is exceeded.

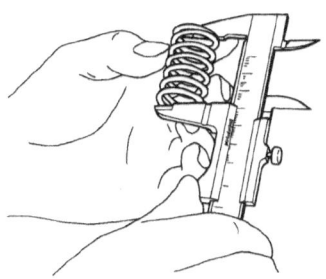

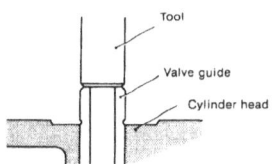

mm (in.)

	YSM8	YSM12
Amount of interference of valve guide	0.015 ± 0.014 (0.00004 ~ 0.00114)	

NOTE: Insert the valve guide until the groove on its outer surface reaches the cylinder head surface.

Chapter 2 Basic Engine
3. Cylinder Head

Also, measure the tension of the spring with a spring tester. If the tension is below the prescribed limit, replace the spring.

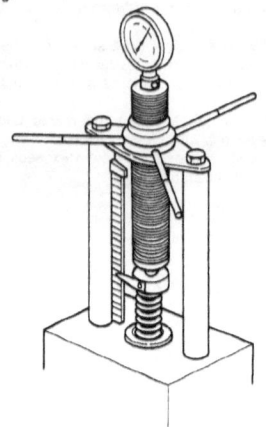

mm (in.)

	YSM8		YSM12	
	Maintenance standard	Wear limit	Maintenance standard	Wear limit
Valve spring free length	41mm (1.6141)	39.5mm (1.5551)	40mm (1.5748)	38.5mm (1.5157)
Length when attached	30.8mm (1.2125)	—	33.3mm (1.3110)	—
Load applied when attached	16.4kg (36.15 lb)	—	15.3kg (33.73 lb)	—

3-4.4 Spring retainer and spring cotter pin
Inspect the inside face of the spring retainer and the outside surface of the spring cotter pin, and the contact area of the spring cotter pin inside surface and the notch in the head of the valve stem. Replace the spring retainer and spring cotter pin when the contact area is less than 70% or when the spring cotter pin has been recessed because of wear.

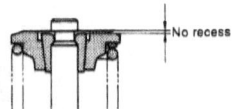

3-4.5 Valve top retainer
Make sure the valve top retainer surface is in contact with the valve rocker arm. If it is worn out, replace it with a new one.

3-5 Precombustion chamber and top clearance
3-5.1 Precombustion chamber
Remove the packing and insulation packing at the precombustion chamber's front and rear chambers, and inspect.
Check for burning at the front end of the precombustion chamber front chamber, acid corrosion at the precombustion chamber rear chamber, and for burned packing.
Replace if faulty.

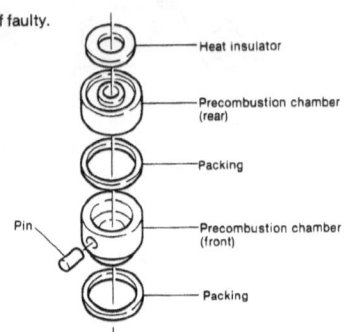

3-5.2 Insulation packing
The insulation packing prevents transmission of heat from the precombustion chamber to the nozzle valve and serves to improve the nozzle's durability.
Always put in a new insulation packing when it has been disassembled.

3-5.3 Top clearance
Top clearance is the size of the gap between the cylinder head combustion surface and the top of the piston at top dead center.
Since top clearance has considerable effect on the combustion performance and the starting characteristic of the engine, it must be checked periodically.

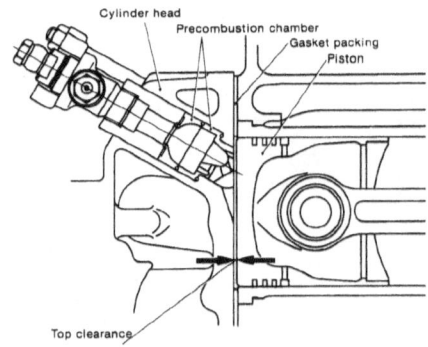

Chapter 2 Basic Engine
3. Cylinder Head

(1) Top clearance measurement
  1) Check the cylinder head mounting bolts and tightening torque.
  2) Remove the fuel injection valve and pre-combustion chamber.
  3) Lower the piston.
  4) Insert quality fuse wire through the nozzle holder hole. (Be careful that the wire does not enter the intake and exhaust valve and the groove in the combustion surface.)
  5) Crush the fuse wire by moving the piston to top dead center by slowly cranking the engine by hand.
  6) Lower the piston by hand cranking the engine and remove the crushed fuse wire, being careful not to drop it.
  7) Measure the thickness of the crushed part of the fuse wire with vernier calipers or a micrometer.

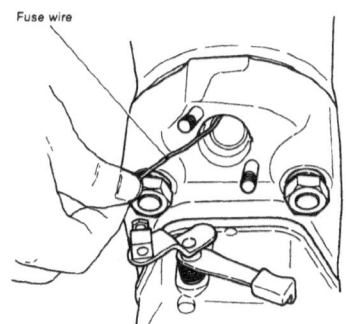
Fuse wire

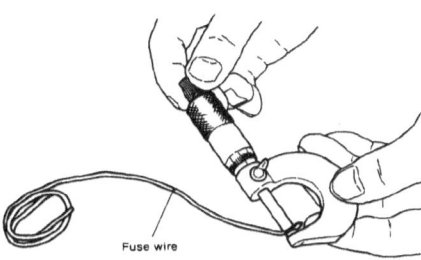
Fuse wire

(2) Top clearance value.

mm (in.)

	YSM8	YSM12
Top clearance	0.6 ~ 0.93 (0.0236 ~ 0.0366)	1.10 ~ 1.50 (0.0433 ~ 0.0551)
Fuse to be used	⌀1.0 (0.039)	⌀1.5 (0.059)

When the top clearance value is not within the above range, check for damaged gasket packing, distortion of the cylinder head combustion surface, or other abnormal conditions.

(3) How to deal with too-large top clearance
When the top clearance is too large, check for the following:
  1) The cylinder head is clamped wrong.
  2) The bearing metal for the crankpin, journal, and piston pin sections is worn.
  3) Check the connecting rod for bending, etc., and if any malfunctioning part is found, replace the connecting rod.

3-6 Intake and exhaust valve rocker arm

Since the intake and exhaust valve rocker arm shaft and bushing clearance and valve head and push rod contact wear are directly related to the valve timing, and have an effect on engine performance, they must be carefully serviced.

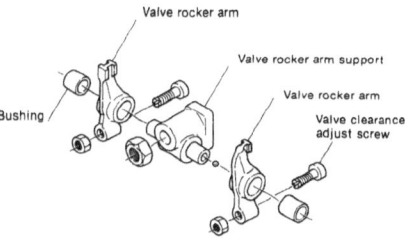
Valve rocker arm
Valve rocker arm support
Valve rocker arm
Bushing
Valve clearance adjust screw

3-6.1 Measuring the valve rocker arm shaft and bushing clearance

Measure the outside diameter of the valve rocker arm shaft and the inside diameter of the bushing, and replace the rocker arm or bushing if the measured value exceeds the wear limit.
Replace a loose valve rocker arm shaft bushing with a new bushing. However, when there is no tightening allowance, replace the valve rocker arm.

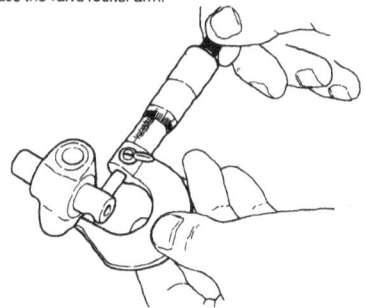

Chapter 2 Basic Engine
3. Cylinder Head

SM/YSM

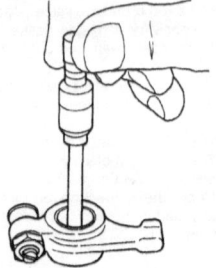
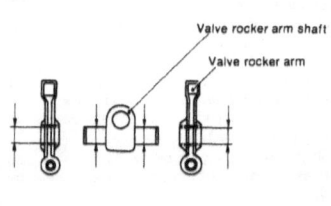

mm (in.)

			Maintenance standard	Clearance at assembly	Maximum allowable clearance	Wear limit
YSM8	Intake and exhaust valve rocker arm shaft outside diameter	A	ø12 $_{-0.018}^{0}$ (0.4717 ~ 0.4724)	0.016 ~ 0.052 (0.00063 ~ 0.00205)	0.15 (0.0059)	ø11.9 (0.4685)
	Intake and exhaust valve rocker arm bushing inside diameter (assembled)	B	ø12 $_{+0.016}^{+0.034}$ (0.4731 ~ 0.4738)			ø12.1 (0.4764)
YSM12	Intake and exhaust valve rocker arm shaft outside diameter	A	ø16 $_{-0.018}^{0}$ (0.6292 ~ 0.6299)	0.016 ~ 0.052 (0.00063 ~ 0.00205)	0.15 (0.0059)	ø15.9 (0.6260)
	Intake and exhaust valve rocker arm bushing inside diameter (assembled)	B	ø16 $_{+0.016}^{+0.034}$ (0.6305 ~ 0.6313)			ø16.1 (0.6339)

3-6.2 Valve rocker arm and valve head contact and wear
Check the valve rocker arm and valve head contact, and replace when there is any abnormal wear or peeling.
NOTE: Correct a trifle stepped wear in the contact surface of the stem and valve rocker arm by using an oil stone, etc.

3-6.3 Valve clearance adjusting screw
Inspect the valve clearance adjusting screw and push rod contact, and replace when there is any abnormal wear or peeling.

3-7 Adjusting intake and exhaust valve head clearance
Adjustment of the intake and exhaust valve head clearance governs the performance of the engine, and must be performed accurately. The intake and exhaust valve head clearance must always be checked and readjusted, as required, when the engine is disassembled and reassembled, and after every 300 hours of operation. Adjust the valve head clearance as described below.

3-7.1 Adjustment
Make this adjustment when the engine is cold.
(1) Remove the valve rocker arm cover.
(2) Crank the engine and set the piston to top dead center (TDC) on the compression stroke.

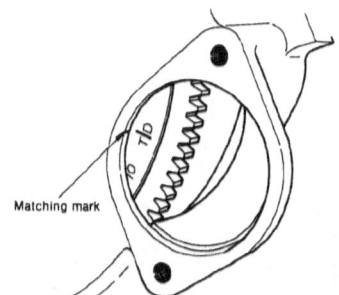

Matching mark

NOTE: Set to the position at which the valve rocker arm shaft does not move even when the crankshaft is turned to the left and right, centered around the TD mark.

Chapter 2 Basic Engine
3. Cylinder Head

_____ SM/YSM

(3) Loosen the valve clearance adjusting screw lock nut, adjust the clearance to the maintenance standard with a feeler gauge, and retighten the lock nut.

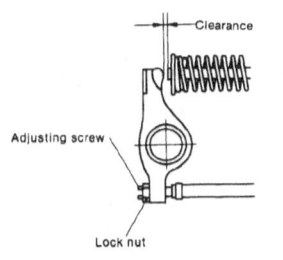

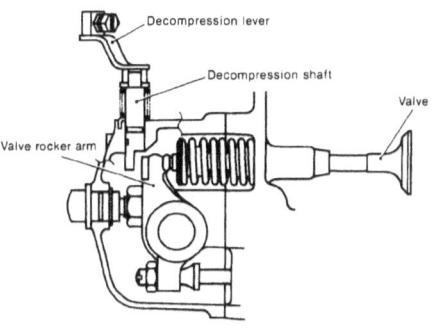

Intake and exhaust valve head clearance (cold engine)	mm (in.) 0.20 (0.00787)

3-7.2 Adjusting without a feeler gauge
Set the head clearance to zero by tightening the adjusting screw, being careful not to tighten the screw too tight. Then adjust the valve clearance to the maintenance standard by backing off the adjusting screw by the angle given below.

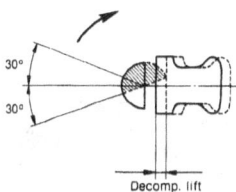

With this engine, there is no need to adjust the decompression lift.

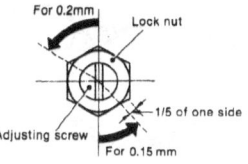

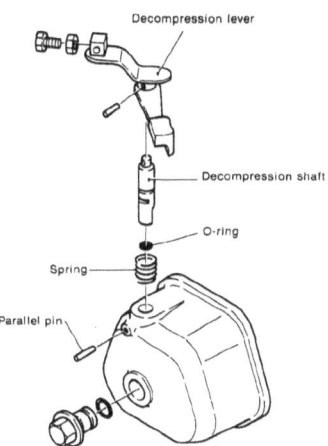

	mm (in.)
Valve clearance adjusting screw	M8 × 1.25
Adjusting screw backoff angle	Approx 58° ~ 60°

NOTE: Calculating the backoff angle.
Calculate the 0.2mm advance angle from 1.25mm advance at one turn = 360°.
$0.2/1.25 \times 360° = 57.6° \fallingdotseq 58°$.
One side (60°) of the hexagonal nut should be used to measure.

3-8 Decompression mechanism
The decompression mechanism is used when the starter motor fails to rotate sufficiently because the battery is weak, and to facilitate starting in cold weather.
When the decompression lever is operated, the valve is pushed down, the engine is decompressed, the engine turns over easily and the flywheel inertia increases, thus making starting easy.

4. Piston

The piston is cast of an Lo-Ex aluminum alloy with a small thermal expansion coefficient and excellent cooling properties. Its ellipsoid shape makes for better contact on the cylinder surface and reduces oil consumption. In addition the lowly constructed land area between the third ring and the oil ring allows the lubricating oil to stay longer, thereby providing better lubrication of the piston and cylinder and reducing oil comsumption. A total of four piston rings are installed, three compression rings and one oil ring, to ensure good compression and lubrication. To improve the rigidity of the piston skirt no ring is installed on the skirt itself so that the piston seldom becomes deformed and retains stable contact.

The piston pin is of the floating type. Both its ends are fastened with a circlips.

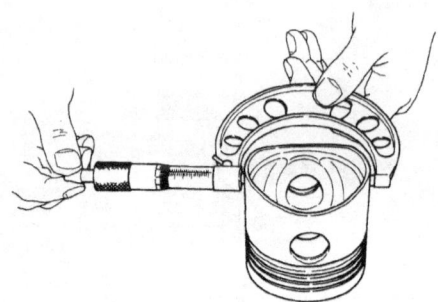

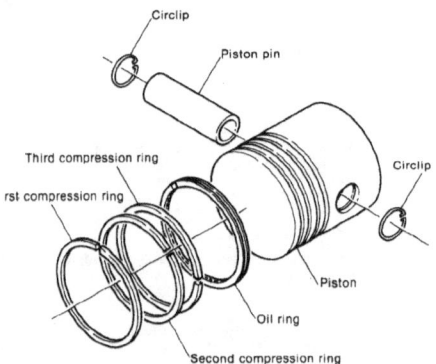

(2) Measure the clearance between the piston ring or oil ring and the ring groove with a thickness gauge.

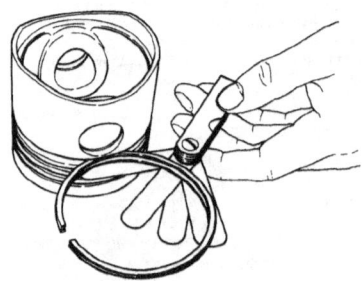

4-2 Piston
4-2.1 Inspection
(1) Measuring important dimensions

Measure each important dimension, and replace the piston when the wear limit is exceeded.

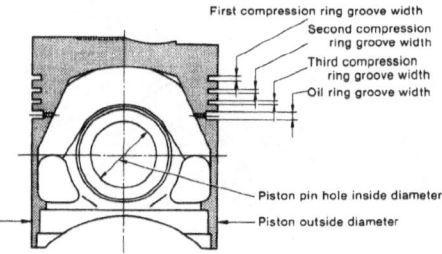

Chapter 2 Basic Engine
4. Piston

SM/YSM

mm (in.)

	YSM8		YSM12	
	Maintenance standard	Wear limit	Maintenance standard	Wear limit
Piston outside diameter (axial direction)	⌀75 $^{-0.125}_{-0.155}$ (2.9467 ~ 2.9478)	⌀74.8 (2.9448)	⌀85 $^{-0.115}_{-0.145}$ (3.3407 ~ 3.3419)	⌀84.8 (3.3386)
Piston pin hole inside diameter	⌀23 (0.9055)	—	⌀28	—
First compression piston ring-to-groove clearance	0.050 ~ 0.080 (0.00196 ~ 0.00314)	0.2 (0.00787)	0.050 ~ 0.095 (0.00197 ~ 0.00374)	0.2 (0.00787)
Second and third compression piston ring-to-groove clearance	0.020 ~ 0.055 (0.00078 ~ 0.00216)	0.2 (0.00787)	0.020 ~ 0.055 (0.00078 ~ 0.00216)	0.2 (0.00787)
Oil ring-to-groove clearance	0.020 ~ 0.055 (0.00078 ~ 0.00216)	0.15 (0.0059)	0.020 ~ 0.055 (0.00078 ~ 0.00216)	0.15 (0.0059)

(3) Piston pin outside contact and ring groove carbon build-up.
Check if the piston ring grooves are clogged with carbon, if the rings move freely, and for abnormal contact around the outside of the piston. Repair or replace the piston if faulty.

4-2.2 Replacing a piston
If the dimension of any part is worn past the wear limit or outside of the piston is scored, replace the piston.
(1) Replacement
  1. Install the piston pin circlip at one side only.
  2. Immerse the piston in 80°C oil for 10 ~ 15 minutes.

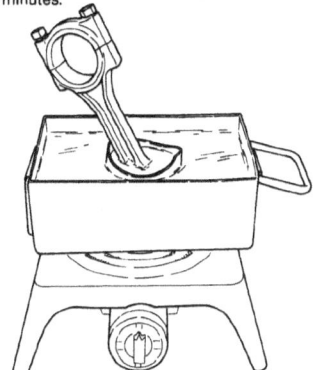

  3. Remove the piston from the hot oil and place it on a bench with the piston head at the bottom.
  4. Insert the small end of the connecting rod into the piston, insert the piston pin with a rotating motion, and install the other piston pin circlip.
Use wooden hammer if necessary.

(2) Precautions
  1. Before inserting, check whether the piston pin is in the connecting rod.
  2. Coat the piston pin with oil to facilitate insertion.
  3. Check that the connecting rod and piston move freely.
  4. Insert the pin quickly, before the piston cools.

4-3 Piston pin and piston pin bushing
4-3.1 Piston pin
Measure the dimensions of the piston pin, and replace the pin if it is worn past the wear limit or severely scored.

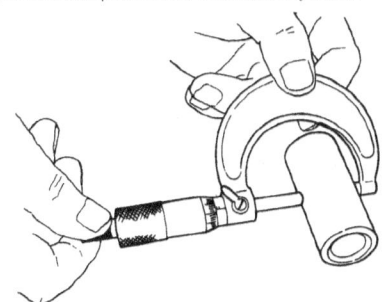

Chapter 2 Basic Engine
4. Piston

— SM/YSM

mm (in.)

	YSM8		YSM12	
	Maintenance standard	Wear limit	Maintenance standard	Wear limit
Piston pin outside diameter	⌀23 $_{-0.009}^{0}$ (0.9052 ~ 0.9055)	⌀22.98 (0.9047)	⌀28 $_{-0.009}^{0}$ (1.1020 ~ 1.1024)	⌀27.98 (1.1016)

mm (in.)

	YSM8	YSM12
Piston pin hole inside diameter	⌀22.995 ~ 23.008 (0.9053 ~ 0.9058)	⌀27.995 ~ 28.008 (1.1022 ~ 1.1027)
Piston pin outside diameter	⌀22.991 ~ 23.000 (0.9052 ~ 0.9055)	⌀27.991 ~ 28.000 (1.1020 ~ 1.1024)
Pin and pin hole tightening allowance	−0.005 ~ 0.017 (−0.0002 ~ 0.0007)	−0.005 ~ 0.017 (−0.0002 ~ 0.0007)
Pin fitting temperature	50° ~ 60°	50° ~ 60°

4-3.2 Piston pin bushing
A copper alloy wound bushing is pressed onto the piston pin.
Since a metallic sound will be produced if the piston pin and piston pin bushing wear is excessive, replace the bushing when the wear limit is exceeded.
The piston pin bushing can be easily removed and installed with a press. However, when installing the bushing, be careful that it is not tilted.

4-4 Piston rings
4-4.1 Piston ring configuration

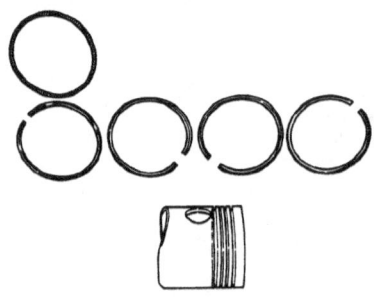

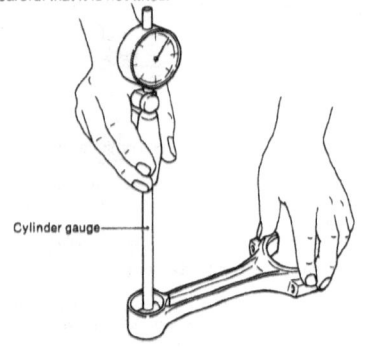

mm (in.)

	YSM8		YSM12	
	Maintenance standard	Wear limit	Maintenance standard	Wear limit
Piston pin bushing inside diameter	⌀23 (0.9055)	⌀23.1 (0.9094)	⌀28 (1.1023)	⌀28.1 (1.1063)

NOTE: "Piston pin bushing inside diameter" is the dimension after pressing onto the connecting rod.

(1) The first compression ring is a barrel face ring that effectively prevents abnormal wear caused by engine loading and combustion gas blowby at initial run-in.

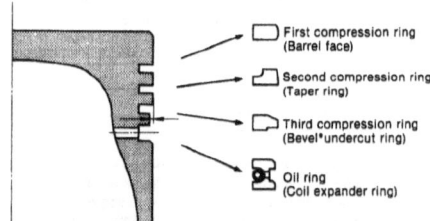

First compression ring (Barrel face)
Second compression ring (Taper ring)
Third compression ring (Bevel*undercut ring)
Oil ring (Coil expander ring)

(2) The second compression ring is a taper ring having a sliding face taper of 30' ~ 1°30'. Since the cylinder liner is straight, and the contact area at initial operation is small, it is easily seated to the cylinder liner.
Moreover, the bottom of the sliding face is sharp, and oil splash is excellent and air-tightness is superb.

Chapter 2 Basic Engine
4. Piston
SM/YSM

(3) Since the third compression ring has a cross-section that combines the shape of a bevel ring and undercut ring, oil splash is superb and oil upflow control is excellent.
The land (A in figure) between the third compression ring and the oil ring has a small 1.0mm outside diameter that effectively improves oil collection and reduces oil consumption.

(4) The oil ring is a chrome-plated coil expander having a small contacting face, and exerts high pressure against the cylinder liner wall. Oil splash at the bottom of the sliding face is excellent, and its oil control effect is high.

4-4.2 Inspection

(1) Piston ring contact
Inspect the piston ring contact, and replace the ring when contact is faulty. Since the oil ring side contact is closely related to oil consumption, it must be checked with particular care.

(2) Measuring the piston ring gap
Insert the piston into the cylinder liner by pushing the piston ring at the head of the piston as shown in the figure, and measure the piston ring gap with a feeler gauge. Measure the gap at a point about 120mm from the top of the cylinder liner.

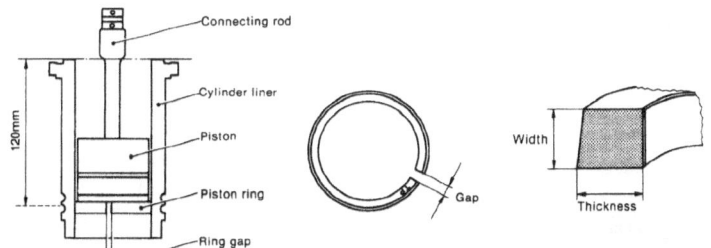

mm (in.)

		YSM8		YSM12	
		Maintenance standard	Wear limit	Maintenance standard	Wear limit
Piston ring (1, 2, 3)	Thickness	3.3 ±0.1 (0.1259 ~ 0.1338)	—	3.6 ±0.1 (0.1378 ~ 0.1457)	—
	Width	$2^{-0.01}_{-0.03}$ (0.0775 ~ 0.0783)	1.90 (0.0748)	$2.5^{-0.01}_{-0.03}$ (0.0972 ~ 0.0980)	2.40 (0.0945)
Oil ring	Thickness	2.6 ±0.2 (0.0945 ~ 0.1102)	—	2.9 ±0.2 (0.1063 ~ 0.1220)	—
	Width	$4.0^{-0.01}_{-0.03}$ (0.1562 ~ 0.1570)	3.90 (0.1535)	$4.0^{-0.01}_{-0.03}$ (0.1562 ~ 0.1570)	3.90 (0.1535)
Piston ring gap (1, 2, 3)		0.2 ~ 0.4 (0.00787 ~ 0.01574)	1.5 (0.0591)	0.3 ~ 0.5 (0.0118 ~ 0.0197)	1.5 (0.0591)
Oil ring gap		0.2 ~ 0.4 (0.00787 ~ 0.01574)	1.5 (0.0591)	0.2 ~ 0.4 (0.00787 ~ 0.01574)	1.5 (0.0591)

(3) Piston ring replacement precautions
When attaching the piston rings to the piston, make sure they are in the correct sequence and face the proper direction.
1) Clean the ring grooves carefully when replacing the rings.
2) When installing the rings, assemble the rings so that the manufacturer's mark near the gap is facing the top of the piston.
3) After assembly, check that the rings move freely in the grooves.

4) The rings must be installed so that the gaps are 180° apart. At this time, be careful that the ring gap is not lined up with the piston side pressure part.

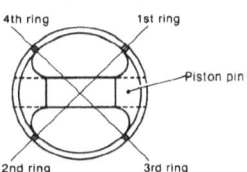

Printed in Japan
A0A1001 8311

Chapter 2 Basic Engine
4. Piston

5) Since the oil ring is equipped with a coil expander, attach it to the piston so that the joint of the ring is shifted 180° from that of the coil expander.

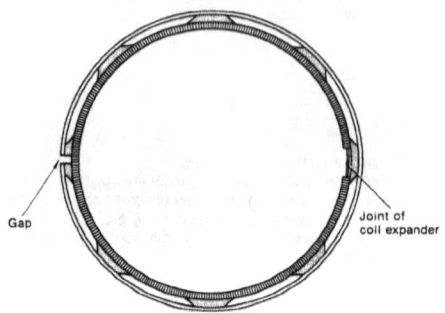

Gap   Joint of coil expander

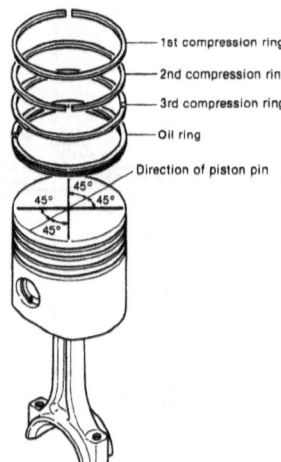

- 1st compression ring
- 2nd compression ring
- 3rd compression ring
- Oil ring
- Direction of piston pin

5. Connecting Rod

5-1 Connecting rod ass'y construction
The connecting rod connects the piston pin and crank pin and transmits the explosive force of the piston to the crankshaft. It is a stamp forging designed for extreme lightness and ample strength against bending. A kelmet bushing split at right angles is installed to the big end of the rod, and a round copper alloy is pressed onto cap.

Pass a test bar through the large end and small end holes of the connecting rod, place the bars on a V-block on a stool and center the large end test bar. Then set the sensor of a dial indicator against the small end test bar and measure twist and parallelity. When the measured value exceeds the wear limit, replace the connecting rod. Twisting and poor parallelity will cause uneven contact of the piston and bushing and shifting of the piston rings, resulting in compression leakage and excessive oil consumption.

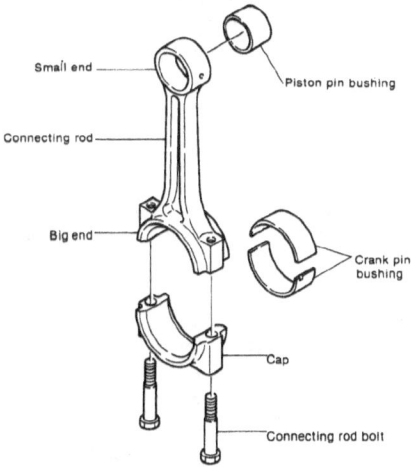

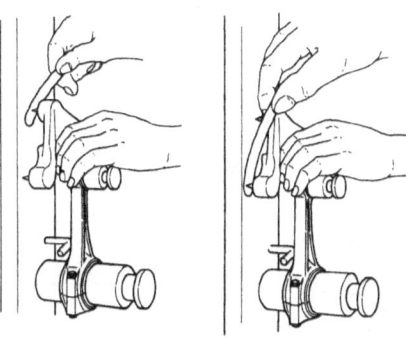

Measuring twist and parallelity

5-2 Inspection
5-2.1 Large and small end twist and parallelity

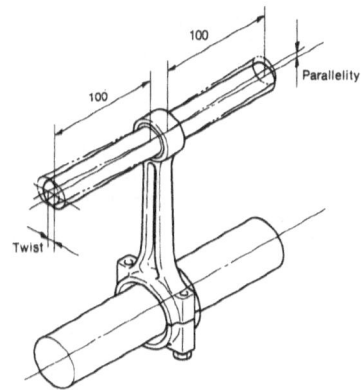

Connecting rod twist and parallelity	mm (in.)
Maintenance standard	0.03/100 or less (0.00118/3.937)
Limit	0.08/100 or less (0.00315/3.937)

5-3 Crank pin bushing
Since the crank pin bushing slides while receiving the load from the piston, an easy-to-replace kelmet bushing with a wear-resistant overlay is used.

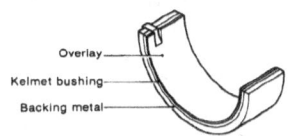

5-3.1 Crank pin bushing inside diameter
Tighten the large end of the connecting rod to the prescribed torque with the connecting rod bolts, and measure the inside diameter of the crank pin bushing. Replace the bushing if the inside diameter exceeds the wear limit or the clearance at the crank pin part exceeds the wear limit.

Chapter 2 Basic Engine
5. Connecting Rod

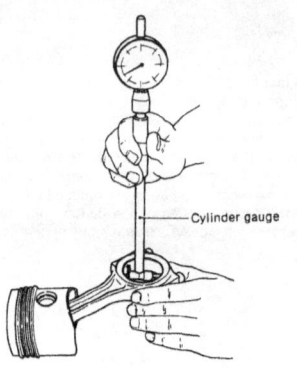

Cylinder gauge

3) Tighten the connecting rod bolt to the prescribed tightening torque.

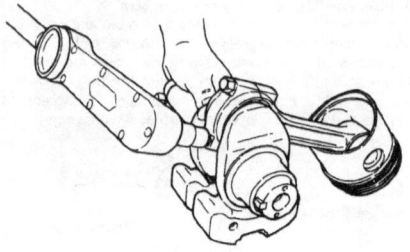

	YSM8	YSM12
Connecting rod tightening torque	4 (28.9)	5.5 (39.8)

kg•m (ft-lb)

mm (in.)

	YSM8		YSM12	
	Maintenance standard	Wear limit	Maintenance standard	Wear limit
Crank pin bushing inside diameter	⌀42.000 ~ 42.042 (1.6535 ~ 1.6551)	⌀42.1 (1.6574)	⌀46.000 ~ 46.042 (1.8110 ~ 1.8126)	⌀46.1 (1.8149)
Crank pin and bushing oil clearance	⌀0.028 ~ 0.086 (0.0011 ~ 0.0033)	⌀0.14 (0.0055)	⌀0.027 ~ 0.090 (0.0010 ~ 0.0035)	⌀0.17 (0.0066)
Connecting rod bolt tightening torque	4kg-m (28.9 ft-lb)		5.5kg-m (39.8 ft-lb)	

NOTE: The crank pin bushing inside diameter must always be measured with the connecting rod bolts tightened to the prescribed torque.

5-3.2 Crank pin and bushing clearance (oil clearance)
Since the oil clearance affects both the durability of the bushing and lubricating oil pressure, it must always be the prescribed value. Replace the bushing when the oil clearance exceeds the wear limit.
(1) Measurement
1) Thoroughly clean the inside surface and crank pin section of the crank pin bushing.
2) Install the connecting rod on the crank pin section of the crankshaft and simultaneously fit a Plasti gauge on the inside surface of the crank pin bearing.

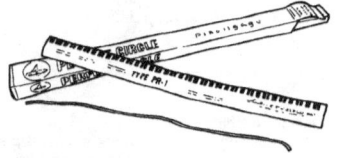

4) Loosen the connecting rod bolt and slowly remove the connecting rod big end cap, then measure the crushed Plasti gauge with a gauge.

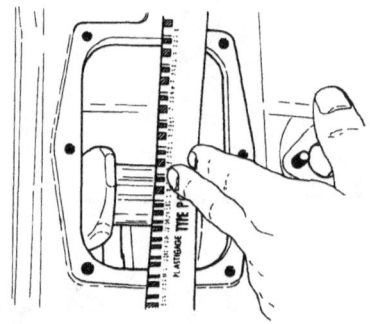

NOTE: Never adjust by shims or machine the crank pin bushing. Always replace the crank pin bushing with a new one.

5) The crank pin and bushing clearance (oil clearance) may also be measured with a micrometer, in addition to measurement with a Plasti gauge. With this method, the outside diameter of the crankshaft crank pin section and the inside diameter of the connecting rod's big end bushing, when the connecting rod bolt has been tightened to the prescribed torque, are

Chapter 2 Basic Engine
5. Connecting Rod

measured, and the difference between the large end bushing inside diameter and crank pin outside diameter is set as the oil clearance.

(2) Measurement precautions
   1) Be careful that the Plasti gauge does not enter the crank pin oil hole.
   2) Be sure that the crankshaft does not turn when tightening the connecting rod bolt.

5-3.3 Crank pin bushing replacement precautions
(1) Thoroughly clean the crank pin bushing and the rear of the crank pin bushing.
(2) Also clean the big end cap, and install the crank pin bushing and check if the bushing contacts the big end cap closely.
(3) When assembling the connecting rod, match the number of the big end section and the big end cap, coat the bolts with engine oil, and alternately tighten the bolts gradually to the prescribed tightening torque. If a torque wrench is not available, put matching marks (torque indication lines) on the bolt head and big end cap before disassembly and tighten the bolts until these two lines are aligned.

5-4 Connecting rod side clearance
After installing the connecting rod on the crankshaft, push the rod to one side and measure the side clearance by inserting a feeler gauge into the gap produced at the other side.
The connecting rod bolts must also be tightened to the prescribed tightening torque in this case.

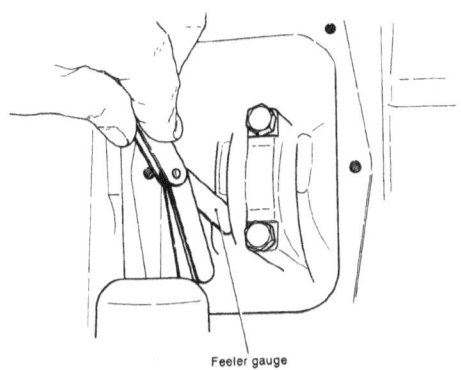
Feeler gauge

	mm (in.)
Connecting rod side clearance	0.25 ±0.1 (0.0059 ~ 0.0137)

5-5 Piston bushing and piston pin
The piston bushing is a round copper alloy bushing driven onto the small end of the connecting rod. During use, the piston pin bushing and piston pin will wear. If this wear becomes excessive, a metallic sound will be produced and the engine will become noisy.

5-5.1
Measure the oil clearance between the piston pin and the piston pin bushing. If it exceeds the prescribed limit, replace the piston pin and its bushing.

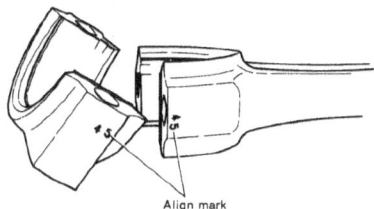
Align mark

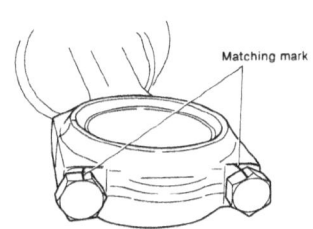
Matching mark

(4) Check that there is no sand or metal particles in the lubricating oil and that the crankshaft is not pitted. Clean the oil holes with particular care.

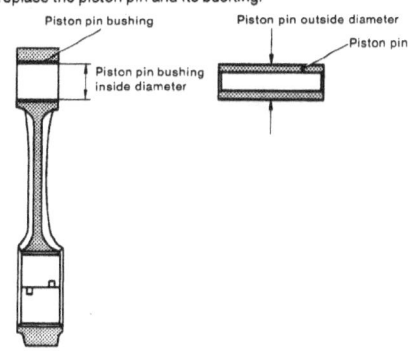
Piston pin bushing | Piston pin outside diameter
Piston pin bushing inside diameter | Piston pin

Chapter 2 Basic Engine
5. Connecting Rod

mm (in.)

	YSM8		YSM12	
	Maintenance standard	Wear limit	Maintenance standard	Wear limit
Piston pin bushing inside diameter	⌀23.025 ~ 23.038 (0.9065 ~ 0.9070)	⌀23.12 (0.9102)	⌀28.025 ~ 28.038 (1.1033 ~ 1.1038)	⌀28.12 (1.1071)
Piston pin and bushing clearance	0.025 ~ 0.047 (0.00098 ~ 0.00185)	0.1 (0.00394)	0.025 ~ 0.048 (0.00098 ~ 0.00189)	0.1 (0.00394)

5-5.2 Replacing the piston pin bushing

(1) When the bushing for the connecting rod piston pin is either worn out or damaged, replace it by using the "piston pin extracting tool" installed on a press.

NOTE: Force the piston pin bushing into position so that its oil hole coincides with the hole on the small end of the connecting rod.

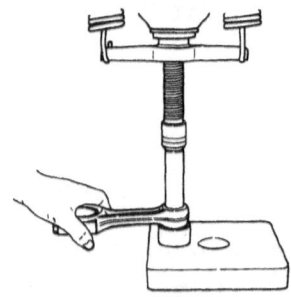

(2) After forcing the piston pin bushing into position, finish the inner surface of the bushing by using a pin honing machine or reamer so that it fits the piston pin to be used.

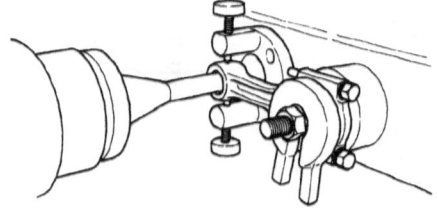

NOTE: Attach the bushing to the piston pin so that a pin, coated with engine oil can be pushed into position with your thumb.

6. Crankshaft

6-1 Crankshaft ass'y and bearing construction

The crankshaft is stamp-forged, and the crank pin and journal sections are high-frequency induction hardened and ground and polished to a high precision finish. Therefore, the contact surface with the bushing is excellent and durability is superb.

The crankshaft is supported by two types of main bearing, namely, the main bearing for the cylinder body and the main bearing for the mounting flange. On one end the flywheel is mounted and on the other end is the crankshaft gear. In order to effect the proper balance, a balancing weight is mounted on each crank arm by serration matching.

The oil passage for the crankshaft journal and pin is shaped (see the diagram) so that the crankshaft can withstand low and high-speed operations.

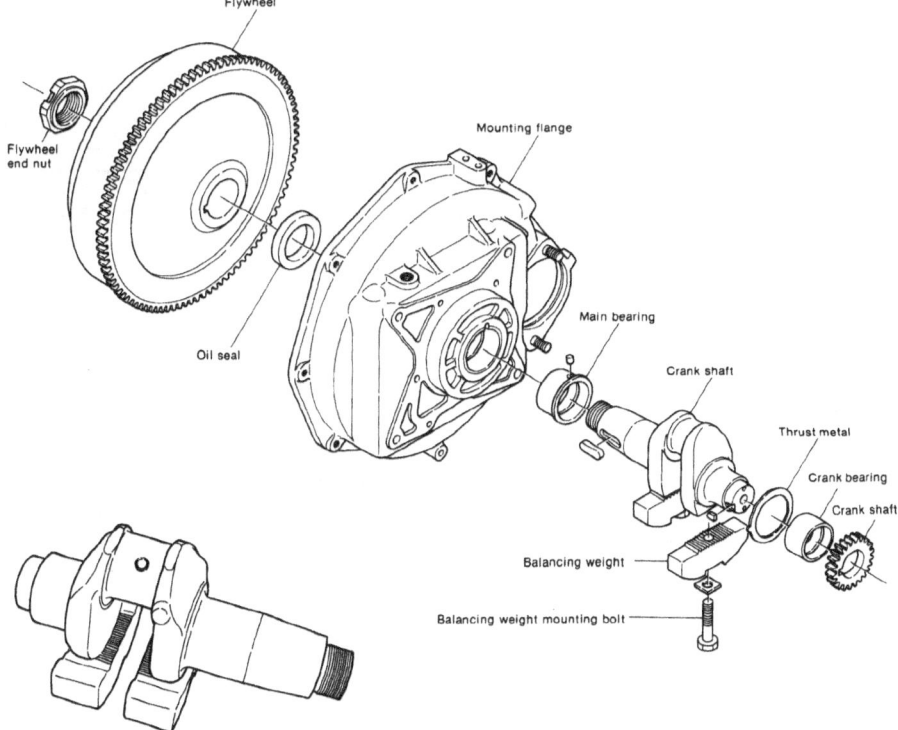

6-2 Inspection
6-2.1 Crank journal and crank pin
(1) Cracking

If cracking of the crank journal or crank pin is suspected, thoroughly clean the crankshaft and perform a color check on the shaft, or run a candle flame over the crankshaft and look for oil seepage from cracks. If any cracks are detected, replace the crankshaft.

(2) Crank pin and crank journal outside diameter measurement.

When the difference between the maximum wear and minimum wear of each bearing section exceeds the wear limit, replace the crankshaft. Also check each bearing section for scoring. If the scoring is light, repair it with emery cloth.

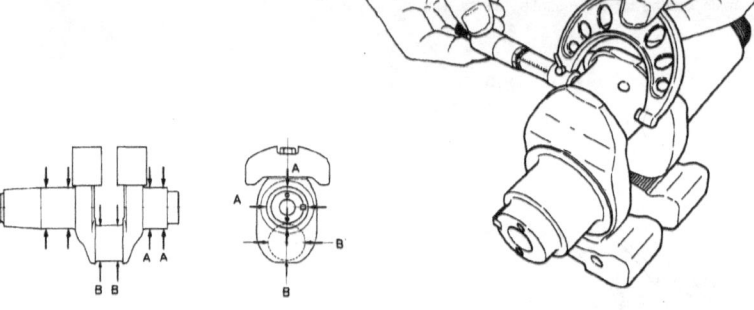

		YSM8		YSM12	
		Maintenance standard	Wear limit	Maintenance standard	Wear limit
Crankshaft journal wear	A A'	⌀43.950 ~ 43.965 (1.7303 ~ 1.7309)	⌀43.85 (1.7264)	⌀51.952 ~ 51.973 (2.0454 ~ 2.0462)	⌀51.85 (2.0413)
Crank pin wear	B B'	⌀41.956 ~ 41.972 (1.6518 ~ 1.6524)	⌀41.87 (1.6484)	⌀45.952 ~ 45.973 (1.8091 ~ 1.8100)	⌀44.87 (1.7665)
Crank journal and bushing oil clearance	Gear side	0.035 ~ 0.105 (0.0014 ~ 0.0041)	0.17 (0.0067)	0.027 ~ 0.088 (0.0011 ~ 0.0035)	0.18 (0.0071)
	Flywheel side	0.045 ~ 0.095 (0.0018 ~ 0.0037)	0.17 (0.0067)	0.037 ~ 0.092 (0.0015 ~ 0.0036)	0.18 (0.0071)
Crank pin and crank pin bushing oil clearance		0.028 ~ 0.086 (0.0011 ~ 0.0034)	0.14 (0.0055)	0.027 ~ 0.090 (0.0011 ~ 0.0035)	0.17 (0.0067)

6-3 Crankshaft side gap
6-3.1 Side gap
The clearance in the axial direction after the crankshaft has been assembled is called the side gap.
If the side gap is too large, contact with pistons will be uneven, the clutch disengagement position will change, and other troubles will occur. If it is too small, the crankshaft sliding resistance will increase and cranking will become stiff.

6-3.2 Measuring side gap
Move the crankshaft to one side, attach dial gauge to the crankshaft tip, and measure the clearance between the crankshaft and the thrust bearing metal. Or, using a thickness gauge, measure the clearance between the thrust bearing metal on the housing side of the main shaft and the crankshaft. If the clearance exceeds the specified limit, replace the thrust bearing metal.

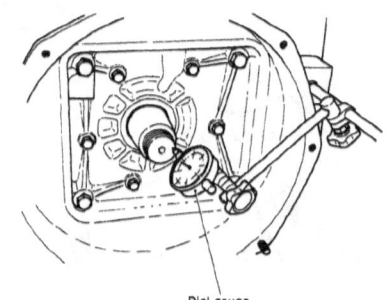

Dial gauge

Chapter 2 Basic Engine
6. Crankshaft

6-3.3 Side gap maintenance standard and wear limit
mm (in.)

	YSM8		YSM12	
	Maintenance standard	Wear limit	Maintenance standard	Wear limit
Crank shaft side gap	0.155~0.315 (0.0061~ 0.0124)	0.45 (0.0177)	0.114~0.294 (0.0045~ 0.0116)	0.45 (0.0177)

6-4 Main bearing
6-4.1 Construction
The main shaft bearing metal is round, made of a copper-lead series sintered alloy, and is highly wear resistant. As for the gear side main shaft bearing metal, the crank bearing metal and the thrust bearing metal are installed separately. With the flywheel side main shaft bearing metal, the above two bearing metals are installed together.

6-4.2 Inspecting the crank bearing
(1) Check the crank bearing metal for scaling, deposited metal and seizure. Also check the condition of the contact surface. If defects are found, replace.
If the bearing metal contact is too unsymmetrical, carefully check all related component parts which might be responsible, and take proper measures.
(2) Determine the oil clearance by measuring the inside diameter of the crankshaft bearing and the outside diameter of the crankshaft.

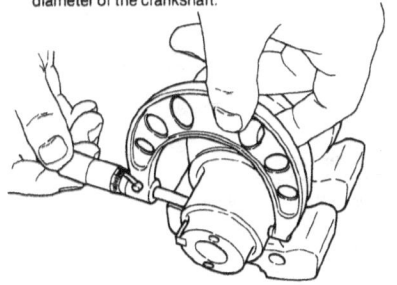

NOTE: Measure the crank bearing at the four points shown in the figure and replace the bearing if the wear limit is exceeded at any of these points.

 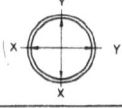

mm (in.)

		YSM8		YSM12	
		Maintenance standard	Wear limit	Maintenance standard	Wear limit
Flywheel side	Main bearing inside diameter	⌀44.010 ~ 44.045 (1.7327 ~ 1.7341)	⌀44.14 (1.7378)	⌀52.010 ~ 52.040 (2.0476 ~ 2.0488)	⌀52.14 (2.0528)
	Crankshaft journal outside diameter	⌀43.950 ~ 43.965 (1.7303 ~ 1.7309)	⌀43.85 (1.7264)	⌀51.952 ~ 51.973 (2.0847 ~ 2.0462)	⌀51.85 (2.0413)
	Oil clearance	0.045 ~ 0.095 (0.0018 ~ 0.0037)	0.17 (0.0067)	0.037 ~ 0.088 (0.0015 ~ 0.0036)	0.18 (0.0071)
Opposite side of flywheel	Main bearing inside diameter	⌀44.000 ~ 44.055 (1.7323 ~ 1.7344)	⌀44.14 (1.7378)	⌀52.000 ~ 52.060 (2.0472 ~ 2.0496)	⌀44.14 (1.7378)
	Crankshaft journal ouside diameter	⌀43.950 ~ 43.965 (1.7303 ~ 1.7309)	⌀43.85 (1.7264)	⌀51.952 ~ 51.973 (2.0847 ~ 2.0462)	⌀51.85 (2.0413)
	Oil clearance	0.035 ~ 0.105 (0.0014 ~ 0.0041)	0.17 (0.0067)	0.027 ~ 0.108 (0.0011 ~ 0.0043)	0.18 (0.0071)

Chapter 2 Basic Engine
6. Crankshaft

6-4.3 Inspecting the thrust metal
Measure the thickness of the thrust metal and replace the metal when wear exceeds the wear limit.

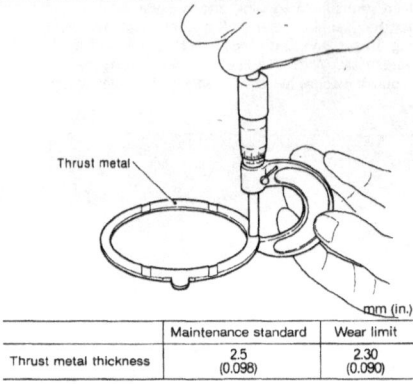

	Maintenance standard	Wear limit
Thrust metal thickness	2.5 (0.098)	2.30 (0.090)

6-4.4 Replacing the crank bearing
Since the crank bearings at both ends of the crankshaft are pressed to the cylinder block and bearing housing with a press, a force of approximately 1.0 ~ 1.5 tons (2200 ~ 3300 lbs) is required to remove them.
Moreover, since the crankshaft will not rotate smoothly and other trouble may occur if the bearing is distorted, it must always be installed with the special tool.

(1) Removal
Assemble the spacer and plate A as shown in the figure, place the puller/extractor against the bearing from the opposite end and pull the bearing by tightening the nut of the special tool. Remove the oil seal before pulling the bearing pressed to the bearing housing.

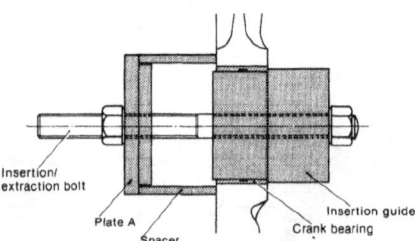

(2) Installation
Coat the outside of the bearing with oil and align the positions of the bearing oil holes. Then press in plate B until it contacts the cylinder block or bearing housing, using the puller/extractor as a guide, as shown in the figure.

After inserting the bearing, measure its outside diameter. If the bearing is distorted, remove it again and replace it with a new bearing.

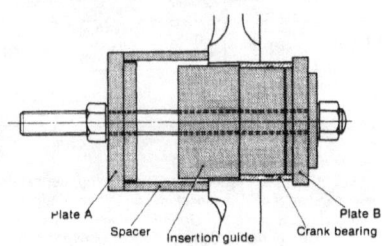

(3) Crank bearing installation precautions
1) Pay careful attention to the crank bearing insertion direction. Insert the bearing so that the side with the outside fillet is at the outside.
2) Align the oil hole of the crank bearing with the oil holes of the cylinder block and bearing housing.
3) After inserting the crank bearing, check that the crankshaft rotates easily with the thrust metal and bearing housing installed.
4) Be careful that the bearing is not tilted during insertion.

6-5 Crankshaft oil seal
6-5.1 Oil seal type and size
T-type oil seal is employed at the flywheel end of the crankshaft.

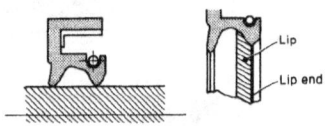

	Size	Part No.
YSM8	44 · 60 · 9	104211-02220
YSM12	52 · 70 · 9	104511-02220

6-5.2 Oil seal insertion precautions
(1) Clean the inside of the housing hole, ascertaining that the hole was not dented when the seal was removed.
(2) Be sure that the insertion direction of the oil seal is correct. Insert so that the main lip mounting the spring is on the inside (oil side).

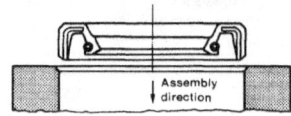

Chapter 2 Basic Engine
6. Crankshaft

(3) Insert the oil seal with a press. However, when unavoidable, the seal may be installed by tapping the entire periphery of the seal with a hammer, using a block. In this case, be careful that the oil seal is not tilted.
Never tap the oil seal directly.

GOOD

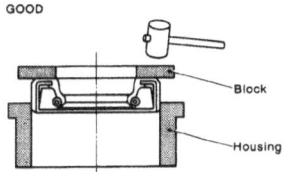

Block
Housing

BAD

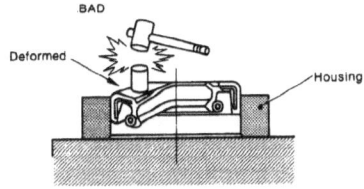

Deformed
Housing

7. Camshaft

7-1 Construction

The camshaft is made of carbon steel. The bearings on the gear case side are ball bearings and its clutch side is directly borne by the block. The camshaft end is provided with a slit for inserting the lubricating oil pump. Its gear side is constructed so that the cam for driving the fuel injection pump can be mounted on it. The cam and its bearings have been treated with induction hardening to give them high hardness, better wear resistance and toughness.

Since the intake and exhaust cam profile is a parabolic acceleration cam with a buffering curve, movement of the valve at high speed is smooth, improving the durability of the intake and exhaust valve seats.

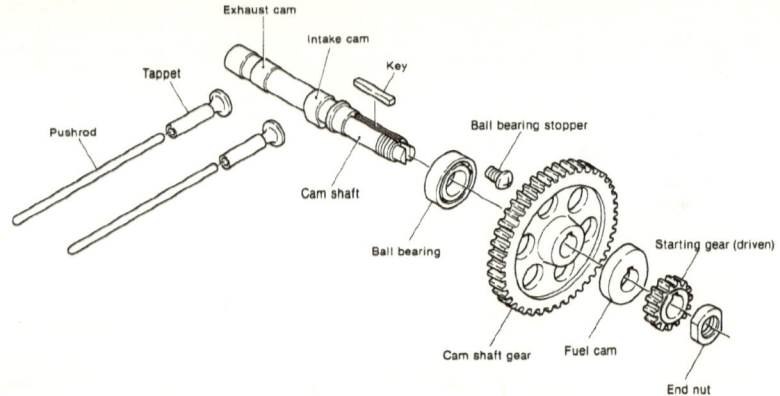

7-2 Valve curve

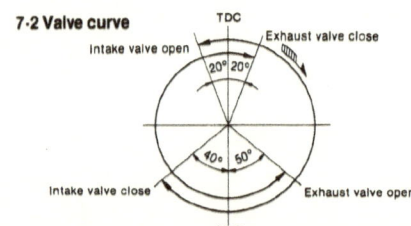

Intake and exhaust valve head clearance	0.20mm (0.00787in.)
Intake valve open b. TDC	20°
Intake valve close a. BDC	40°
Exhaust valve open b. BDC	50°
Exhaust valve close a. TDC	20°

7-3 Inspection

Since the cam surface is tempered and ground, there is almost no wear. However, measure the height of the intake and exhaust cams, and replace the camshaft when the measured value exceeds the wear limit.

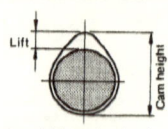
Intake and exhaust cam

Fuel cam

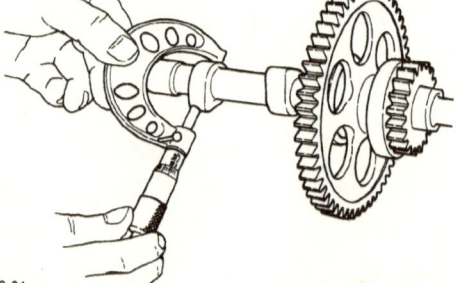

Chapter 2 Basic Engine
7. Camshaft

mm (in.)

		YSM8		YSM12	
		Maintenance standard	Wear limit	Maintenance standard	Wear limit
Camshaft height	Intake and exhaust cam	30.8 (1.2125)	30.5 (1.2007)	34.5 (1.3582)	34.2 (1.3464)
	Fuel cam	45 (1.771)	44.9 (1.7677)	60 (2.3622)	59.9 (2.3582)

7-4 Camshaft ball bearing

The camshaft bearing is a single row deep groove ball bearing. The construction and material of this ball bearing such that it can withstand the radial load, thrust loads in both directions, and a combination of both these loads. Replace the main camshaft bearing if their components have the following defects: balls, inner or outer race, cage, etc., have flaws, impressions, etc.; components that will not rotate smoothly; components that produce noise; components that loose; components that have discolored due to seizure; etc.
1. When the bearings are rotated by hand, they should not rang up anywhere.
2. When they are rotated rapidly, they should not produce any abnormal sound.

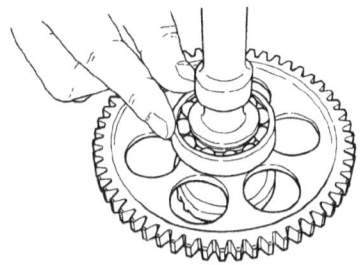

7-5 Tappets

These mushroom type tappets feature a special iron casting with chill-hardened contact surfaces for high wear resistance. The center of the cam surface width and the center of the tappet are offset to prevent eccentric wear of the contact surface.

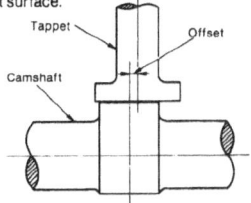

7-5.1 Tappet disassembly precautions
Intake and exhaust must be clearly indicated when disassembling the camshaft and tappets.

7-5.2 Tappet stem wear and contact
Measure the outside diameter of the tappet stem, and replace the tappet when the wear limit is exceeded or contact is uneven.

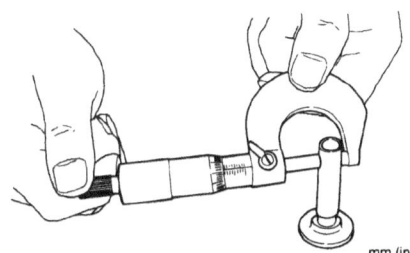

mm (in.)

	YSM8		YSM12	
	Maintenance standard	Wear limit	Maintenance standard	Wear limit
Outside diameter of tappet stem	ø9.980 ~ 9.995 (0.39291 ~ 0.39350)	9.95 (0.39173)	ø10.980 ~ 10.995 (0.43228 ~ 0.43287)	10.95 (0.43110)
Inside diameter of tappet guide (cylinder block)	ø10.000 ~ 10.027 (0.3937 ~ 0.39476)	—	ø11.000 ~ 11.027 (0.43307 ~ 0.43413)	—
Oil clearance	ø0.005 ~ 0.047 (0.00019 ~ 0.00185)	0.1 (0.00393)	ø0.005 ~ 0.047 (0.00019 ~ 0.00185)	0.1 (0.00393)

Chapter 2 Basic Engine
7. Camshaft

7-5.3 Tappet and cam contact surface
Since the tappet and cam are offset, the tappet rotates in an up and down movement during operation, so there is no uneven contact.
Since eccentric wear will occur if cam tappet contact is poor, replace the tappet if there is any uneven contact or deformation.

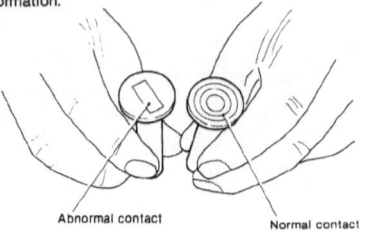

Abnormal contact   Normal contact

NOTE: If the sliding surface of the tappet and the cam is damaged, check the camshaft also.

7-6 Push rods
The push rods are sufficiently rigid and strong to prevent bending.
Place the push rod on a stool or flat surface and measure the clearance between the center of the push rod and the flat surface, and replace the push rod if the wear limit is exceeded.

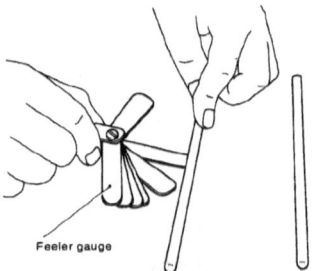

Feeler gauge

Check both ends for wear and peeling, and replace the push rod if faulty.

mm(in.)

	Maintenance standard	Wear limit
Push rod bend	0.03 or less (0.00118 or less)	0.3 (0.0118)

7-7 Fuel cam assembly precautions
Install the fuel cam by aligning it with the key of the camshaft. If the installation direction is not correct, the fuel injection timing will be considerably off and the engine will not start.
When assembling the fuel cam, be sure that the "0" mark side of the cam is opposite the camshaft gear.

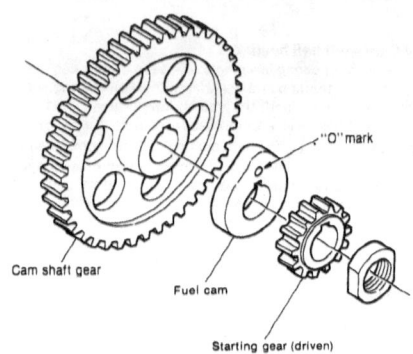

Cam shaft gear   Fuel cam   "O" mark   Starting gear (driven)

8. Timing Gear

8-1 Timing gear train construction

The gear case is cast with the cylinder body in a monoblock casting and is formed by the cylinder side cover. It is mounted along with the lubricating oil pump, lubricating oil filter, fuel control device and P.T.O. shaft (which drives the fuel feed pump), the cooling water pump and alternator. The camshaft gear is a steel forging with a hardened tooth face that has been precision, ground and finished. It is driven by the crank gear which is mounted on the crankshaft.

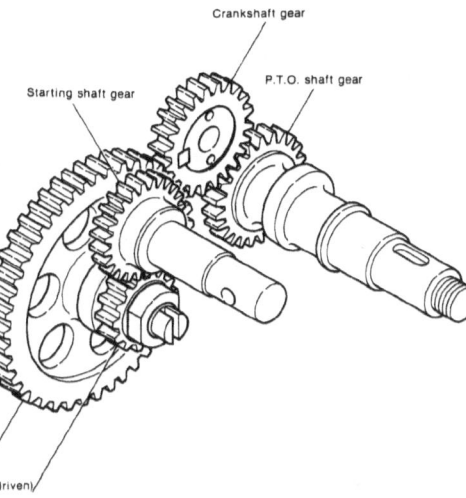

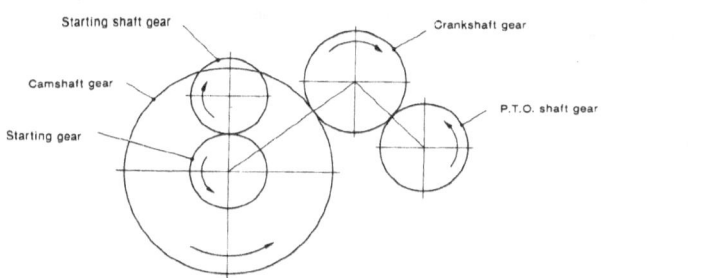

		YSM8				YSM12		
	Module	Number of teeth	Tooth width	Center-to-center distance	Module	Number of teeth	Tooth width	Center-to-center distance
P.T.O. shaft gear	2.5	23	10.5 (0.4134)	P.T.O. shaft gear ~ Crankshaft gear ...58 (2.2835) Crankshaft gear ~ Camshaft gear ...86.75 (3.4154) Starting gear ~ Starting shaft gear ...43.225 (1.7018)	2.5	23	10.5 (0.4134)	P.T.O. shaft gear ~ Crankshaft gear ...62.5 (2.4606) Crankshaft gear ~ Camshaft gear ...101.25 (3.9862) Starting gear ~ Starting shaft gear ...50 (1.9685)
Crankshaft gear	2.5	23	11 (0.4331)		2.5	27	11 (0.4331)	
Camshaft gear	2.5	46	10 (0.3937)		2.5	54	11 (0.4331)	
Starting gear (driven)	2.5	15	10 (0.3937)		2.5	20	10 (0.3937)	
Starting shaft gear	2.5	20	9.7 (0.3819)		2.5	20	9.7 (0.3819)	

8-2 Disassembly and reassembly
Timing mark
A timing mark is provided on the crankshaft gear and camshaft gear to adjust the timing between opening and closing of the intake and exhaust valves and fuel injection when the piston is operated.
Always check that these timing marks are aligned when disassembling and reassembling the timing gear.

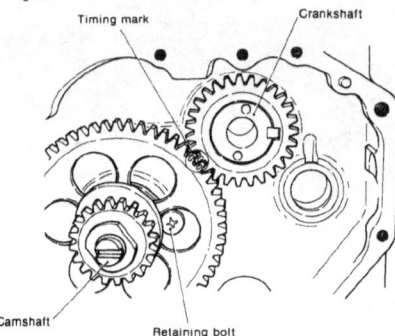

8-3 Inspection
8-3.1 Backlash
Unsuitable backlash will cause excessive wear or damage at the tooth top and abnormal noise during operation. Moreover, in extreme cases, the valve and fuel injection timing will deviate and the engine will not run smoothly.

When the backlash exceeds the wear limit, repair or replace the gears as a set.

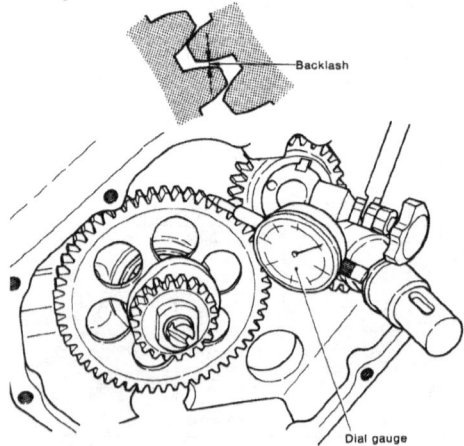

mm (in.)

	Maintenance standard	Wear limit
Crankshaft gear and camshaft gear backlash	0.08 ~ 0.16 (0.0031 ~ 0.0062)	0.3 (0.0118)
Crankshaft gear and P.T.O.shaft gear backlash		

Measuring backlash
(1) Lock one of the two gears to be measured and measure the amount of movement of the other gear by placing a dial gauge on the tooth surface.
(2) Insert a piece of quality solder between the gears to be measured and turn the gears. The backlash can be measured by measuring the thickness of the crushed part of the solder.

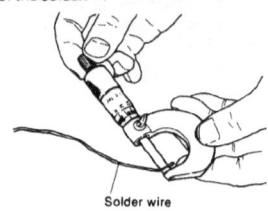
Solder wire

8-3.2 Inspecting the gear tooth surface
Check the tooth surface for damage caused by pitching and check tooth contact. Repair if the damage is light. Also inspect the gears for cracking and corrosion.
When gear noise becomes high because of wear or damage, replace the gears as a set.

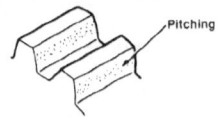
Pitching

CHAPTER 3
FUEL SYSTEM

1. Construction 3-1
2. Injection Pump 3-2
3. Injection Nozzle 3-15
4. Fuel Filter 3-20
5. Fuel Feed Pump 3-21
6. Fuel Tank 3-24

Chapter 3 Fuel System

1. Construction

The fuel system consists mainly of an injection pump, injection pipe, and an injection nozzle, plus a fuel tank, feed pump, fuel filter and other associated parts. The injection pump is driven by a fuel cam mounted on one end of the camshaft and is controlled by a governor. Fuel stored in the fuel tank is fed to the fuel filter through the feed pump. (The feed pump is indispensable when the fuel tank is installed lower than the injection pump.)

Dirt and other impurities in the fuel are removed by the filter and the clean fuel is sent to the injection pump, which applies the necessary pressure for injection to the fuel and atomizes the fuel by passing it through the injection nozzle. The injection pump also controls the amount of fuel injected and the injection timing depending on the engine load and speed by means of a governor.

The injection pump feeds the fuel to the injection nozzle through a high pressure pipe. The pressurized fuel is atomized and injected by the injection nozzle into the precombustion chamber.

Fuel that overflows the injection nozzle is returned to the fuel filter through the fuel return pipe. The quality of the equipment and parts comprising the fuel injection system directly affects combustion performance and has a considerable effect on engine performance. Therefore, this system must be inspected and serviced regularly to ensure top performance.

1-1 Fuel system diagram

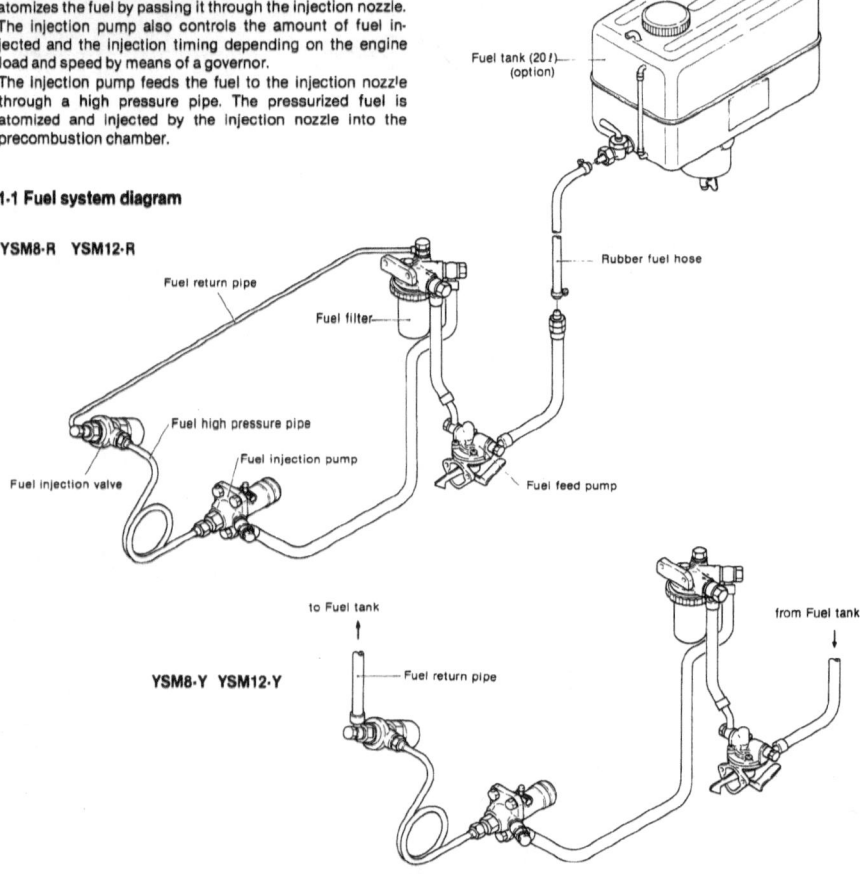

2. Injection Pump

The injection pump is the most important part of the fuel system. This pump feeds the proper amount of fuel to the engine at the proper time in accordance with the engine load.

This engine uses a Bosch type injection pump. It is designed and manufactured by Yanmar, and is ideal for the fuel system of this engine.

Since the injection pump is subjected to extremely high pressures and must be accurate as well as deformation and wear-free, stringently selected materials are used and precision-finished after undergoing heat treatment.

The injection pump must be handled carefully. Since the delivery valve and delivery valve holder and the plunger and plunger barrel are lapped, they must be changed as a pair.

2-1 Construction

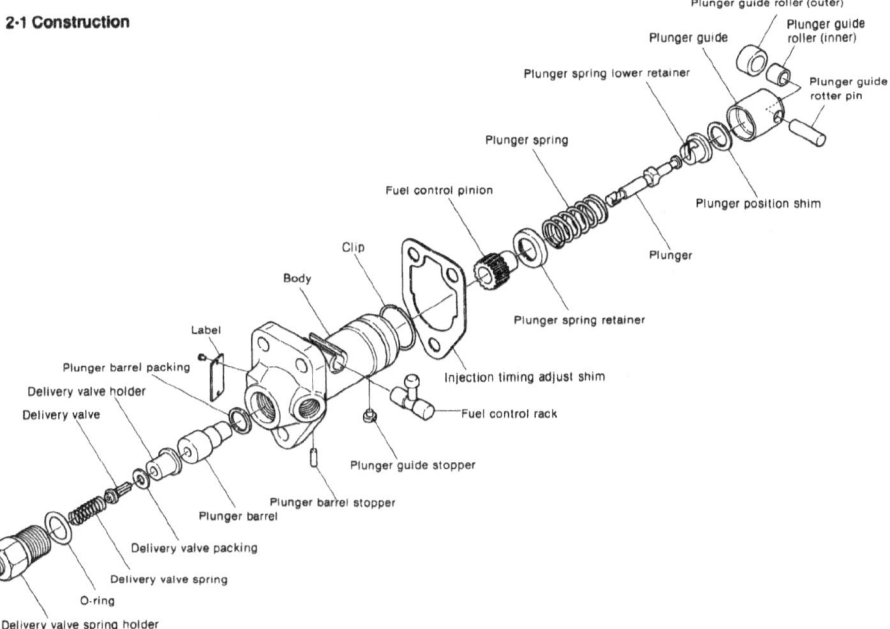

Chapter 3 Fuel System
2. Injection Pump

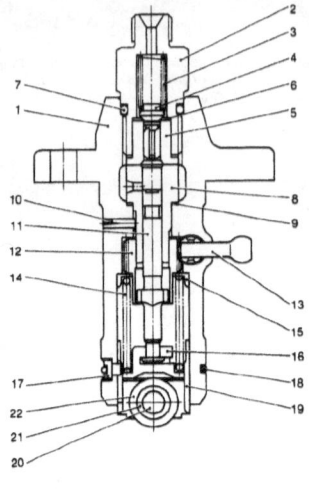

1. Body
2. Delivery valve spring holder
3. Delivery valve spring
4. Delivery valve
5. Delivery valve holder
6. Delivery valve packing
7. O-ring
8. Plunger barrel
9. Plunger barrel packing
10. Plunger barrel stopper
11. Plunger
12. Fuel control pinion
13. Fuel control rack
14. Plunger spring
15. Plunger spring retainer
16. Plunger spring lower retainer
17. Plunger guide stopper
18. Clip
19. Plunger guide
20. Plunger guide roller pin
21. Plunger guide roller (inner)
22. Plunger guide roller (outer)

2-2 Specifications

mm (in.)

		YSM8-R(Y)	YSM12-R(Y)
Fuel cam lift		7 (0.2756)	
Plunger	Diamater × stroke	ø6 × 7 (0.2362 × 0.2756)	
	Configuration	(Injection amount increases at starting)	
Fuel adjusting rack sliding resistance (pump standstill)		less than 60 (0.132)	
Plunger upper clearance (mounting dimension 76.0 ±0.05mm)		1.0 (0.0394)	
Plunger position shim		0.1, 0.2, 0.3 (0.0394, 0.0787, 0.1181) (3 kinds)	
Plunger spring	Free length	35.0 (1.3780)	
	Mounted length	27.0 (1.0630)	
	Mounting load	10.4 kg (22.9280lb.)	
Delivery valve spring	Free length	31.0 (1.2205)	
	Mounted length	23.96 (0.9433)	
	Mounting load	2.885 kg (6.3603 lb.)	

2·3 Fuel Injection pump

The fuel injection pump force-feeds the fuel by means of the plunger (1) which operates at a constant stroke. Since the plunger is lap fitted into the plunger barrel (2) for super precison, it can be replaced only as a set. The cylindrical surface of the plunger has an obliquely cut lead (3) and a groove which connects the lead to the plunger head. The plunger has an intake hole (4) through which the fuel passes and is force-fed by the plunger. Then the fuel opens the delivery valve (5), goes through the fuel injection tube, and is injected into the spiral-vortex type pre-combustion chamber from the injection valve. The plunger is fitted with the fuel control gear (6), and its flange (7) fits into the groove which is longitudinally cut into the inner surface of the lower end of the control gear. The fuel control gear is in mesh with the fuel control rack, the motion of which rotates the plunger to constantly vary the amount of fuel injected from zero to maximum.

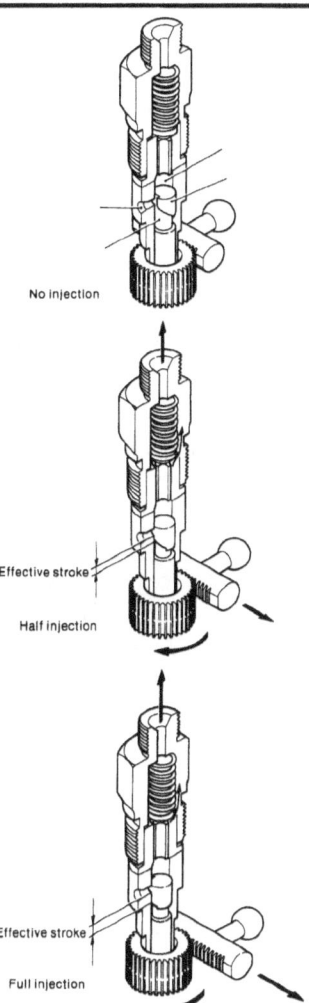

No injection

Effective stroke
Half injection

Effective stroke
Full injection

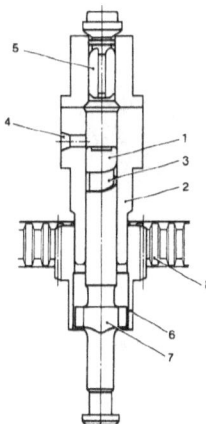

2·3.1 Fuel control

When the plunger (1) is at bottom dead center, the oil, which comes in through the oil hole, fills the delivery chamber (3) to above the plunger; the oil pressure then builds up as the plunger rises and closes the oil hole, and by opening the delivery valve, is force-fed toward the fuel injection tube. As the plunger, pushed by the plunger guide, rises further, the pressure of the oil between the delivery chamber and the nozzle also increases. When this oil pressure builds up to 155 to 165 kg/cm^2, the nozzle opens, and the fuel oil is injected into the spiral vortex type combustion chamber. However, if the plunger keeps rising and the lead groove (4) lines up with the oil hole (2), the oil under high pressure in the delivery chamber passes the lead from the longitudinal groove up the lead and is driven back into the suction chamber from the oil hole. At the same force feeding of the fuel is suspended.

As a result of the above action, the plunger is rotated by the fuel control rack and the angle of this rotation changes the effective stroke of the plunger and controls the discharge of the pump. Also, when the fuel control rack lines up the longitudinal groove on the plunger with the oil hole, the oil hole does not close, despite the rise of the plunger, but rather the fuel is driven back to the suction chamber. As a result the fuel is not force-fed but the amount of injection

Chapter 3 Fuel System
2. Injection Pump

is reduced to zero. At this time the fuel control rack is at the cylinder side end; when it reaches the opposite side end the maximum amount of fuel is injected. Before the maximum injection level is reached, the fuel injection control shaft regulates the amount of fuel injected to the normal operation level.

2-3.2 Action of the delivery valve and the sucking-back of fuel

The delivery valve on top of the plunger prevents the fuel within the injection tube from flowing backward toward the plunger side and also serves to suck back the fuel to prevent the backward dripping of the nozzle valve. When the notch (lead) of the plunger comes up to the oil hole of the plunger barrel, the feeding pressure acting on the fuel oil drops, and the delivery valve falls due to the force of the spring. After the sucking-back collar (1) has first shut off the fuel injection tube and the delivery chamber the delivery valve drops further until it comes into contact with the seat surface. (2) corresponding to the amount of fall (i.e., increase in volume), the fuel oil pressure within the injection tube drops, speeding up the closure of the nozzle valve, and sucking up the fuel before it drips back, This enhances the durability of the nozzle and improves fuel oil combustion.

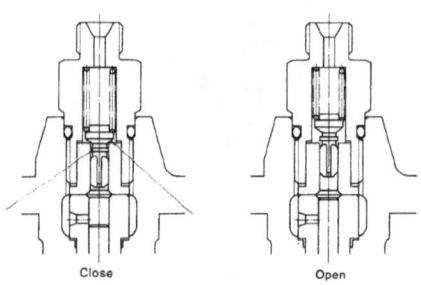

Action of the delivery valve

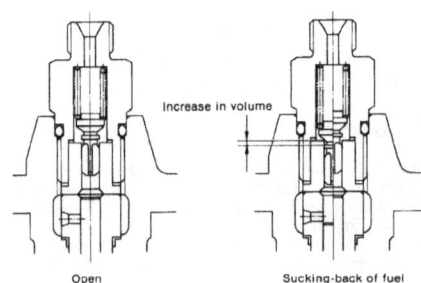

Function of the delivery valve

2-4 Disassembly
2-4.1 Removal of Fuel Injection Pump
(1) Remove the parts in the follming order.
   1) Fuel injection pipe and fuel pipe
   2) Oil port
   3) Fuel limiter end nut

NOTE: After removing the fuel oil pipe, screw in the pipe-connecting bolt so that no dust gets into the pump.

(2) Loosen the fuel limiter lock nut, and pull out the fuel limiter about 10 mm.
(3) Loosen the four fuel injection pump lock nuts evenly and remove the pump.

NOTE: During removal be careful not to bump the fuel injection rack and the full injection timing plate against the cylinder block.

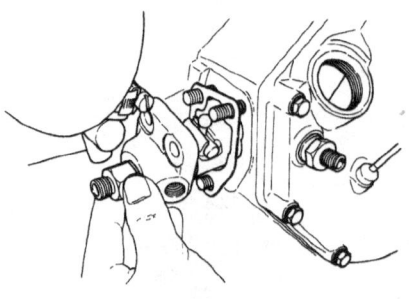

Pump removal

2-4.2 Disassembly of fuel injection pump

NOTE: 1) Before disassembly wash the pump in clean oil, and after assembly arrange all parts carefully.
2) Make sure the work area is exceptionally clean.

(1) Remove the plunger guide stopper pin with needle nose pliers.

Chapter 3 Fuel System
2. Injection Pump
SM/YSM

(2) Remove the plunger guide stopper.
The stopper can be removed by pushing the plunger guide down with the palm of your hand.
(3) Remove the plunger guide.
NOTE: Be careful not to lose the plunger adjusting shim which is located inside the plunger guide.

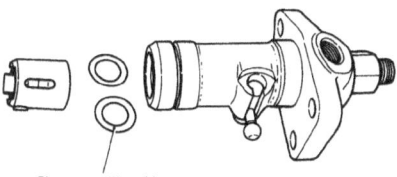

Plunger position shim

(4) Remove the plunger and plunger spring lower retainer be careful not to damage the plunger.
(5) Remove the plunger spring, fuel control pinion and plunger spring upper retainer, using your fingers or tweezers.

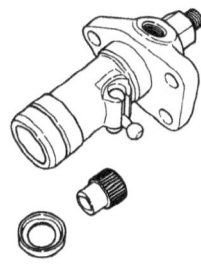

(6) Remove the fuel control rack.
(7) Remove the delivery valve holder; be careful not to damage the O-ring.
(8) Remove the delivery valve spring.
(9) Remove the delivery valve.

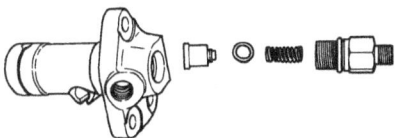

(10) Remove the plunger barrel by pushing it toward the delivery valve side.

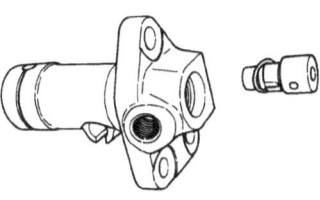

NOTE: 1. Line up the plunger valve and the plunger, and put them in order.
2. Immerse the delivery valve, plunger, etc. in clean oil.
3. Do not loosen or remove the injection control plate, etc.

2-5 Inspecting injection pump parts

2-5.1 Rinse each component part in clean light oil before inspecting it.

NOTE: Do not touch the sliding surface of the plunger and the delivery valve with your fingers during handling.

2-5.2 Control rack and pinion
(1) Check control rack teeth and sliding surface for damage and abnormalities. If found, replace.
NOTE: When replacing control rack, adjust fuel discharge amount with a fuel injection pump tester and stamp a rack mark.
(2) Replace pinion if teeth are damaged or worn unevenly.

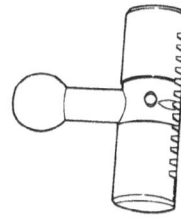 

Chapter 3 Fuel System
2. Injection Pump _____ SM/YSM

2-5.3 Plunger

(1) Inspect the plunger for wear, scoring and discoloration around the lead. If any problems are found, conduct a pressure test and replace the plunger and plunger barrel assembly.

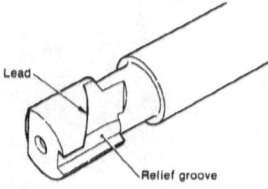

(2) Inspect the outside sliding surface of the plunger with a magnifying glass. Lap or replace the plunger and plunger barrel assembly when corrosion, hairline cracks, staining and/or scoring are detected.
(3) Check the clearance between the plunger collar and control pinion groove. Replace these parts when wear exceeds the specified limit.
(4) After cleaning the plunger, tilt it approximately 60°, as shown in the figure, and slowly slide it down. Repeat this several times while rotating the plunger. The plunger should slide slowly and smoothly. If it slides too quickly, or binds along the way, repair or replace it.

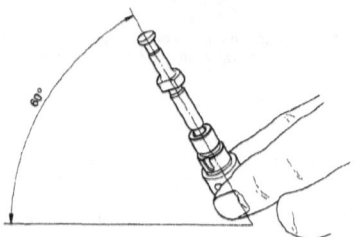

2-5.4 Delivery valve

(1) Replace the delivery valve if the return collar and seat are scored, dented or worn.

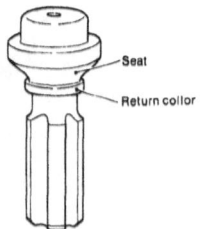

(2) Raise the delivery valve and put a finger over the hole on the valve seat bottom. Let go of the delivery valve. If it sinks quickly and stops at the position where the suck-back collar closes the valve seat hole, the delivery valve may be considered normal. If this is not the case, replace the delivery valve as a set.

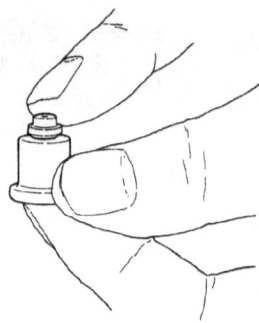

(3) Place your finger over the hole in the bottom of the valve seat and insert the valve into the valve body. If the valve returns to its original position when you remove your finger, the valve is okay. If some defect is found, replace with a new valve.
(4) If the valve closes completely by its own weight when you remove your finger from the hole on the bottom of the valve seat, the valve is okay. If it doesn't close perfectly replace with a new valve.

NOTE: When using a brand-new set, wash off the rust-proof oil with clean oil or gasoline. Then, wash once more with clean oil, and follow the steps outlined above.

2-5.5 Plunger spring and delivery valve spring

Inspect the plunger spring and delivery valve spring for fractured coils, rust, inclination and permanent strain. Replace the spring when faulty. (See 2-2)

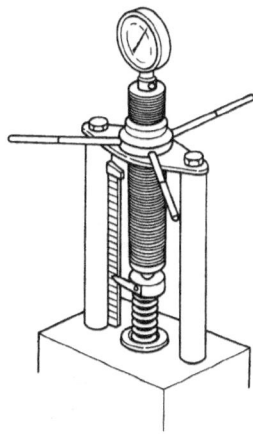

2-6 Assembling the fuel injection pump

NOTE: 1. After inspection, divide the components into two groups, i.e. the components to be replaced, and those that are reusable. Rinse the components and store the two groups separately.
2. Replace the packing with a new one.

(1) While lining up the plunger barrel positioning groove with the dowel of the main unit, attach the plunger barrel to the main unit.

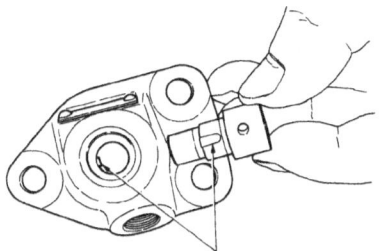

Attaching the plunger barrel to the main unit

(2) Attach the delivery valve seat and the delivery valve to the main unit.

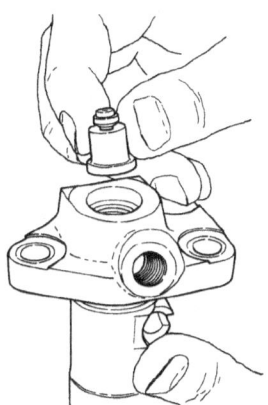

Attaching the delivery valve to the main unit

2-5.6 Plunger guide

Check the tappet roller (inside and outside) and roller pin for damage and uneven wear, and replace if required.
Measure the clearance between the plunger and plunger guide. If the clearance exceeds the limit, replace.

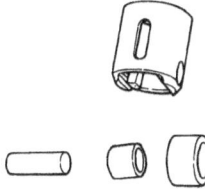

mm (in.)

Clearance limit	0.3 (0.0118)

NOTE: If the delivery valve tip projects noticeably above the top of the main unit of the pump, the plunger barrel has been installed incorrectly, and must be re-attached.

Chapter 3 Fuel System
2. Injection Pump

(3) Attach the delivery valve packing and the delivery valve spring to the main unit and carefully tighten the delivery valve holder.

NOTE: Tighten the delivery valve holder with a torque wrench after attaching the plunger and while checking the fuel control rack for sliding motion.

kg-cm (lb-ft)

Tightening torque	400 to 450 (28.92 ~ 32.54)

(4) With the matching mark of the fuel control rack directed towards the lower part of the main unit of the pump, attach the fuel control rack to the main unit.

NOTE: Make sure the fuel control rack moves smoothly along its entire stroke.

(5) By aligning the matching mark on the fuel control pinion with that on the fuel control rack, attach the fuel control pinion to the main unit.

NOTE: After attaching the fuel control pinion to the main unit, check its meshing by moving the fuel control rack.

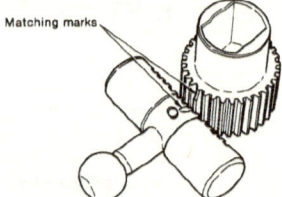

Matching marks on the fuel control pinion and fuel control rack

(6) Insert the plunger spring retainer and attach the plunger spring to the main unit.

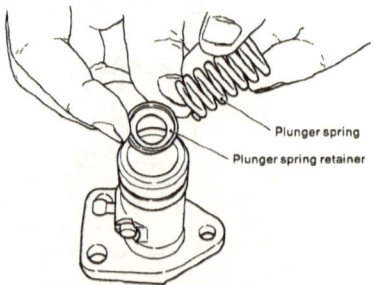

Attaching the plunger spring to the main unit

NOTE: The plunger spring retainer should face the underside of the pump.

(7) After aligning the matching mark on the plunger flange with that on the fuel control pinion, attach the plunger to the main unit.

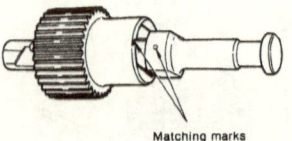

Matching marks

Attaching the plunger to the main unit

NOTE: By inverting and standing the main unit of the pump upright attach the plunger to it carefully.

(8) Mount the plunger lower retainer onto the plunger.

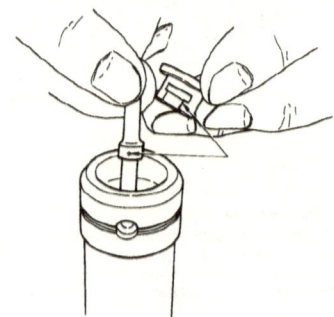

Socket for the lower part of the plunger spring

(9) Insert the plunger adjusting shims.

NOTE: 1. Insert the same number of shims with the same thickness as those inserted before disassembling the pump. After re-assembling the pump, measure and adjust the top clearance of the plunger.

(10) While adjusting the direction of the detent (stopper) hole for the plunger guide, insert the plunger guide carefully.
When the detent hole is lined up with the plunger guide, insert the detent. Then mount the retaining ring (clip).

Attaching the plunger guide to the main unit

(11) After attaching tighten the delivery valve holder with a torque wrench.

kg·cm (lb·ft)

Tightening torque	550 to 600 (39.77 ~ 43.38)

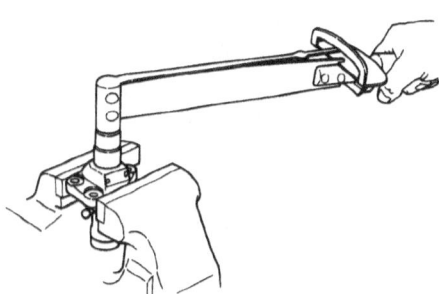

Tighting the delivery valve holder

2·7 Inspection after reassembly

When the engine doesn't run smoothly and the injection pump is suspected as being the cause, or when the pump has been disassembled and parts replaced, always conduct the following tests.

2·7.1 Control rack resistance test

After reassembling the pump, wash it in clean fuel, move the rack and check resistance as follows:

(1) This test is performed to determine the resistance of the control rack. When the resistance is large, the engine will run irregularly or race suddenly.
(2) Place the pump on its side, hold the control rack up and allow it to slide down by its own weight. The rack should slide smoothly over its entire stroke. Place the pump on end and perform the above test again; check for any abnormalities.[Resistance below 60g (0.132 lbs)]
(3) Since a high sliding resistance is probably a result of the following, disassemble the pump and wash or repair it.

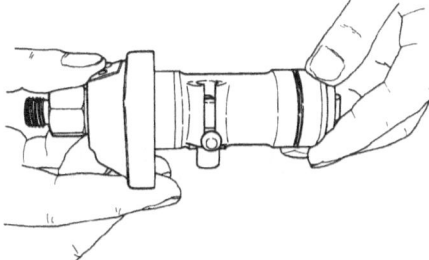

(a) Resistance of the rotating and sliding parts of the plunger assembly is too high.
(b) Delivery valve holder is too tight (plunger barrel distorted).
(c) Control rack or control pinion teeth and control rack outside circumference are dirty or damaged.
(d) Injection pump body control rack hole is damaged.
(e) Plunger barrel packing is not installed correctly and the barrel is distorted. (Since in this case fuel will leak into the crankcase and dilute the lubricating oil, special care must be taken).

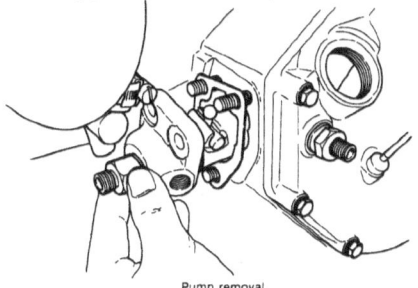

Pump removal

Chapter 3 Fuel System
2. Injection Pump

2-7.2 Fuel injection timing
Fuel injection timing is adjusted by timing shims inserted between the pump body and gear case pump mounting seat.
Adjusting the injection timing
(1) Remove the injection pipe from the pump.
(2) Install a measuring pipe.
(3) Bleed the air from the injection pump.

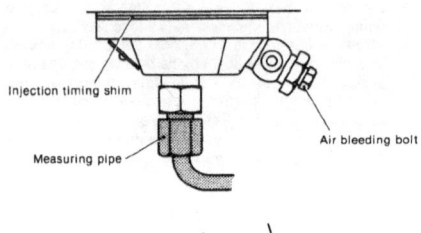

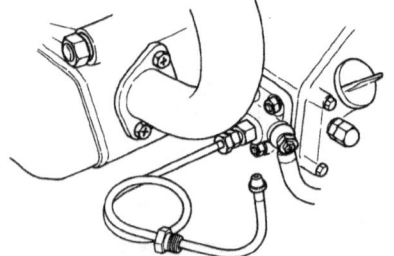

(4) Set the control rack to the middle fuel injection position.
(Pull the lever when setting the accelerator lever.)
(5) Turn the crankshaft slowly by hand, and read the timing mark (TD) on the flywheel the instant fuel appears at the measuring pipe.
(FiD + Fuel injection from delivery valve.)

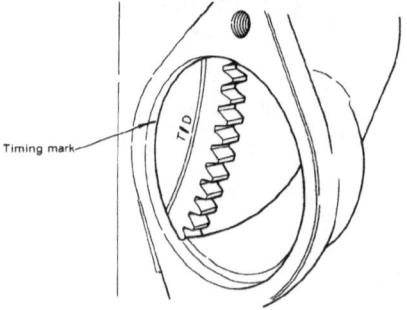

(6) If the injection timing is off, add adjusting shims when the timing is fast, and remove shims when the timing is slow.

Fuel injection timing	b. TDC 25° ±1°
Injection timing shim	Thickness 0.1 mm (0.004 in.), 0.3 mm (0.012 in.) Injection timing change 1° (crankshaft) per 0.1 mm

(8) Finally, turn the crankshaft slowly and confirm that it turns easily. If it is stiff or does not rotate, the plunger head gap is too small.

2-8 Injection pump adjustment
The injection pump is adjusted with an injection pump tester after reassembly.

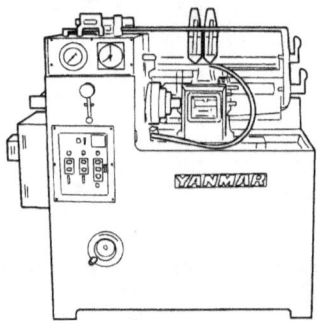

2-8.1 Setting pump on tester
(1) After the injection pump has been disassembled and reassembled, install it on a pump tester (cam lift: 7mm (0.276in.).
(2) Confirm that the control rack slides smoothly. If it does not, inspect the injection pump and repair it so that the rack does slide smoothly.

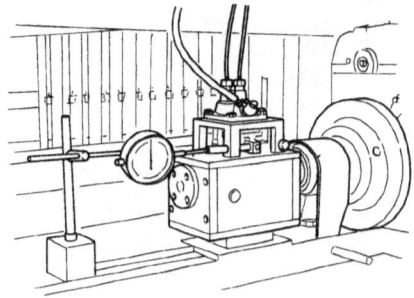

Chapter 3 Fuel System
2. Injection Pump

(3) Run the pump tester at low speed, loosen the air bleeder screw, and bleed the air from the injection pump.

2-8.2
Measuring the sliding resistance of the fuel control rack
Measure the sliding resistance of the fuel control rack with a spring scale (balance).
1. Number of pump rotations/sliding resistance: 0rpm/ less than 60 g.

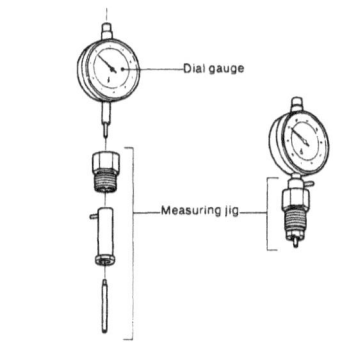

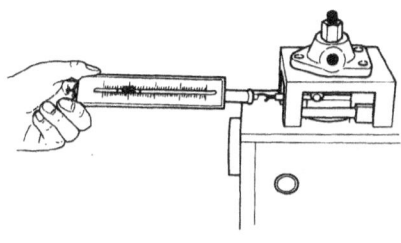

Measuring the sliding resistance of the fuel control rack

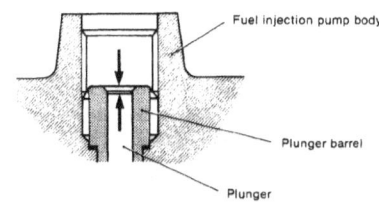

NOTE: If the sliding resistance is unsatisfactory, disassemble, inspect and repair the fuel control rack.

2-8.3 Adjusting the plunger head gap
(1) Set the pump installation dimension (end of plunger barrel when the roller is on the cam base cycle) at 83mm (3.268in.), remove the delivery valve holder and delivery valve, and set the plunger to top dead center by turning the camshaft. Measure the difference in height (head gap) between the end of the plunger and the end of the plunger barrel using a dial gauge.

mm (in.)

Plunger head gap	1.15 ~ 1.25 (0.0453 ~ 0.0492)

(2) Using the plunger head gap measuring jig
 1) Install a dial gauge on the measuring jig.
 2) Stand the measuring jig on a stool and set the dial gauge pointer to O.
 3) Remove the pump delivery valve and install the measuring jig.
 4) Turn the camshaft to set the plunger to top dead center and read the dial gauge. The value given is the plunger head gap.

(3) When the plunger head gap is larger than the prescribed value, remove the plunger guide and insert plunger shims between the plunger spring lower retainer and the plunger guide. Adjust both pumps in the same manner.
Plunger shim thickness: 0.1mm (0.004in.),
0.2mm (0.008in.)

Chapter 3 Fuel System
2. Injection Pump

_____ SM/YSM

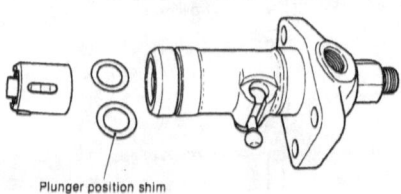

Plunger position shim

(4) After rechecking adjustment, install the delivery valve.
Delivery valve holder tightening torque: 4.0 ~ 4.5kg-m
(29. ~ 32.6 lb-ft)

2-8.4 Plunger pressure test

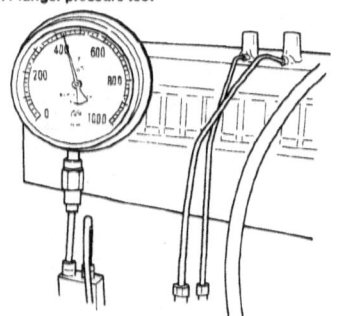

(1) Install a 1,000kg/cm² (14,223 lb/in.²) pressure gauge to the delivery valve holder.

(2) Fix the fuel control rack at the discharge stop position. By developing an engine speed of 200 rpm, shift the control rack. When the built-up pressure exceeds 300 kg/cm² in the vicinity of the matching mark, there should be no sudden pressure drops.
(3) When the pressure has reached 300 kg/cm², set the rack to the discharge reducing position and stop the tester. (4.266 lb/in²)

NOTE: The delivery valve must be of high quality.

Pressure gauge AVT 1/2 × 150 × 1,000 kg/cm²

2-8.5 Testing the delivery valve for oil tightness
(1) Follow procedures similar to those used for the plunger test. When the pressure gauge indication exceeds 120 kg/cm², stop the rotation and set the fuel control rack to the 0 mm position. (1707 lb/in²)
(2) Measure the time required for the pressure gauge indication to drop from 100 kg/cm² to 90 kg/cm² at 10 kg/cm².

Time required at 10 kg/cm² (142.2 lb/in²)	less than 5 sec.

(3) If both the plunger and the delivery valve fail the test, replace them.

2-8.6 Adjusting the amount of injection
Performance of pump

	YSM8	YSM12
Pump speed	1600 rpm	1500 rpm
Plunger diameter × stroke	ø6 × 7 mm (0.2362 × 0.2756 in.)	ø6 × 7 mm (0.2362 × 0.2756 in.)
Injection nozzle type	YDN-0SDYD1	YDN-0SDYD1
Pressure for fuel injection	160 kg/cm² (2276 lb/in.²)	160 kg/cm² (2276 lb/in.²)
Amount of injection at rack mark position	27 ±0.5 cc	42 ±0.5 cc
Stroke	1000	1000

NOTE: Maintain the pressure for feeding oil to the injection pump at 0.5 kg/cm².

Chapter 3 Fuel System
2. Injection Pump

SM/YSM

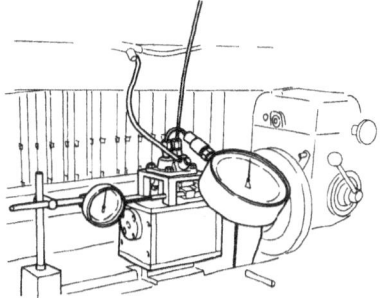

Measuring the fuel injection volme

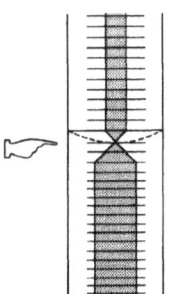

Measuring the degree

3. Injection Nozzle

3·1 Construction

The injection nozzle atomizes the fuel sent from the injection pump and injects it into the precombustion chamber in the prescribed injection pattern to obtain good combustion through optimum fuel/air mixing.

The main parts of the injection nozzle are the nozzle holder and nozzle body. Since both these parts are exposed to hot combustion gas, they must be extremely durable.

Moreover, since their operation is extremely sensitive to the pressure of the fuel, high precision is required. Both are made of quality alloy steel that has been specially heat treated and lapped, so they must always be handled as a pair.

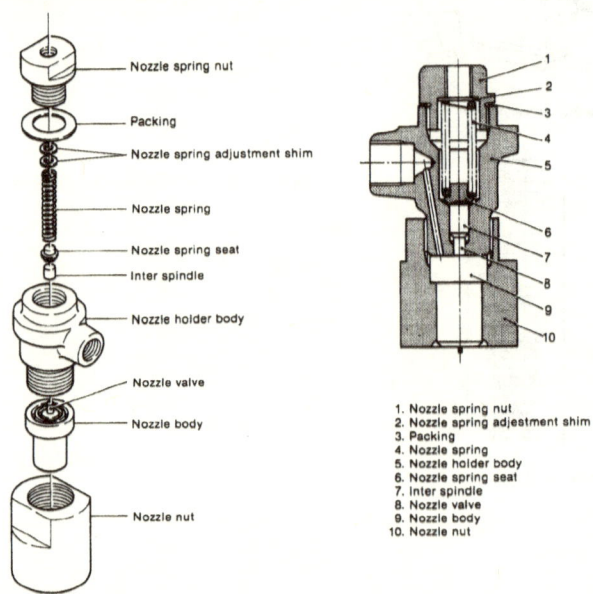

1. Nozzle spring nut
2. Nozzle spring adjestment shim
3. Packing
4. Nozzle spring
5. Nozzle holder body
6. Nozzle spring seat
7. Inter spindle
8. Nozzle valve
9. Nozzle body
10. Nozzle nut

3·2 Specifications for nozzle valve

Model		YDN-OSDYD1
Nozzle	Type of nozzle valve	Throttle
	Valve opening pressure	160 ±5 kg/cm² (2205 ~ 2347 lb/in.²)
	Diameter of injection nozzle	∅1 mm (0.0394 in.)
	Angle of injection	5° ~ 10°
Nozzle spring	Free length	30.0 mm (1.1811 in.)
	Mounted length	28.7 mm (1.1299 in.)
	Mounted load	14.14 kg
Nozzle spring adjusting plate (for adjusting nozzle opening pressure)		0.1, 0.2, 0.3, 0.4 mm (4 kinds)

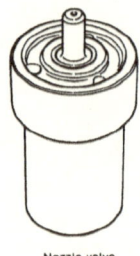

Nozzle valve

Chapter 3 Fuel System
3. Injection Nozzle

3-3 Yanmar throttle nozzle

The semi-throttle nozzles used in this engine are designed and manufactured by Yanmar. A semi-throttle nozzle resembles a pintle nozzle, except that with the former the nozzle hole at the end of nozzle and nozzle body are longer and the end of the nozzle is tapered. This nozzle features a "throttling effect": relatively less fuel is injected into the precombustion chamber at the initial stage of injection, and the volume is increased as the nozzle rises. This type of throttle nozzle ideal for small, high-speed engines.

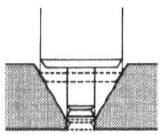
Pintle nozzle

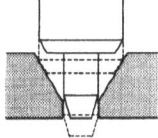
Yanmar semi-throttle nozzle

3-4 Nozzle operation

The nozzle is pushed down to its lowest position by the pressure-adjusting nozzle spring and contacts the valve seat of the nozzle body.

Under high pressure, fuel from the fuel pump passes through the hole drilled in the nozzle holder, enters the circular groove at the end of the nozzle body and then enters the pressure chamber at the bottom of the nozzle body.

When the force acting in the axial direction on the differential area of the nozzle at the pressure chamber overcomes the force of the spring, the nozzle is pushed up and the fuel is injected into the precombustion chamber through the throttle hole.

The nozzle is closed again when the pressure in the nozzle body's pressure chamber drops below the force of the spring.

This cycle is repeated at each opening and closing of the injection pump delivery valve.

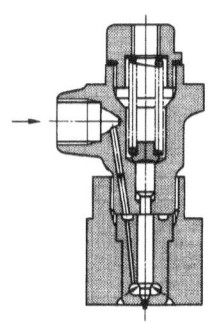

3-5 Disassembly and reassembly
3-5.1 Disassembly sequence

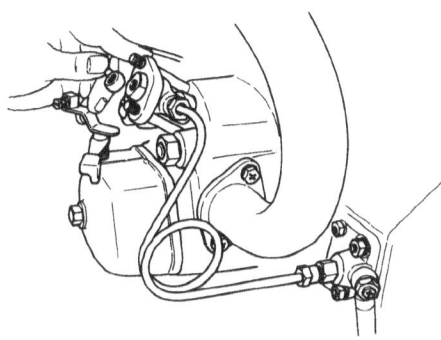

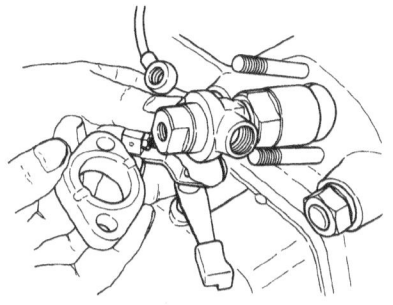

(1) Remove the carbon from the nozzle end.
(2) Loosen the nozzle spring holder.
(3) Remove the nozzle holder body from the nozzle mounting nut.

Chapter 3 Fuel System
3. Injection Nozzle

(4) Remove the nozzle body and nozzle ass'y from the nozzle mounting nut.
(5) Remove the nozzle spring retainer from the nozzle holder body, and remove the nozzle spring retainer, inter-spindle etc.

Reassemble in the reverse order of disassembly, paying special attention to the following items.

3-5.2 Disassembly and reassembly precautions

(1) The disassembled parts must be washed in fuel oil, and carbon must be completely removed from the end of the nozzle body, the nozzle body and the nozzle mounting nut fitting section.
If reassembled with any carbon remaining, the nozle will not tighten evenly, causing faulty injection.

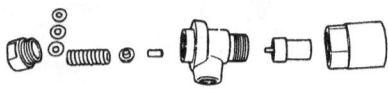

(2) Precautions when using a new nozzle.
First immerse the new nozzle in rust-preventive oil, and then seal it on the outside with seal peel. After removing the seal peel, immerse the nozzle in diesel oil and remove the rust-preventive oil from both the inside and outside of the nozzle.
Stand the nozzle holder upright, lift the nozzle about 1/3 of its length: it should drop smoothly by it own weight when released.

(3) The nozzle must be assembled to the nozzle holder with the nozzle spring retainer loosened.
If the nozzle is installed with the nozzle spring tightened, the nozzle mounting nut will be tightened unevenly and oil will leak from between the end of the nozzle holder body and the end of the nozzle mounting nut, causing faulty injection.

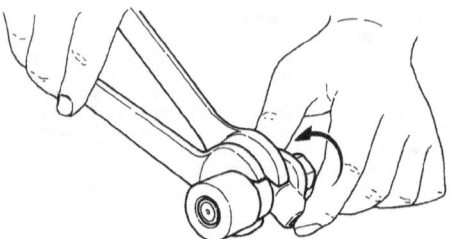

		kg-cm (lb-ft)
Nozzle tightening torque	Nozzle nut	1000 (72.36)
	Nozzle spring nut	700 ~ 800 (50.65 ~ 57.89)

(4) When installing the injection nozzle on the cylinder head, tighten the nozzle holder nuts alternately, being careful to tighten them evenly. Tightening torque: 2 kg-m (14.5 ft-lb)
Moreover, the nozzle holder must be installed with the notch side on the nozzle side.

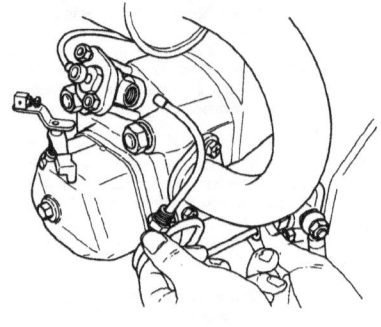

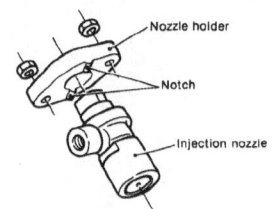

Chapter 3 Fuel System
3. Injection Nozzle

3-6 Injection nozzle inspection and adjustment
3-6.1 Carbon and corrosion on the nozzle body
Inspect the end and sides of the nozzle body for carbon build-up and corrosion. If there is considerable carbon build-up, check the properties of the fuel used, etc.
Replace the body if heavily corroded.

3-6.2 Checking nozzle action
Wash the nozzle in clean fuel oil and hold the nozzle body upright, then lift the nozzle about 1/3 of its length with one hand. The nozzle is in good condition if it drops smoothly by its own weight when released. If the nozzle slides stiffly, repair or replace it.

3-6.4 Nozzle seat oil tightness check
After injecting fuel several times by operating the lever of the nozzle tester, wipe the oil off the injection port. Then raise the pressure to 20 kg/cm^2 (284.5 lb/in.^{2}) (140kg/cm^2 (1991 lb/in.^{2})) lower than the prescribed injection pressure. The nozzle is faulty if oil drips from the nozzle. In this case, clean, repair or replace the nozzle.

3-6.5 Checking the spray condition
Adjust the nozzle injection pressure to the prescribed value and check the condition of the spray while operating the tester at 4—6 times/sec. Judge the condition of the spray by referring to the below figure.

3-6.3 Adjusting the nozzle injection pressure
Install the injection nozzle to the high pressure pipe of a nozzle tester and slowly operate the lever of the tester. Read the pressure the instant injection from the nozzle begins.
If the injection pressure is lower than the prescribed pressure, remove the nozzle spring holder and adjust the pressure by adding nozzle spring shims.
The injection pressure increases about 10 kg/cm^2 (142.2 lb/in.^{2}) when a 0.1 mm (0.004in.) shim is added.

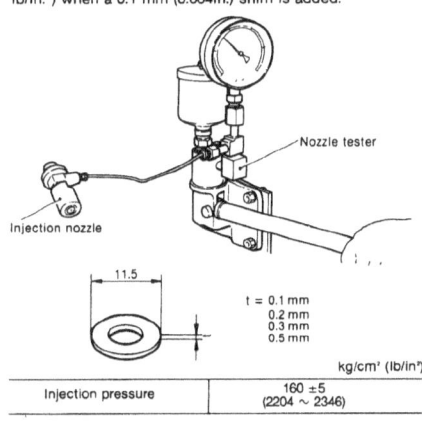

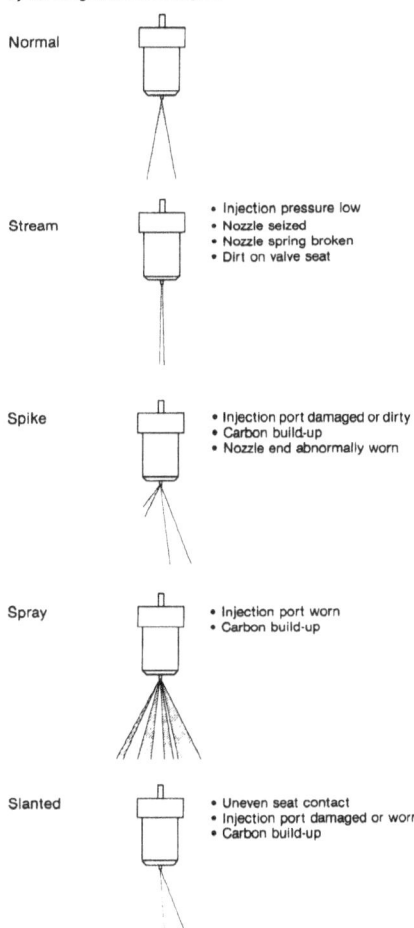

Normal

Stream
- Injection pressure low
- Nozzle seized
- Nozzle spring broken
- Dirt on valve seat

Spike
- Injection port damaged or dirty
- Carbon build-up
- Nozzle end abnormally worn

Spray
- Injection port worn
- Carbon build-up

Slanted
- Uneven seat contact
- Injection port damaged or worn
- Carbon build-up

Injection pressure	160 ±5 (2204 ~ 2346) kg/cm^2 (lb/in^2)

Chapter 3 Fuel System
3. Injection Nozzle

3-6.6 Inspecting the nozzle spring
Inspect the nozzle spring for fractured coils, corrosion, and permanent strain, and replace the spring when faulty.

3-6.7 Inspecting the nozzle spring retainer and inter-spindle
Inspect the nozzle spring retainer and inter-spindle for wear and peeling of the contact face, and repair or replace the spring if faulty.

Chapter 3 Fuel System
4. Fuel Filter

4. Fuel Filter

4-1 Construction
The fuel filter is installed between the feed pump and injection pump, and serves to remove dirt and impurities from the oil fed from the fuel tank through the feed pump.

The fuel filter incorporates a replaceable filter paper element. Fuel from the fuel tank enters the outside of the element and passes through the element under its own pressure. As it passes through, the dirt and impurities in the fuel are filtered out, allowing only clean fuel to enter the interior of the element. The fuel exits from the outlet at the top center of the filter and is sent to the injection pump.

An hexagonal head bolt for air bleeding and a threaded hole for fuel return are provided in the fuel filter body. The surplus fuel at the injection nozzle is returned to the fuel filter and then to the injection pump.

4-2 Inspection
The fuel filter must be periodically inspected. if there is water and sediment in the filter, remove all dirt, rust, etc. by washing the filter with clean fuel.

The normal replacement interval for the element is 100 hours, but the element should be replaced whenever it is dirty or damaged, even if the 100-hour replacement period has not elapsed.

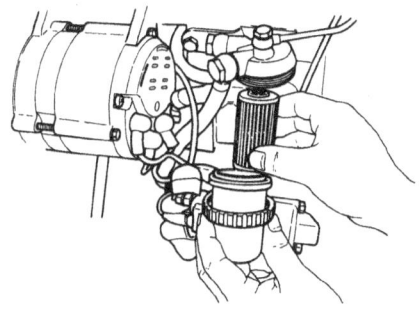

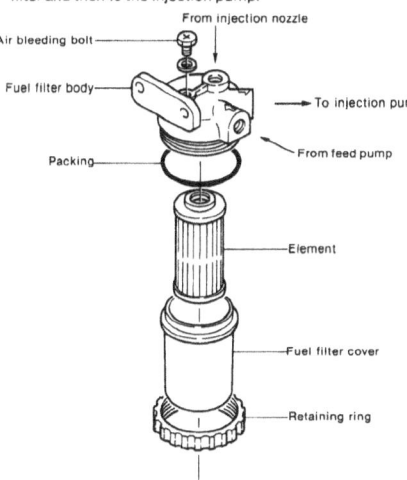

Filter cleaning	Every 50 hours
Filter element replacement	Every 100 hours
Part No.	104800—55710

5. Fuel Feed Pump

5-1 Construction

The fuel pump feeds the fuel from the fuel tank to the injection pump through the fuel filter. When the fuel tank is installed at a higher position than the fuel filter and injection pump, the fuel will be fed by its head pressure, but if the fuel tank is lower than the filter and injection pump, a fuel pump is required.

The fuel pump of this engine is a diaphragm type and is installed on the gear case side of the cylinder body. The diaphragm is operated by the movement of a lever by the fuel feed pump cam at the P.T.O. shaft.

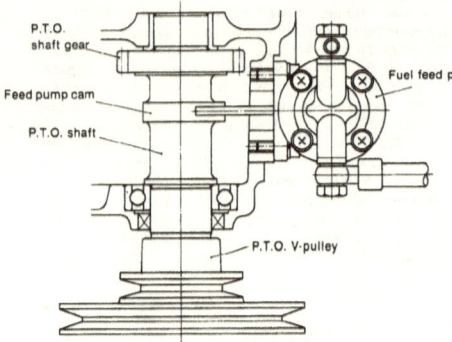

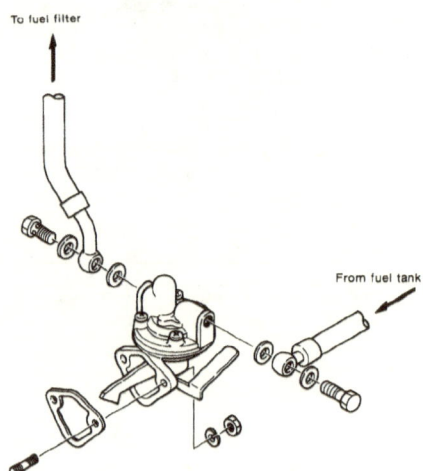

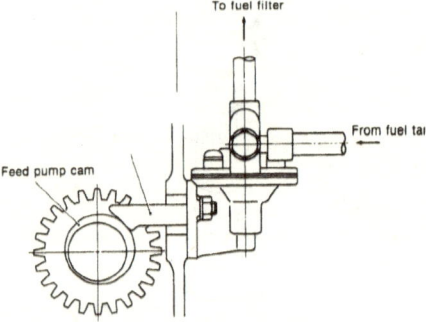

5-2 Disassembly and Reassembly

5-2.1 Disassembly

Clean the outside of the pump, scribe a matching mark on the upper body and lower body of the pump, disassemble and put the components in order.

Component parts of fuel feed pump

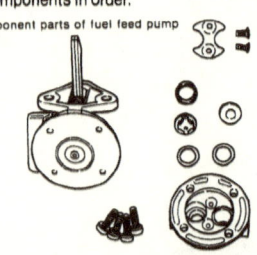

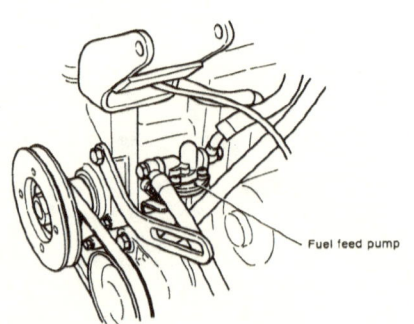

Chapter 3 Fuel System
5. Fuel Feed Pump

5-2.2 Reassembly
Assemble the pump by reversing the disassembling procedures. Pay close attention to the following:
1. Clean the components, blow compressed air against them, and inspects. Replace any defective components.
2. Replace the packings, etc. with new ones.
3. When mounting the valves, be careful not to mix up the inlet and outlet valves. Also, don't forget the valve packing.

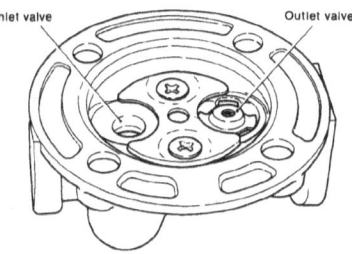

Inlet valve   Outlet valve

4. Make sure the diaphragm mounting hole is in the correct position and gently attach the diaphragm to the pump body.
5. Line up the matching marks on the pump body, and clamp on the pump body evenly.

5-3 Inspecting and adjusting the fuel feed pump
5-3.1 Checking the pump for fuel oil leaks
After removal, immerse the pump in kerosene, stop its outlet port with a finger and, by operating the rocker arm, check for bubbles.
If any bubbles are present, this indicates a defective point which should be replaced.

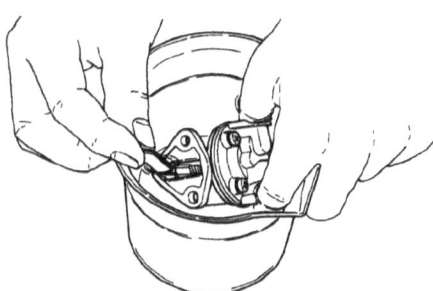

5-3.2 Checking the pump for engine oil leaks
Check pump mounting bolts for looseness and the pump packing for breaks. Retighten any loose bolts and replace defective packing.

5-3.3 Measuring the sucking power
Attach a piece of vinyl hose to the inlet port, keep the pump at a specified height (head) above the fuel oil level, and operate the rocker arm by hand. If the fuel oil spurts out from the outlet port, the pump is all right. A simpler method of testing pump power is as follows: cover the inlet port with a finger and, by operating the rocker arm by hand, estimate the pump's sucking power by judging the suction on the finger, Although this is not an exact method, it can at least confirm that the diaphragm, valves, etc. are operating.

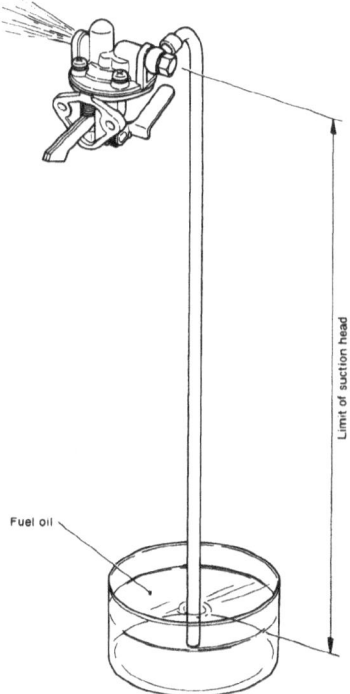

Fuel oil

Limit of suction head

5-3.4 Aging, breakdown and cracking of the diaphragm

Since the diaphragm constantly in motion, the cloth on its flexible parts becomes thin, cracked, and sometimes breaks down after long periods of use. A broken diaphragm causes fuel oil leakage and often fragments of the diaphragm get into the engine oil, either seriously hampering fuel oil discharge or blocking it altogether.

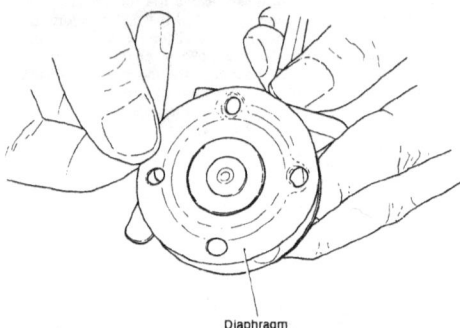

Diaphragm

5-3.5 The contact area and mounting condition of valve

Test the valve seat as follows: Remove the valve and blow into the valve seat from the direction in which the valve spring is mounted. If air leaks, replace the seat with a new one. If fuel oil leaks as a result of dust, foreign objects, etc. caught in the valve seat, rinse it and clean it by blowing air into it.

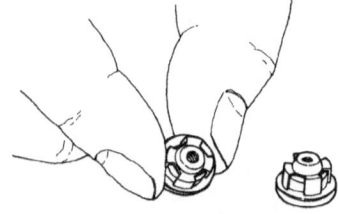

5-3.6 Diaphragm spring and rocker arm spring

Check the diaphragm spring and rocker arm spring for permanent deformation, and the rocker arm and rocker pin for wear. If any of these components are defective, replace them with new ones.

NOTE: When it becomes necessary to replace any of these parts, the entire fuel feed pump assembly should be replaced.

6. Fuel Tank (Option)

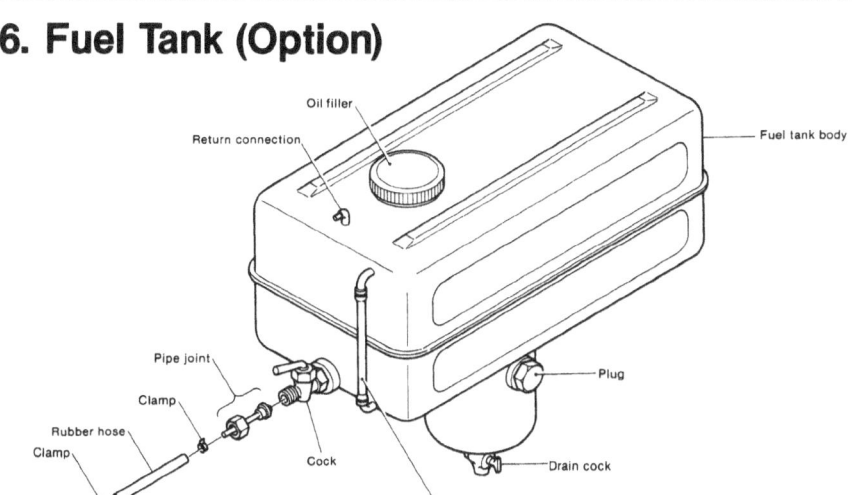

Material	Steel plate
Capacity	20ℓ
Thread of outlet cock	PF 1/2
Size of rubber hose	ø7/ø13 × 2000 mm (0.2756/0.5118 × 78.74in.)

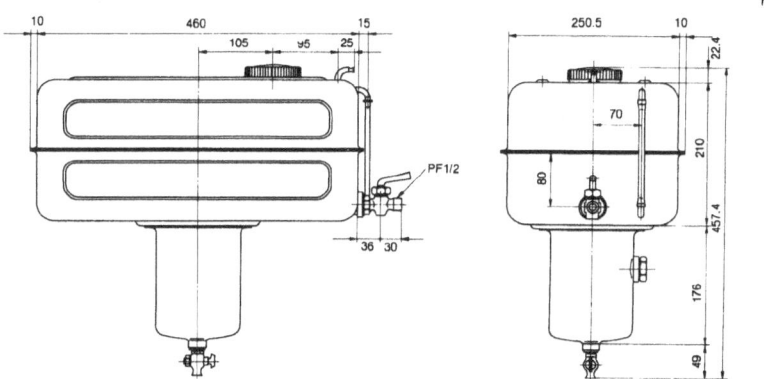

Draining the fuel oil tank

In order to keep the injection system from developing repeated troubles, drain the fuel oil tank at intervals of every 100 hours and after servicing the fuel injection valve and fuel injection pump.

When mounting the fuel oil tank, be careful not to mix up its pipe joints and bolts with those of other components, and after attaching the fuel oil tank, test it for oil leakage.

CHAPTER 4
GOVERNOR

1. Governor... 4-1
2. Injection Limiter..................................... 4-4
3. Adjusting the Governor Link.......................... 4-5
4. Adjusting the No-Load Speed......................... 4-6
5. Engine Stop Lever.................................... 4-7

Chapter 4 Governor
1. Governor ──────────────────────────────── SM/YSM

1. Governor

The governor serves to keep engine speed constant by automatically adjusting the amount of fuel supplied to the engine according to changes in the load. This protects the engine against sudden changes in the load, such as sudden disengagement of the clutch, the propeller leaving the water in rough weather, or other cases where the engine is suddenly accelerated.

This engine employs an all-speed governor in which the centrifugal force of the governor weight, produced by rotation of the crankshaft, and the load of the regulator spring are balanced.
The governor is remotely controlled by a wire. Refer to the "Control System" chapter for details.

1-1 Construction

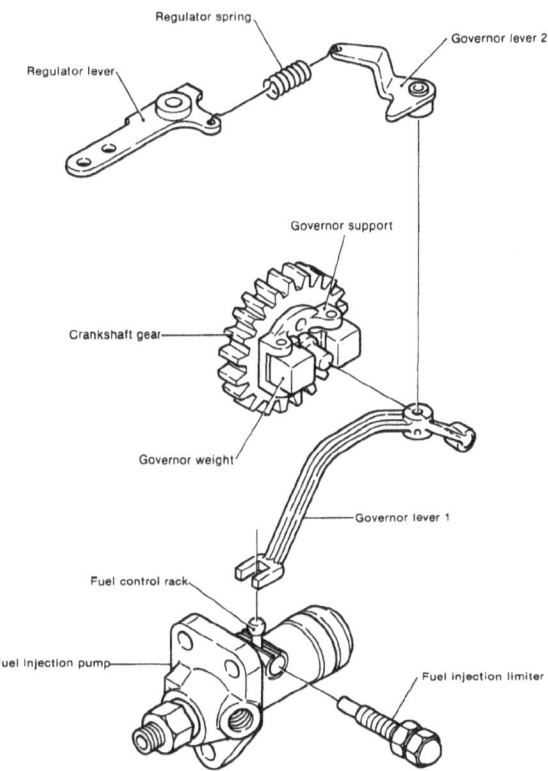

Chapter 4 Governor
1. Governor

SM/YSM

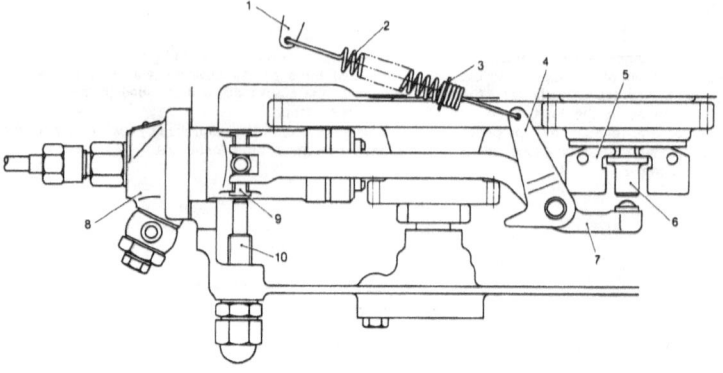

1 Regulator lever
2 Regulator spring
3 Spring hook
4 Governor lever 2
5 Governor weight
6 Governor spindle
7 Governor lever 1
8 Fuel injection pump
9 Fuel control rack
10 Fuel injection limiter

1·2 Operation

The position of the two governor weights (open and closed) is regulated by the speed of the engine. The centrifugal force of the governor weights pivots around the governor weight pin and is changed to axial force that acts on the spindle. This force is transmitted to governor lever 2 through governor lever 1, and lever 1 shifts the fuel control rack to increase or decrease the fuel supply. The governor lever is stabilized at the point at which the force produced by the governor weight is balanced with the load of the regulator spring connecting the regulator lever and governor lever 2.

When the speed is reduced by application of a load, the force of the regulator spring pushes the governor spindle in the "fuel increase" direction, stabilizing the engine speed by changing the position of the regulator lever.

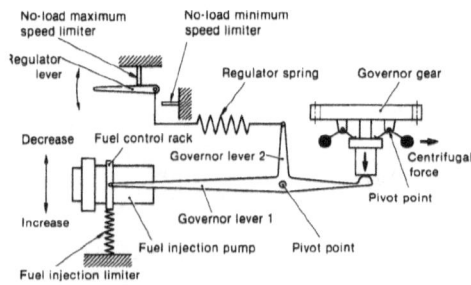

1·3 Performance

	YSM8	YSM12
No-load maximum speed	3400 rpm	3150 rpm
No-load minimum speed	$650 ^{+50}_{-0}$ rpm	

1·4 Parts inspection and replacement

1·4.1 Regulator spring
(1) Inspect the spring for coil damage, corrosion and hook deformation, and replace if faulty.
(2) Measure the spring's dimensions.

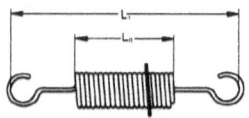

		YSM8	YSM12
Free length	L_0	25mm (0.9843in.)	25mm (0.9843in.)
	L_1	93mm (3.6614in.)	141mm (5.5512in.)

1·4.2 Governor spindle
(1) Check the governor spindle for smoothness of movement through the hole in the governor weight support.
(2) Check the governor spindle flange where it comes into contact with the governor weight for contact margin and wear.
(3) Check the governor spindle tip where it comes into contact with the governor lever for contact margin and wear.

Chapter 4 Governor
1. Governor

─────────── SM/YSM

(4) Measure the clearance between the governor spindle and the governor weight support.

1-4.4 Governor lever shaft
(1) Replace the governor lever shaft if there is play between the shaft and needle bearing, play when the lever is moved, or if the shaft does not move smoothly.
(2) Repair or replace the shaft if there is play between lever 1 or lever 2 and the shaft, or if the taper pin is loose.
(3) Inspect the contact and wear of the end of lever 1.

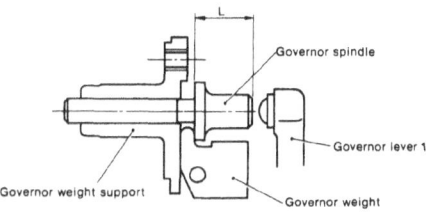

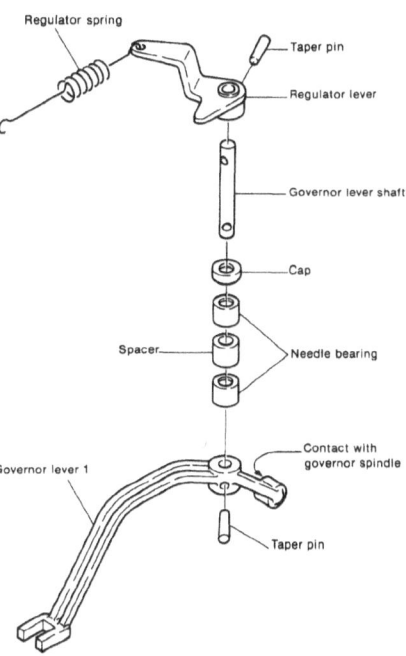

mm (in.)

	Standard dimension	Clearance when assembled	Wear limit
Outside diameter of governor spindle	7 (0.2756)	0.068 ~ 0.113 (0.0027 ~ 0.0044)	0.025 (0.0098)
Diameter of hole in governor weight support	7 (0.2756)		
Length (L) of governor spindle	17 (0.6693)	—	16 (0.6299)

1-4.3 Governor weight
(1) Check the governor weight for smoothness of movement.
(2) Check the surface when it comes into contact with the governor spindle for contact margin and wear. If wear is excessive, replace it as a unit.

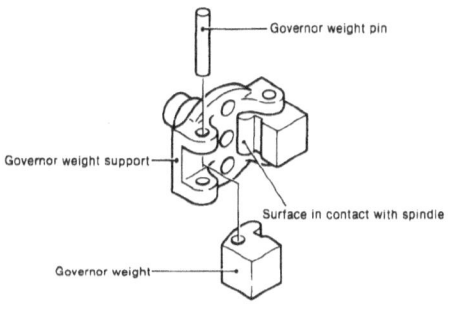

Printed in Japan
A0A1001 8311

2. Injection Limiter

2-1 Construction
Since surplus power is required from the standpoints of sudden overloads and durability, the engine is equipped with an injection control shaft that limits the amount of fuel injected into the precombustion chamber to a fixed amount. Moreover, since the injection control spring (torque spring) affects engine performance by adjusting engine torque, care must be exercised in its handling and adjustment, and governor adjustment must be performed accurately.

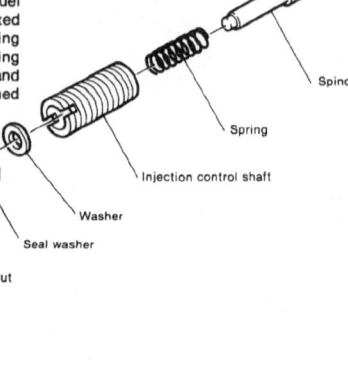

2-2 Inspection
(1) Hold the end of the spindle, and check it for smooth movement.
(2) Replace the spring if it is damaged, corroded or permanently strained.

3. Adjusting the Governor Link

Note: Adjust the governor link carefully after disassembling and reassembling the engine.

Adjusting procedures
(1) Remove the oiler port cap.
(2) Push the governor lever 2 toward the left until it resists slightly to make sure of the rack mark.

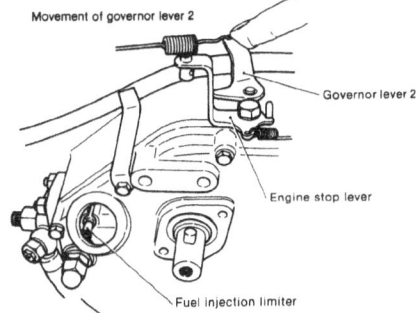

Movement of governor lever 2
Governor lever 2
Engine stop lever
Fuel injection limiter

Note: 1. Do not push the governor lever too far.
2. Make sure the control rack mark from the oiler port is in the correct position. If it does not line up with the reference surface adjust it as follows:

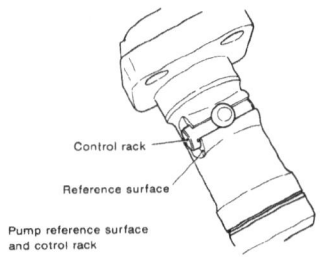

Control rack
Reference surface
Pump reference surface and cotrol rack

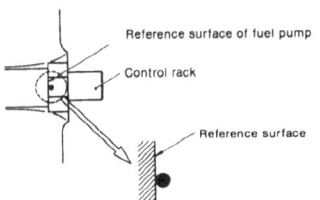

Reference surface of fuel pump
Control rack
Reference surface

(3) Remove the cap nut of the fuel injection limiter and loosen its lock nut.
(4) While pushing the governor lever toward the left, move the fuel injection limiter so that it lines up the control rack mark with the reference surface.

Note: Be sure to correctly align the rack mark with the reference surface.

(5) While holding the fuel injection limiter steady, tighten the lock nut and mount the cap nut.

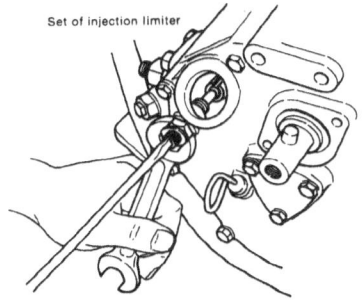

Set of injection limiter

Note: Do not tighten the lock nut excessively.
(6) Attach the lid of the oiler port.

4. Adjusting the No-Load Speed

4-1 Adjusting the no-load maximum speed

The maximum speed is set with the adjusting bolt on the regulator handle. When re-adjusting, provide the speed values listed below.

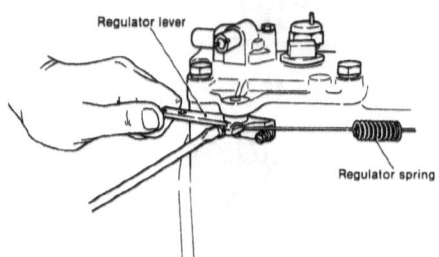

Setting of no-load maximum speed of PTO shaft

	YSM8	YSM12
No-load maximum speed	3400 rpm	3150 rpm
Maximum speed of PTO shaft end	3400 rpm	3700 rpm

4-2 Adjusting the idling speed
(for YSM8R and YSM12R only)

Adjust the idling speed with the adjusting bolt on the regulator handle so that it provides the speed values listed below.

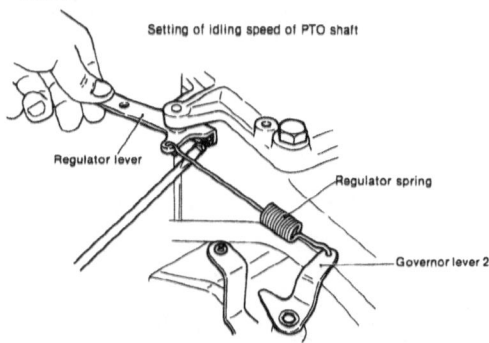

Setting of idling speed of PTO shaft

	YSM8R	YSM12R
Idling speed	700 rpm	700 rpm
Idling speed of PTO shaft end	700 rpm	820 rpm

5. Engine Stop Lever

With this device, governor lever 2 is moved by the engine stop lever, regardless of the position of the regulator lever, so as to adjust the fuel control rack and reduce the supply of fuel.
This device can be remote-controlled.

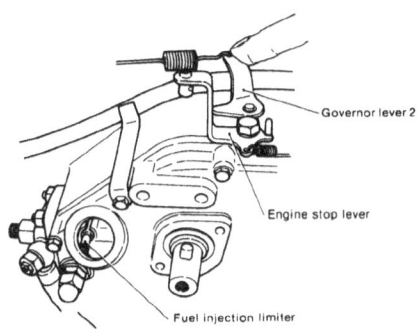

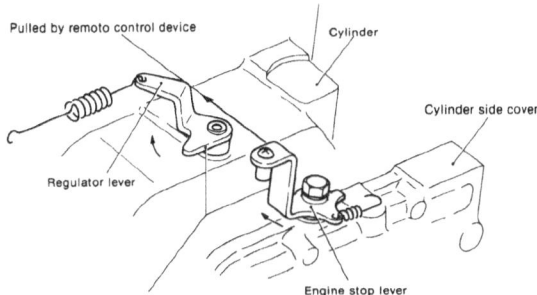

CHAPTER 5
INTAKE AND EXHAUST SYSTEM

1. Intake And Exhaust System 5-1
2. Intake Silencer 5-2
3. Exhaust System 5-3

Chapter 5 Intake and Exhaust System
1. Intake and Exhaust System SM/YSM

1. Intake and Exhaust System

1-1 YSM8-R, YSM12-R

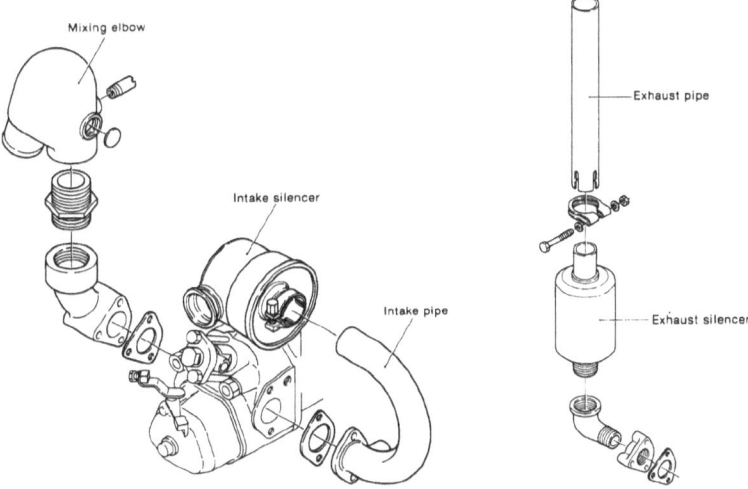

1-2 YSM8-Y, YSM12-Y

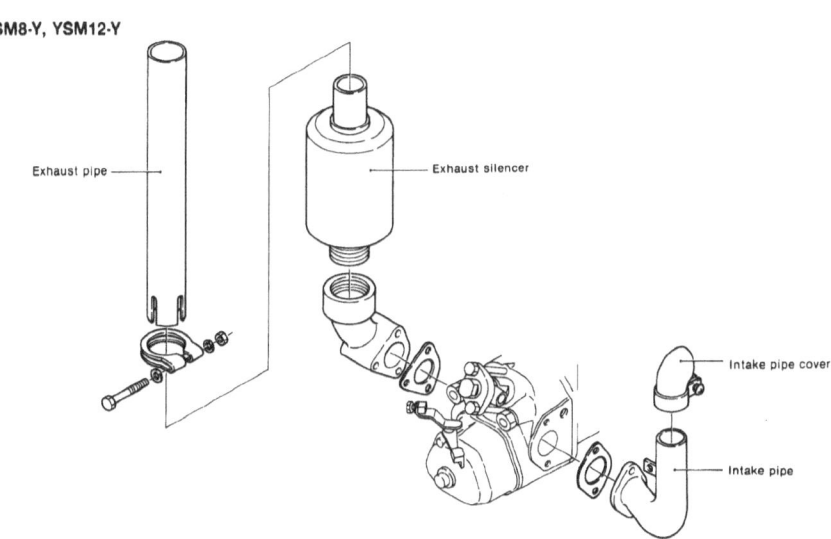

Chapter 5 Intake and Exhaust System
2. Intake Silencer ──────────────────────────────── SM/YSM

2. Intake Silencer

2-1 Construction
A round polyurethane sound absorbing type intake silencer is employed to silence the intake air sucked into the cylinder head from the intake port.
Besides providing a silencing effect, the silencer also acts as an air cleaner.

2-2 Inspection
When the intake silencer is disassembled, remove the internal polyurethane element and inspect it for clogging.

2-3 Element replacement
Replace the element as follows:
Every 300 hours of operation in dusty places
Every 500 hours of operation in ordinary places
After one year of operation even through the specified number of operating hours has not been reached.

3. Exhaust System

3-1 Mixing elbow (R-type)

The high temperature, high pressure exhaust gas emitted intermittently from the cylinder at the speed of sound enters the mixing elbow. It is then mixed with the cooling water to lower its temperature and muffle it, and is discharged.

3-2 Mixing elbow inspection (R-type)

Check for carbon build-up and for corrosion inside the pipe, and repair or replace the pipe if faulty.
Moreover, inspect the mixing elbow mounting threads for cracking and corrosion.
This section is affected by exhaust gas and vibration.

3-3 Exhaust silencer (Y-type)

The exhaust silencer employed is the expansion type.

3-4 Checking the exhaust silencer (Y-type)

Check the threaded parts at both ends of the exhaust silencer for corrosion, cracking, etc.

CHAPTER 6
LUBRICATION SYSTEM

1. Lubrication System 6-1
2. Oil Pump 6-3
3. Oil Filter 6-6
4. Oil Pressure Regulator Valve 6-7

1. Lubrication System

Engine parts are lubricated by a trochoid pump forced lubrication system. To keep the engine exterior uncluttered and to eliminate vibration damage to piping, exterior piping has been minimized by transporting the lubricating oil through passages drilled in the cylinder and cylinder head.

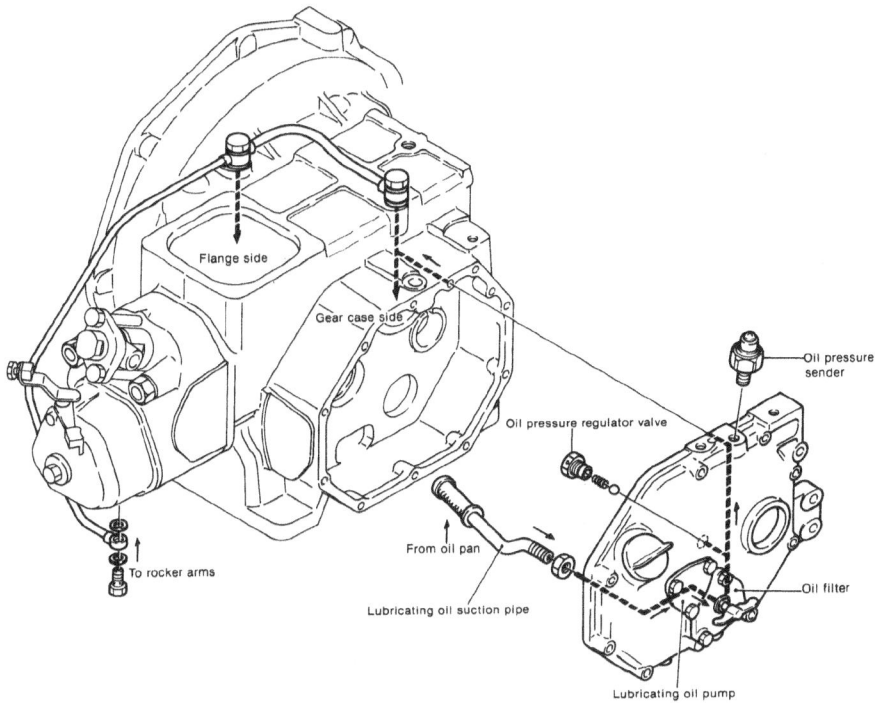

Chapter 6 Lubrication System
1. Lubrication System

The lubricating oil is drawn back up through the lubricating oil suction pipe by the trochoid pump and fed to the oil filter, where impurities are filtered out. Then it is adjusted to the prescribed pressure by the oil pressure regulating valve.
One portion of the lubricating oil under regulated pressure is sent to the gear-side main bearing through the holes drilled in the cylinder side cover and the cylinder body. The other portion is sent to the mounting side main bearing and rocker arm through the lubricating oil pipe.
The lubricating oil, after lubricating the gear-side main bearing, splash-lubricates the PTO shaft bearing metal and various other gears.
The lubricating oil which is sent to the main bearing on the mounting flange side goes through the crankshaft and lubricates the crankpin bearing metal. It then splash-lubricates the piston, cylinder and piston pin.
From the rocker arm shaft, the lubricating oil flows through the small hole in the rocker arm to lubricate the push rods and part of the valve head.
The oil that has dropped to the push rod chamber from the rocker arm chamber lubricates the tappets, cam and cam bearing, and returns to the oil pan.
Moreover, an oil pressure switch is provided in the lubricating system to monitor normal circulation and pressure of the lubricating oil. When the lubricating oil pressure drops 0.1 kg/cm² (1.428 lb/in.²), the oil pressure switch illuminates the oil pressure lamp on the instrument panel to notify the operator.

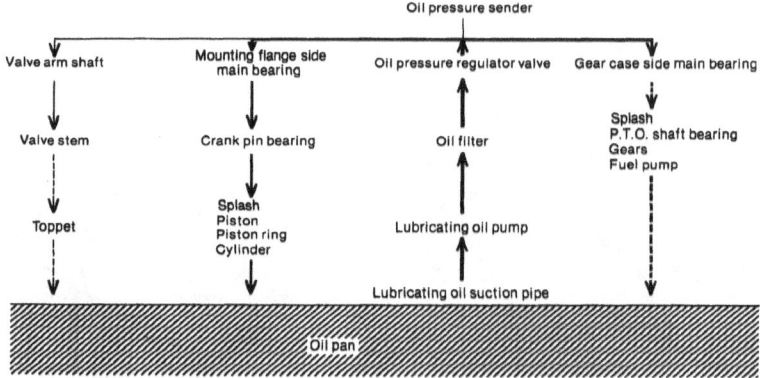

2. Oil Pump

2-1 Construction

The oil pump is a compact, low pressure variation trochoid pump comprising a trochoid curve inner rotor and outer rotor. Pumping pressure is provided by the change in volume between the two rotors caused by rotation of the rotor shaft.

The oil pump is installed on the cylinder side cover and is driven by a rotor shaft fitted to the slit in the end of the camshaft.

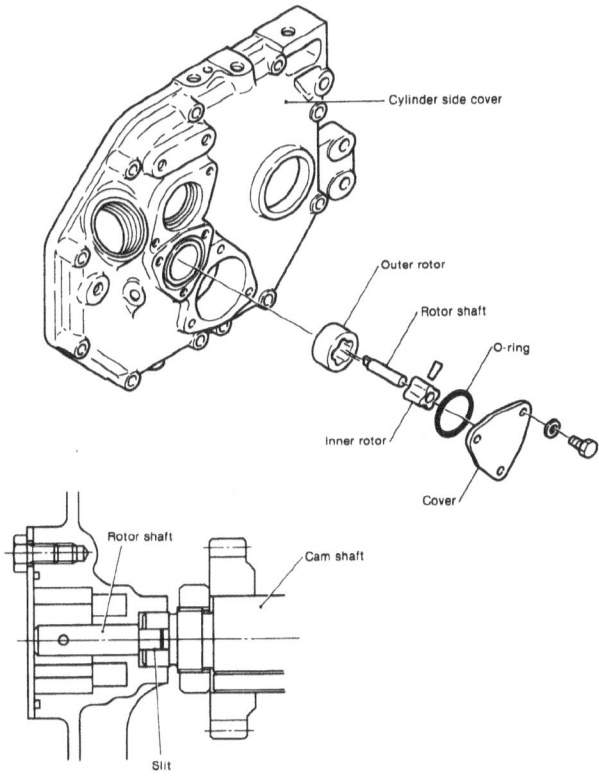

2-2 Specifications

	YSM8	YSM12
Lubricating oil feed volume	200 ℓ/hr (at 3200 rpm)	220 ℓ/hr (at 3000 rpm)
Lubricating oil pressure	2.5 kg/cm² ~ 3.5 kg/cm² (35.56 ~ 49.78 lb/in.²)	

Chapter 6 Lubrication System
2. Oil Pump

2-3 Inspection
When the discharge pressure of the oil pump is extremely low, check the oil level. If it is within the prescribed range, the oil pump must be inspected.

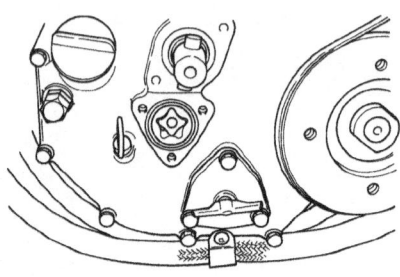

Lubricating oil pump

The lubricating oil pump is constructed integrally with the cylinder side cover and can be checked easily by removing its lid.

(1) Outer rotor and pump body clearance
Measure the clearance by inserting a feeler gauge between the outside of the outer rotor and the pump body casing. If the clearance exceeds the wear limit, replace the outer rotor and pump body as a set.

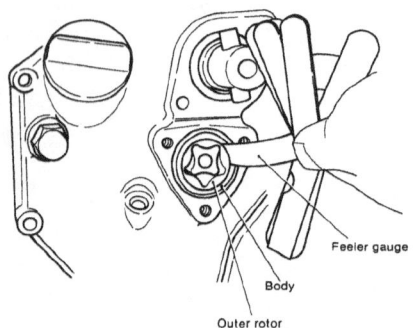

(2) Outer rotor and inner rotor clearance
Fit one of the teeth of the inner rotor to one of the grooves of the outer rotor and measure the clearance at the point where the teeth of both rotors are aligned. Replace the inner rotor and outer rotor ass'y if the wear limit is exceeded.

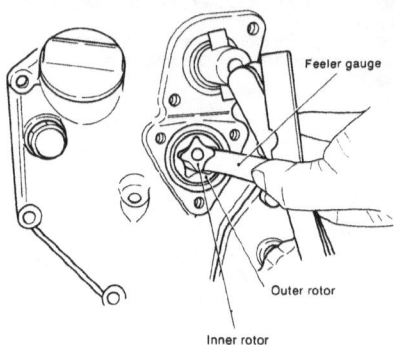

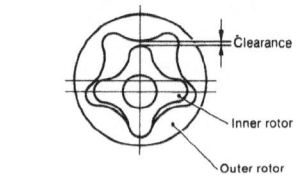

	mm (in.)
Maintenance standard	0.050 ~ 0.105 (0.00197 ~ 0.00413)
Wear limit	0.15 (0.00591)

(3) Pump body and inner rotor, outer rotor side clearance
Install the inner rotor and outer rotor into the pump body casing so that they fit snugly.
Check the clearance by placing a ruler against the end of the body and inserting a feeler gauge between the ruler and the end of the rotor. Replace as a set if the wear limit is exceeded.

	mm (in.)
Maintenance standard	0.050 ~ 0.105 (0.00197 ~ 0.00413)
Wear limit	0.15 (0.00591)

Chapter 6 Lubrication System
2. Oil Pump

SM/YSM

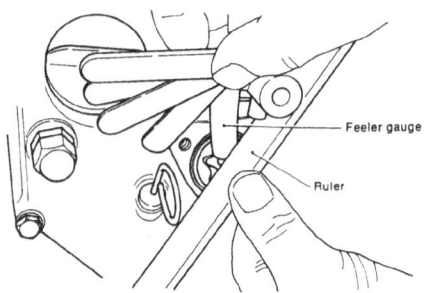

Feeler gauge
Ruler

(5) Rotor shaft and body clearance
Measure the outside diameter of the rotor shaft and the inside diameter of the body shaft hole, and replace the rotor shaft and body as an ass'y if the clearance exceeds the wear limit.

mm (in.)

	Maintenance standard	Clearance when assembled	Maximum allowable clearance
Rotor shaft outside diameter	$29 \, ^{-0.020}_{-0.040}$ (1.14016 ~ 1.14094)	0.12 ~ 0.161 (0.0047 ~ 0.0063)	0.35 (0.0138)
Rotor shaft hole inside diameter	$29.1 \, ^{+0.021}_{0}$ (1.14566 ~ 1.14649)		

mm (in.)

Maintenance standard	0.06 ~ 0.10 (0.00236 ~ 0.00393)
Wear limit	0.13 (0.00511)

(4) Flatness of lubricating oil pump lid surface
Check the lubricating oil pump lid surface for flatness. If it is bent, replace the lid.

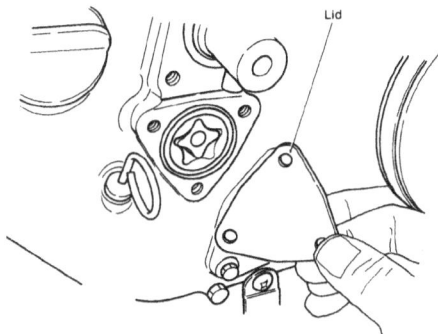

Lid

3. Oil Filter

3-1 Construction of lubricating oil filter

The lubricating oil filter is the auto-clean type, which features high efficiency and ease of maintenance. The lubricating oil from the periphery of the element is filtered through the 150-mesh openings and is sent from the center to the various parts through the hole in the gearcase.

3-3 Checking the lubricating oil filter

(1) Cleaning the lubricating oil filter
Since the filter element can be cleaned simply by turning the handle, make sure it is turned periodically.
(2) Rinsing the lubricating oil filter
Periodically remove the filter and rinse its element in a clean cleansing oil while turning the handle.

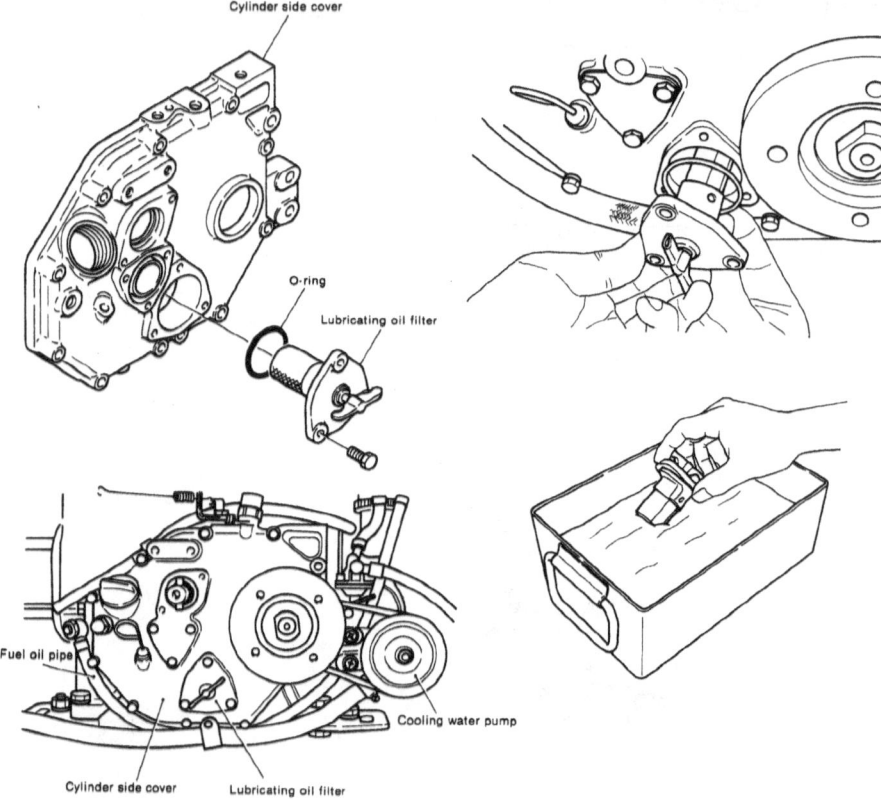

3-2 Specifications for lubricating oil filter

Filtering opening	150 meshes
Filtering capacity	300 ℓ/H

4. Oil Pressure Regulator Valve

4-1 Construction

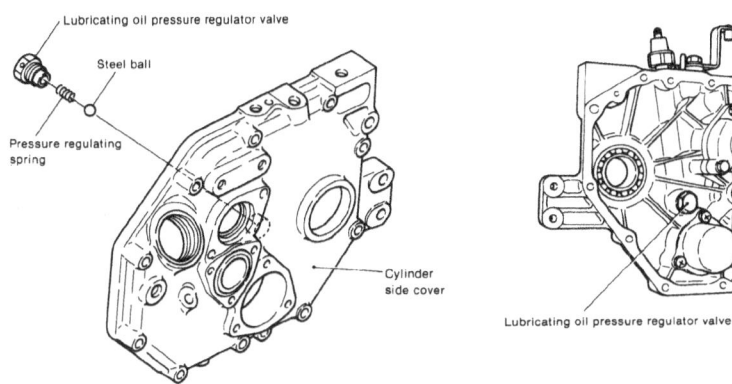

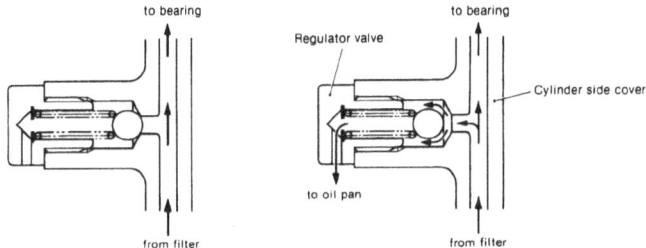

The lubricating oil pressure regulator valve is installed between the drilled holes for connecting the oil filter to the bearing inside the cylinder side cover. It adjusts the oil pressure to a specified value during engine operation. If the pressure of the oil sent from the oil filter is greater than the spring force, the steel ball is pushed out of the valve seat through the gap thus produced and sends the oil toward the oil pan.

Standard Pressure	$2.5 \sim 3.5$ kg/cm² ($35.56 \sim 49.78$ lb/in²)

CHAPTER 7
COOLING SYSTEM

1. Cooling System 7-1
2. Water Pump 7-3
3. Thermostat 7-6
4. Anticorrosion Zinc 7-7
5. Scale Removing 7-8
6. Kingston Cock 7-9
7. Bilge Pump 7-10
8. Bilge Strainer 7-12

1. Cooling System

1. YSM8-R, YSM12-R

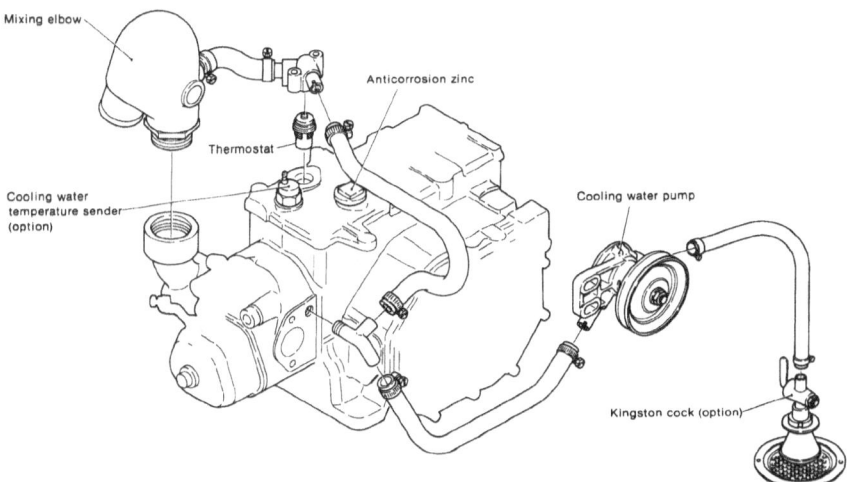

2. YSM8-Y, YSM12-Y

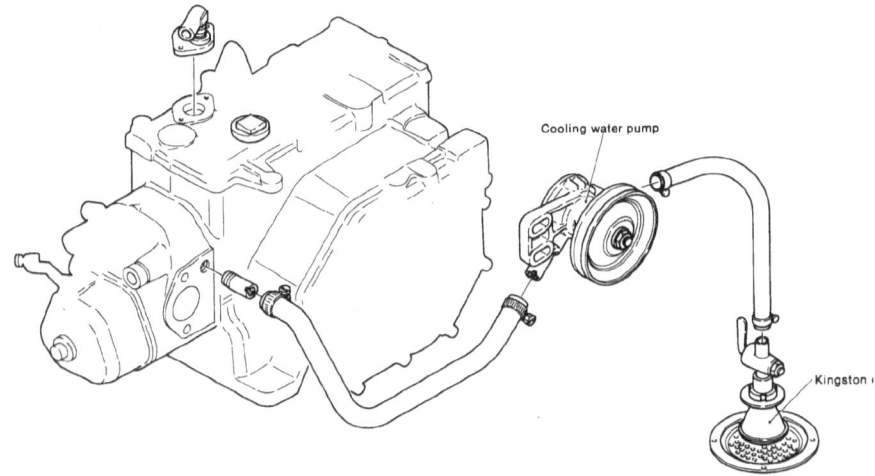

Chapter 7 Cooling System
1. Cooling System

SM/YSM

1-1 Composition

(1) A sea water direct cooling system incorporating a rubber impeller pump is employed.
(2) A themostat is installed on the water-outlet of cylinder jacket and a bypass circuit is provided to keep the cooling water temperature constant at all times.
This not only prevents overcooling at initial operation, but also improves the combustion performance and increases the durability of moving parts by keeping the temperature constant. (R-type)
(3) Anticorrosion zinc is provided at the cylinder jacket to prevent electrolytic corrosion of the cylinder jacket and cylinder head by the sea water.
(4) A cooling water temperature sender is installed so that an abnormal rise in the cooling water temperature is indicated at the lamp on the instrument panel. (R-type)
(5) A tandem type bilge pump for bilge pumping is also available.
(6) A scoop strainer is provided at the water intake kingston cock to remove dirt and vinyl from the water.
(7) Rubber hoses are used for all interior piping. This eliminates pipe brazing damage due to engine vibration and simplifies the engine's mounting.

1-2 Cooling water route (R-type)

The cooling water is sucked up by the water pump through a kingston cock installed on the hull. The water delivered from the water pump is branched in two directions at the cylinder intake coupling: one part of the water enters the cylinder head and the other bypasses the mixing elbow.
The water that enters the cylinder head cools the cylinder head and then rises to the cylinder through the passage and cools the cylinder liner jacket. From the cylinder liner, the water enters the mixing elbow through the thermostat mounting. At the mixing elbow, this water is mixed with the exhaust gas and is discharged out of the vessel.

The temperature of the seawater which is sucked up by the cooling water pump to be used as cooling water is kept constant by the thermostat installed on the upper lid of the cylinder. If the temperature should rise abnormally, it is detected by the temperature sender installed on the upper lid of the cylinder and warning device.

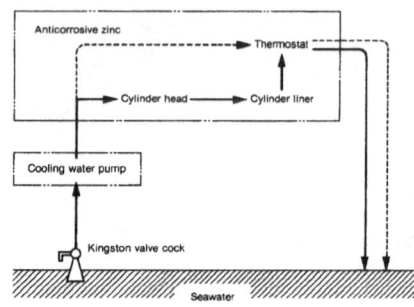

-------- indicates the path of seawater with a temperature below the proper value.
———— indicates the path of seawater with a temperature above the proper value.

2. Water Pump

2-1 Construction and operation

The water pump is a rubber impeller type pump driven from the crankshaft by a V-belt.
The rubber impeller, which has ample elasticity, is deformed by the offset plate inside the casing, causing the water to be discharged. This pump is ideal for small, high-speed engines.

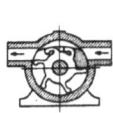

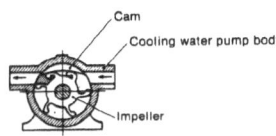

2-2 Cooling water pump (without bilge pump)

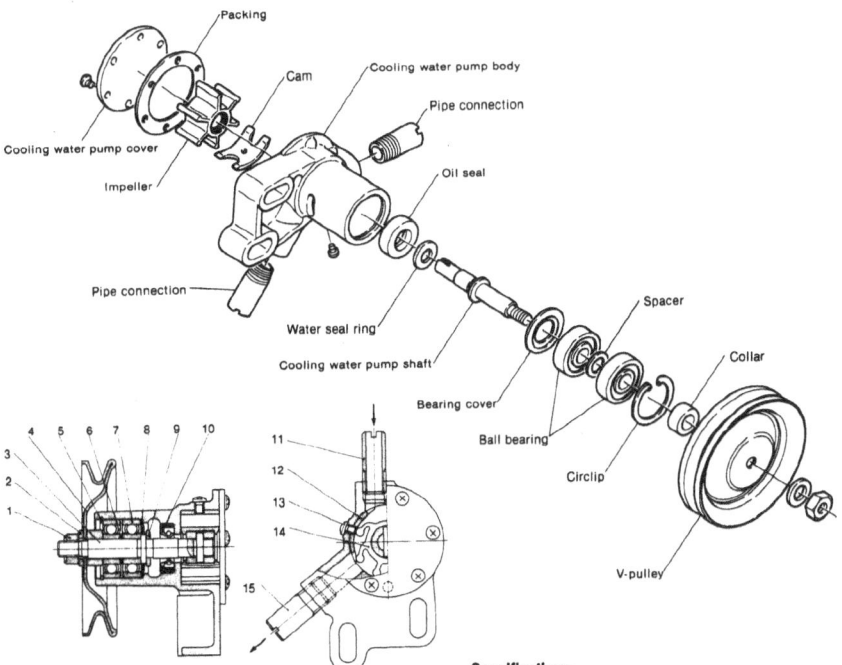

1 Nut
2 Washer
3 Cooling water pump shaft
4 V-pulley
5 Circlip
6 Spacer
7 Ball bearing
8 Bearing cover
9 Water seal ring
10 Oil seal
11 Pipe connection (inlet)
12 Cam
13 Set screw
14 Impeller
15 Pipe connection (outlet)

Specifications m (in.)

Rated speed	2000 rpm
Suction head	1 (39.37)
Total head	3 (78.74)
Delivery Capacity	550 ℓ/hr.

Chapter 7 Cooling System
2. Water Pump

SM/YSM

2-3 Disassembly

(1) Loosen the water pump mounting bolts, remove the V-belt and remove the water pump ass'y from the cylinder.

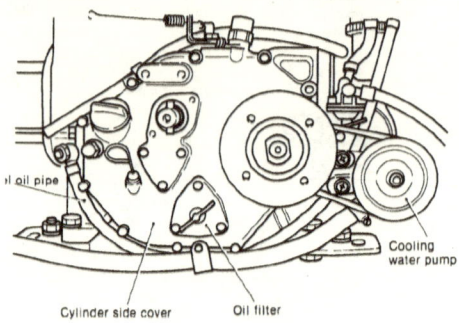

(2) Remove the V-pulley mounting bolt and V-pulley.
(3) Remove the snap ring for fastening the bearing.
(4) Remove the lid for the pump chamber.
(5) Pull out the drive shaft by tapping it with a copper hammer from the impeller side toward the pulley side.
(6) Remove the rubber impeller.
(7) Extract the seal from the pump.
(8) From the drive shaft remove the two bearings, one nylon packing and one rubber seal.

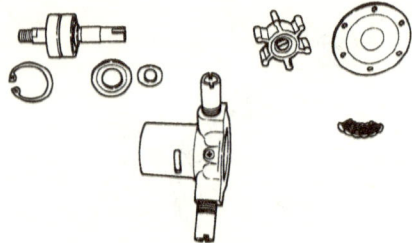

Disassembling the cooling water pump

2-4 Reassembly precautions

(1) Before inserting the rubber impeller into the casing, coat the sliding face, pump shaft and impeller fitting section with grease or Monton X.

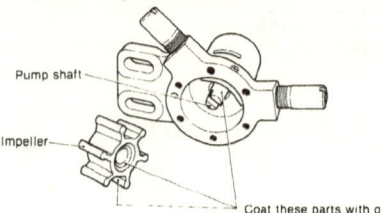

(2) Be sure that the direction of curving of the impeller is correct.
The impeller is curved in the direction opposite the direction of rotation.

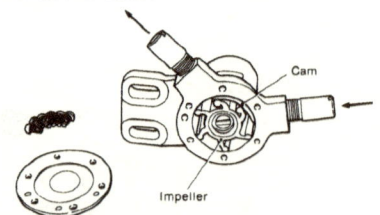

(3) Adjust the V-belt tension.
If the V-belt tension is slack, the discharge of the cooling water will diminish; if it is too tight, the play of the pump bearings and the wear of the wear plate will be accelerated. Adjust the tension to the specified value. Check the deflection of the V-belt by pressing it in the center with your fingers.

mm (in.)

V-Belt deflection	5 to 7 (0.1968 ~ 0.2755)

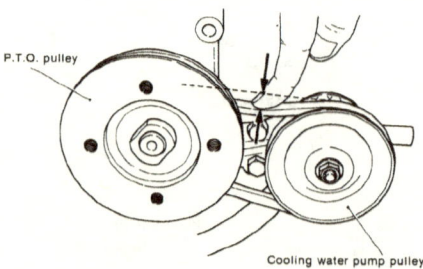

NOTE: Mount the belt in the direction of pump rotation

Chapter 7 Cooling System
2. Water Pump

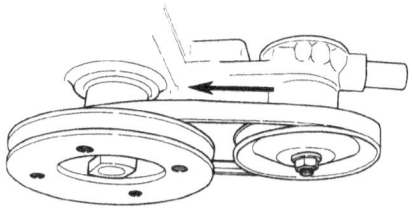

(4) If the sliding surface of the V-belt is cracked or worn or is stained with oil, etc., replace it with a new one.

V-belt for driving cooling water pump	size	19
	code No.	104511 ~ 78780

(5) Check after assembly
After assembly, attach the belt and run the engine to ascertain whether or not it provides the specified discharge.

2-5 Handling precautions
(1) Never operate the water pump dry as this will damage the rubber impeller.
(2) Always turn the engine in the correct direction of rotation as turning the engine in the opposite direction will damage the rubber impeller.
(3) Inspect the pump after every 1,500 hours of operation and replace if faulty.

2-6 Inspection
(1) Inspect the rubber impeller for fractures, cracks and other damage, and replace if faulty.

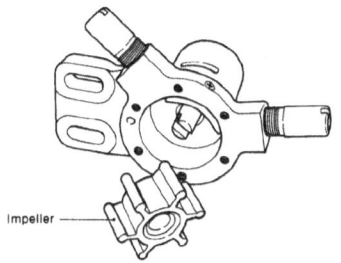

Impeller

(2) Check the pump chamber lid and the impeller sliding surface of the main unit for wear. If they are defective, replace them.

mm (in.)

		Maintenance standard	Clearance at assembly	Maximum allowable clearance	Wear limit
Water pump	Impeller width	19±0.1 (0.744 ~ 0.752)			
	Housing width	18.9 (0.7441) (without packing) 19.2 (0.7559) (with packing)	0.2 (0.0079)	0.4 (0.0157)	
	Wear plate wear				0.2 (0.0079)

(3) Water pump impeller shaft oil seal section wear.

mm(in.)

	Maintenance standard	Wear limit
Oil seal section shaft diameter	10.0 (0.3937)	9.9 (0.3898)

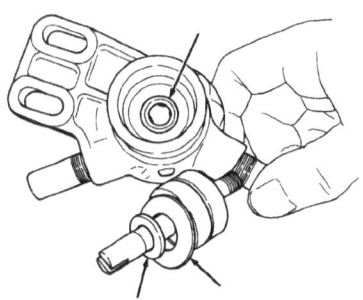

If water leaking from the scupper increases while the engine is running, or if the components are found to be defective when disassembled, replace them.

(4) Inspect the bearing for play and check for seizing at the impeller shaft fitting section. Replace the bearing if there is any play.

Chapter 7 Cooling System
3. Thermostat

3. Thermostat

3-1 Construction and operation

The thermostat remains closed until the cooling water temperature reaches a fixed temperature. Until the cooling water reaches this fixed temperature, it collects at the cylinder head and the water flowing from the water pump is discharged through the bypass circuit. When the cooling water temperature exceeds a fixed temperature, the thermostat opens and the cooling water flows through the main circuit of the cylinder and cylinder head. The thermostat serves to prevent overcooling and improve combustion performance by maintaining the cooling water temperature at a specified level. The thermostat of this engine is installed at the cooling water outlet on the cylinder body.

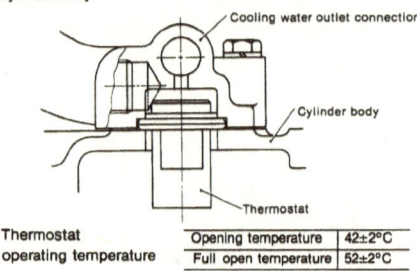

Thermostat operating temperature	Opening temperature	42±2°C
	Full open temperature	52±2°C

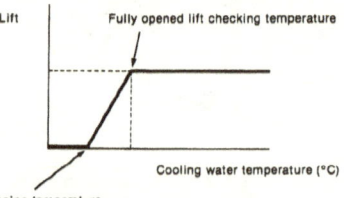

Characteristic of Thermostat

When the seawater temperature is below 42°C, the pumped-up seawater is discharged outside directly from the thermostat section, and circulation of the cooling water into the cylinder is stopped until the water temperature rises. When the water temperature reaches 52°C, the thermostat valve is opened fully.

3-2 Inspection

(1) Remove the water outlet coupling at the top of cylinder body to remove and inspect the thermostat. Remove any dirt or foreign matter that has built up in the thermostat, and check the spring, etc. for damage and corrosion.

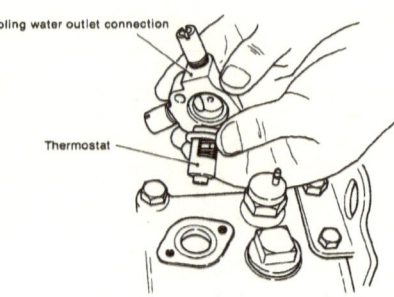

(2) Testing the thermostat
Place the thermostat in a container filled with water. Heat the container with an electric heater. If the thermostat valve begins to open when the water temperature reaches about 42°C and becomes fully open at 52°C, the thermostat may be considered all right. If its behaviour differs much from the above, or if it is found to be broken, replace it.

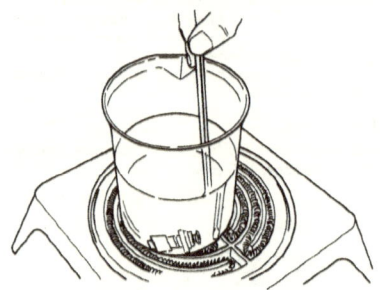

(3) In general, inspect the thermostat after every 300 hours of operation. However, always inspect it when the cooling water temperature has risen abnormally and when white smoke is emitted for a long period of time after the engine starts.

(4) Replace the thermostat when it has been in use for a year, or after every 2000 hours of operation.

Part No. code of thermostat	105582 ~ 49200

(5) Attaching the thermostat to the colling water system
Before attaching the thermostat to the system, be sure to check its packing and make sure there are no leaks.

4. Anticorrosion Zinc

4-1 Principles

Anticorrosion zinc is installed to prevent electrolytic corrosion by sea water.

When different metals, i.e., iron and copper, are placed in an highly conductive liquid, such as sea water, the iron gradually rusts. The anticorrosion zinc provides protection against corrosion by corroding in place of the cylinder, cylinder liners and other iron parts.

Anticorrosion zinc is provided at the cylinder water jacket.

Replace the anticorrosion zinc after 50% corrosion.

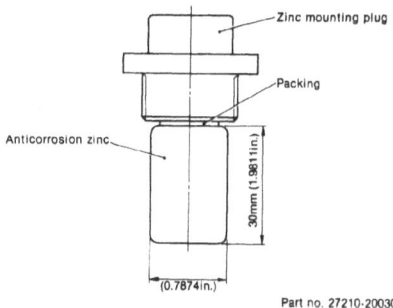

Part no. 27210-200300

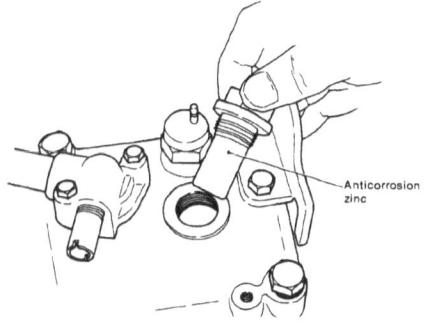

Replace the anticorrosion zinc by pulling the old zinc from the zinc mounting plug and screwing in the new zinc.

4-2 Inspection

Generally, replace the anticorrosion zinc after every 500 hours of operation. However, since this period depends on the properties of the sea water and operating conditions, periodically inspect the anticorrosion zinc and remove the oxidized film on its surface.

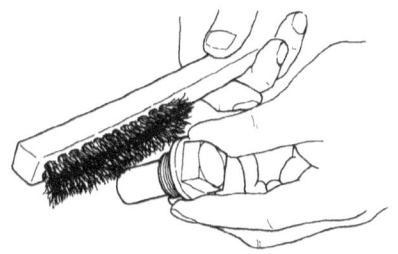

5. Deposit Removing

If deposit formed on the cooling water passageways the flow of the cooling water will be hampered, giving rise to engine trouble. So it is necessary to remove deposit from the passageways by running fresh water through them.

6. Kingston Cock

6-1 Construction
The Kingston cock, installed on the bottom of the hull, controls the intake of cooling water into the boat. The Kingston cock serves to filter the raw water so that mud, sand, and other foreign matter in the water does not enter the water pump.
Numerous holes are drilled in the raw water side of the Kingston cock, and a scoop strainer is installed to prevent sucking in of vinyl, etc.

6-3 Inspection
When the cooling water volume has dropped and the pump is normal, remove the vessel from the water and check for clogging of the Kingston cock.
Moreover, when water leaks from the cock, disassemble the cock and inspect it for wear, and repair or replace it.

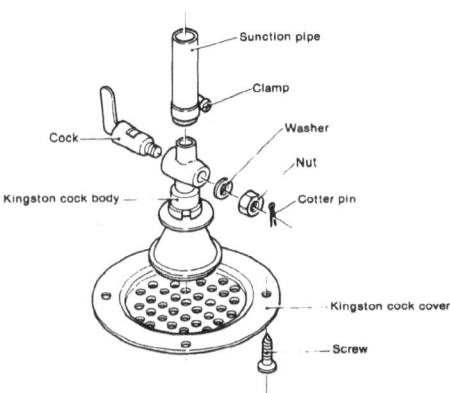

6-2 Handling precautions
Caution the user to always close the Kingston cock after each day of use and to confirm that it is open before beginning operation.
If the Kingston cock is left open, water will flow in reverse and the vessel will sink if trouble occurs with the water pump.
Moreover, if the engine is operated with the Kingston cock closed, the cooling water will not be able to come in, resulting in engine and pump trouble.

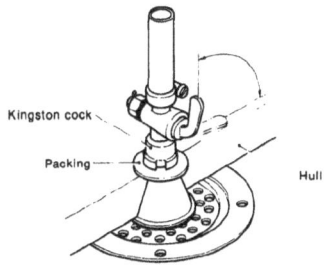

7. Bilge Pump

7-1 Construction of bilge pump

The construction of the bilge pump is similar to that of rotary rubber impeller type cooling water pump. It is mounted on the lid side of the cooling water pump. By inserting the impeller shaft into the slit of the impeller shaft of the cooling water pump, it is driven by the PTO V pulley simultaneously with the cooling water pump.

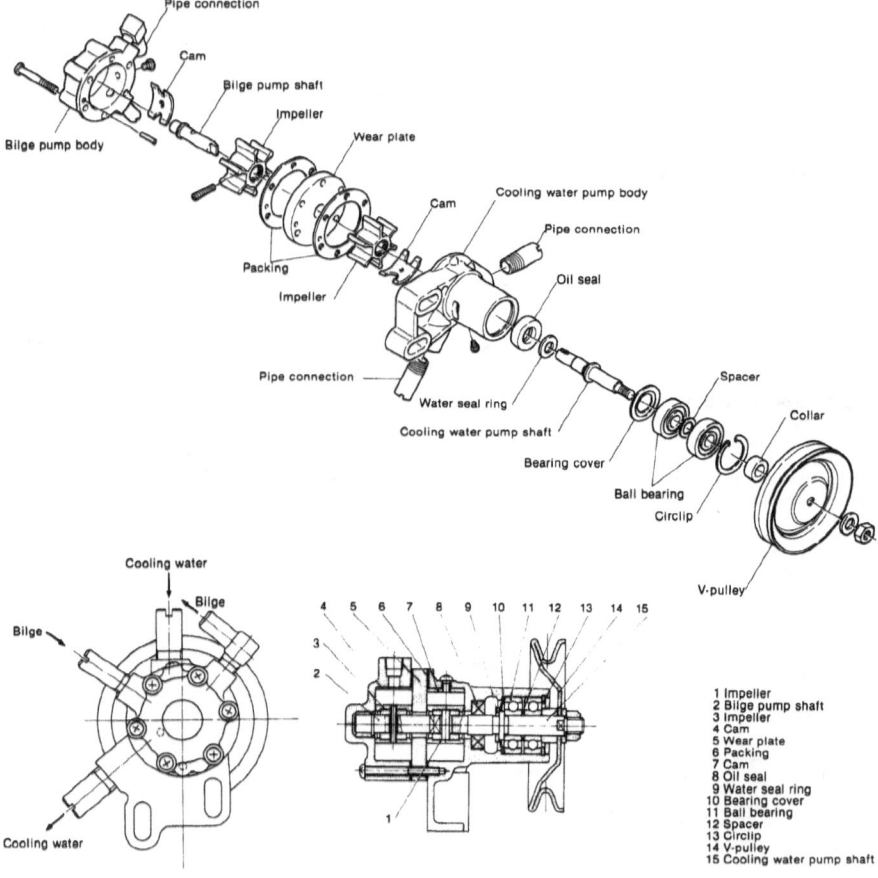

1 Impeller
2 Bilge pump shaft
3 Impeller
4 Cam
5 Wear plate
6 Packing
7 Cam
8 Oil seal
9 Water seal ring
10 Bearing cover
11 Ball bearing
12 Spacer
13 Circlip
14 V-pulley
15 Cooling water pump shaft

Chapter 7 Cooling System
7. Bilge Pump

SM/YSM

7·2 Specifications

m (in.)

Rated speed	2000 rpm
Suction head	1 (39.37)
Total head	2 (78.74)
Delivery capacity	150 ℓ/hr.

7·3 Disassembling the bilge pump
(1) By removing the fitting bolt for the bilge pump, remove the bilge pump as a unit.
(2) Remove the packing and the wear plate.
(3) Pull out the impeller and impeller shaft from the pump.
(4) By removing the setscrew remove the impeller from the impeller shaft.
(5) Remove the cam from the bilge pump.

7·4 Inspection
(1) Inspect the rubber impeller for fractures, cracks and other damage, and replace if faulty.
(2) Rubber impeller side wear and wear plate clearance.

mm (in.)

		Maintenance standard	Clearance at assembly	Maximum allowable clearance	Wear limit
Bilge pump	Impeller width	19 ±0.1 (0.744 ~ 0.752)	0.2 (0.0079)	0.4 (0.0157)	
	Housing width	18.9 (0.7441) (without packing) 19.2 (0.7559) (with packing)			
	Wear plate wear				0.2 (0.0079)

(3) Inspect the bearing for play and check for seizing at the impeller shaft fitting section. Replace the bearing if there is any play.
(4) Bilge pump impeller shaft and bushing clearance measurement.

mm (in.)

		Maintenance standard	Clearance at assembly	Maximum allowable clearance
Wear plate	Impeller shaft outside diameter	9.5 (0.3740)	0.005 ~ 0.045 (0.0002 ~ 0.0018)	0.2 (0.0079)
	Bushing inside diameter	9.5 (0.3740)		
Bilge pump body	Impeller shaft outside diameter	9.5 (0.3740)	0.005 ~ 0.045 (0.002 ~ 0.0018)	0.2 (0.0079)
	Bushing inside diameter	9.5 (0.3740)		

8. Bilge Strainer

8-1 Construction
Water collected in the bilge is sucked up and discharged to the outside of the vessel by the bilge pump. The bilge strainer serves to filter slagged oil, iron particles and other dirt mixed in the bilge. If the bilge strainer becomes clogged, the bilge pump will operate dry, reducing the durability of the impeller.

8-2 Inspection
Since the bilge strainer moves around the bilge and frequently becomes clogged with dirt and other foreign matter, periodically pull it from the bilge and wash it with clean water.

YSM8-Y, YSM12-Y
YSM8-R, YSM12-R : OPTION

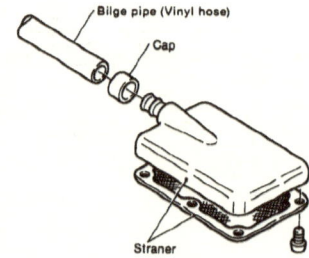

CHAPTER 8
STARTING SYSTEM

1. Starting System Construction 8-1
2. Electric Starting System 8-2
3. Overdrive Hand-Operated System 8-3
4. Chain-Overdrive Hand-Operated System 8-5

1. Starting System Construction

Model	Standard specifications	special specifications
YSM8-R YSM12-R	Overdrive hand-operated starting system and electric starting system installed side by side	Chain-overdrive hand-operated starting system
YSM8-Y YSM12-Y	Overdrive hand-operated starting system	Chain-overdrive hand-operated starting system

Chapter 8 Starting System
2. Electric Starting System —————————————————————— *SM / YSM*

2. Electric Starting System (for details see Chapter 11, "Electrical Equipment")

In the electric starting system the pinion of the starting motor installed on the flywheel housing meshes with the ring gear to rotate the crankshaft. The generator for charging battery is driven by the PTO shaft V-pulley.

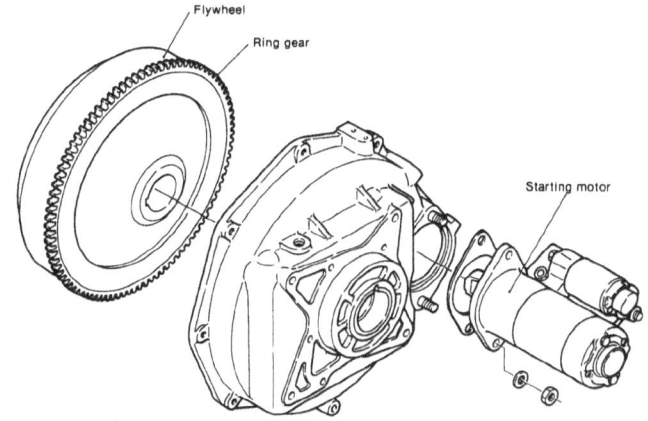

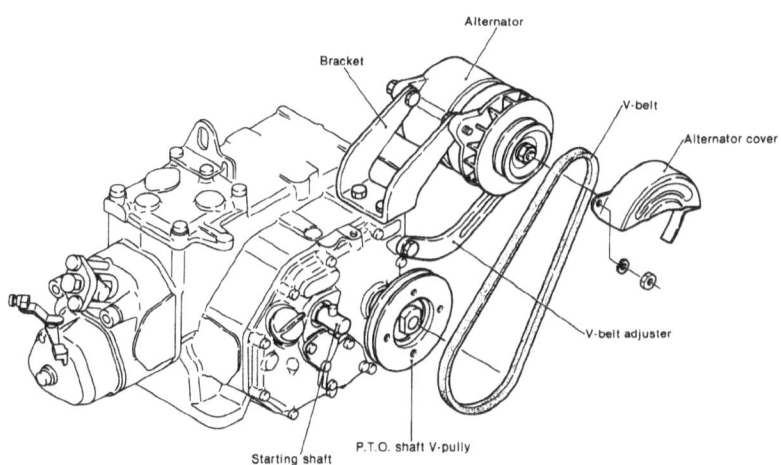

3. Overdrive Hand-Operated System

3-1 Overdrive hand-operated system construction

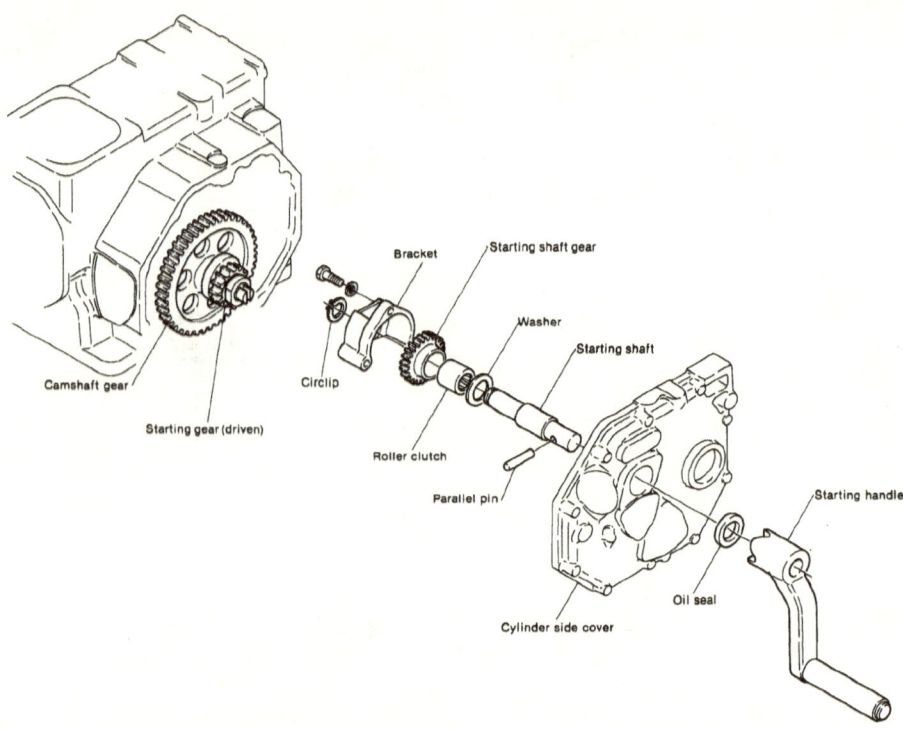

In the overdrive hand-operated starting system the hand-operated starting shaft mounted on the cylinder side cover is rotated by the starting handle. The turning force is them transmitted to the driven gear mounted on the camshaft which rotates the crankshaft. Between the starting shaft and the starting shaft gear the roller clutch is installed. As for cranking during start up, the starting shaft rotates the starting shaft gear. But once the engine starts running the starting shaft is freed and will not rotate despite the rotation of the starting shaft gear.

Chapter 8 Starting System
3. Overdrive Hand-Operated System   *SM/YSM*

3-2 Specifications for overdrive hand-operated starting system

		YSM8	YSM12
Overdrive ratio =	$\dfrac{\text{rotation of crankshaft}}{\text{rotation of starting shaft}}$	2.67	2.0
Direction of starting handle rotation		Clockwise (bow side)	

3-3 Disassembling the overdrive hand-operated starting unit

1. Remove the cylinder side cover.
2. Extract the parallel pin.
3. Remove the bracket mounting and the starting unit as a unit from the cylinder side cover.
4. Remove the circlip and pull out the starting shaft, gear and roller clutch from the bracket.

3-4 Inspection of each component

1. Inspection of roller clutch
2. Inspection of gears
   Check all teeth surfaces. if any cracks, etc. are detected, replace the gear.
3. Inspection of starting shaft
   Check the roller clutch section and bearing section for burning, wear, etc. If any noticeable defects are detected, replace.
4. If the parallel pin is bent or loose, repair or replace.
5. Check the oil seal. If there are any surface scratches, replace.

4. Chain-Overdrive Hand-Operated System

4-1 Construction of chain-overdrive hand-operated system

In the chain-overdrive hand-operated system the sprocket wheel, which is mounted on the starting shaft in an overdrive hand-operated system, is connected by a chain to the sprocket wheel of a separate starting shaft, mounted on the upper part of the engine, so it can be started by the starting handle.

Since the speedup ratio between the chain overdrive hand-operated system and the overdrive hand-operated system is 1:1, the force required for the rotation of the former is equal to that required for rotation of the latter. Despite this fact the chain-overdrive hand-operated system has been adopted for increased ease of operation of the starting handle, by elevating the handle rotating position, and for increased range of operation, by making cranking possible from both the bow and the stern.

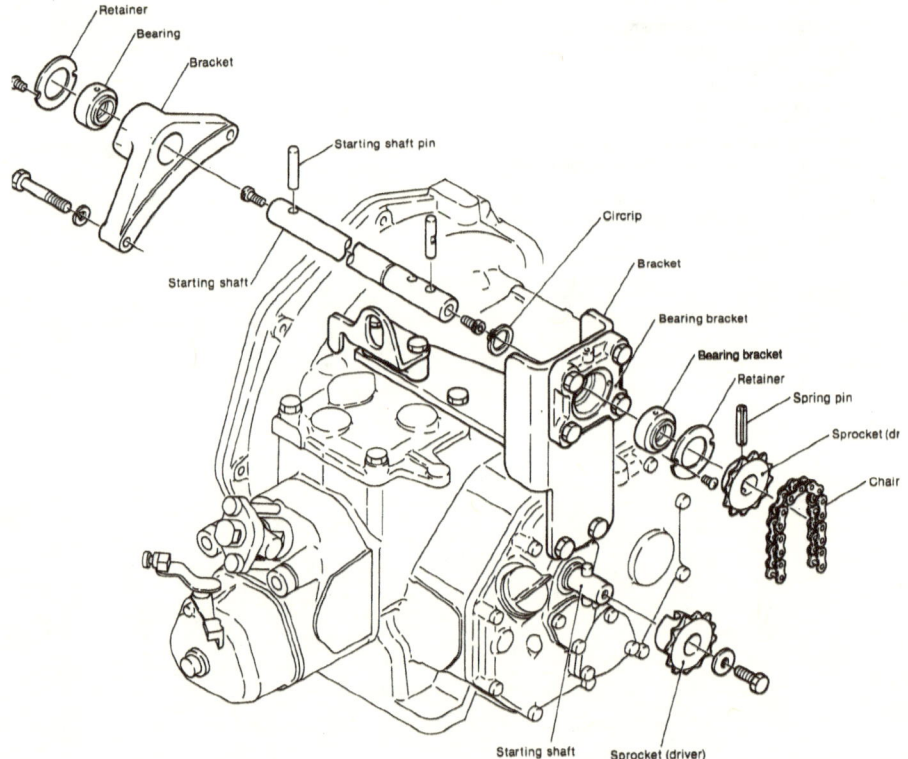

Chapter 8 Starting System
4. Chain-Overdrive Hand-Operated System

4-2 Specifications for chain-overdrive hand-operated system

		YSM8	YSM12
Overdrive ratio		2.67	2.00
Direction of rotation	Bow side start	Clockwise	
	Stern side start	Counterclockwise	
Nominal No. of roller chain		43	
Pitch of roller chain		12.7 mm (1/2")	
Length of standard roller chain		42 links	42 links

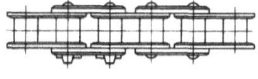

4-3 Adjusting the tension on the chain

Adjust the tension on the chain by raising or lowering the position of the bearing box.

Adjusting the range using a long hole in the bearing box	±3.5 mm
Tension adjustment values	Install the chain so that the sprocket rotates easily.

If the chain has stretched to the point that its tension can not be adjusted by raising or lowering the bearing box, shorten the chain.
When shortening the chain, use coupling links or offset links.

CHAPTER 9
REDUCTION AND REVERSING GEAR

1. Construction... 9-1
2. Installation... 9-6
3. Handling the Reduction and Reversing Gears... 9-7
4. Inspection and Servicing... 9-8
5. Disassembling the Reduction and Reversing Gears... 9-14
6. Reassembling the Reduction and Reversing Gears... 9-17

Chapter 9 Reduction and Reversing Gear
1. Construction
SM/YSM

1. Construction

1-1 Specifications

Engine model			YSM8	YSM12
Reduction system			Two-stage reduction, spur gear	
Reversing system			Constant mesh gear	
Clutch			Wet type single-disc, mechanically operated.	
Reduction ratio		Forward	1.95, 2.93	1.98, 3.06
		Reverse	1.95, 2.93	1.98, 3.06
Direction of rotation	Input shaft		Counter clockwise as viewed from stern	
	Output shaft	Forward	Counter clockwise as viewed from stern	
		Reverse	Clockwise as viewed from stern	
Lubricating oil			SAE 20/30	
Lubricating oil capacity			0.7ℓ (0.185 U.S. Gal.) (total)/0.2ℓ (0.053 U.S. Gal.) (effective)	
Dry weight			21.5kg (47.3 lbs.)	23.5kg (51.7 lbs.)

1-2 Construction

(1) Cross-section

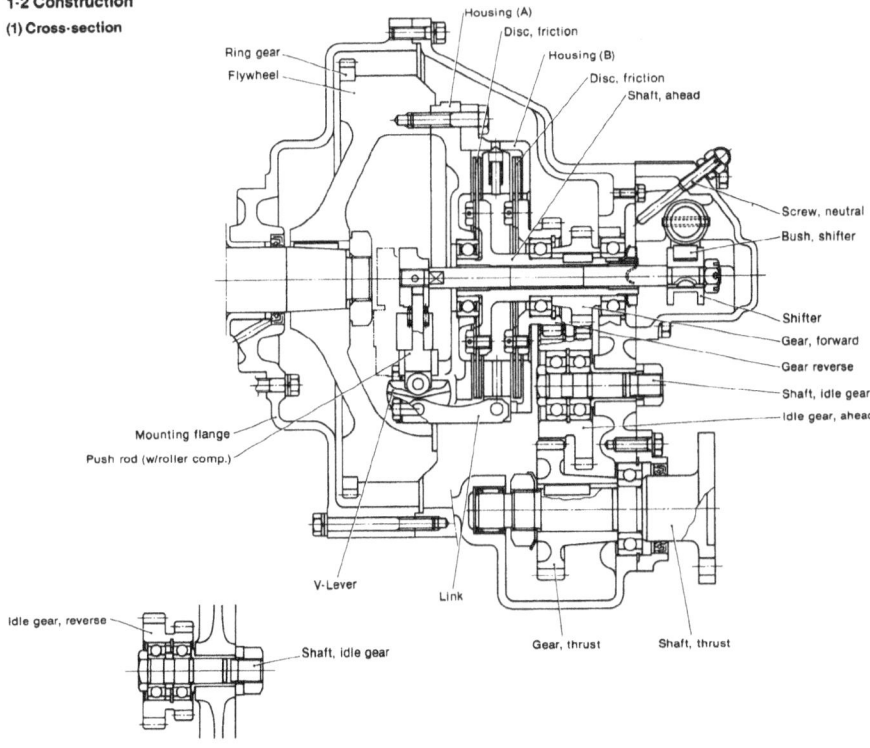

Chapter 9 Reduction and Reversing Gear
1. Construction

SM/YSM

(2) Drawing

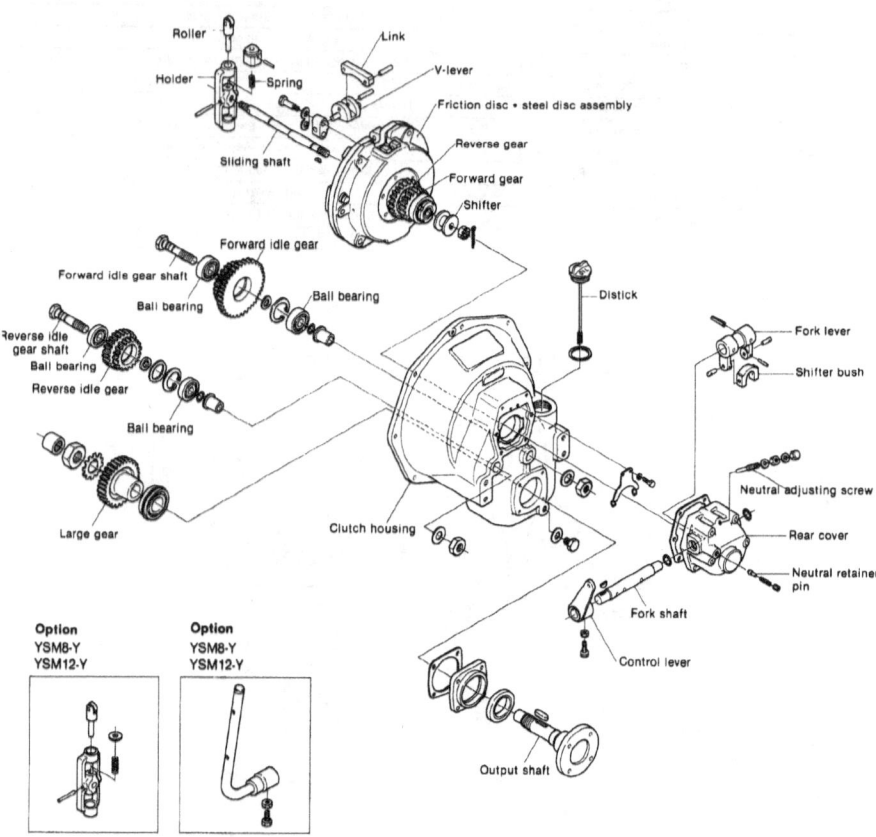

Chapter 9 Reduction and Reversing Gear
1. Construction

1-3 Power transmission system

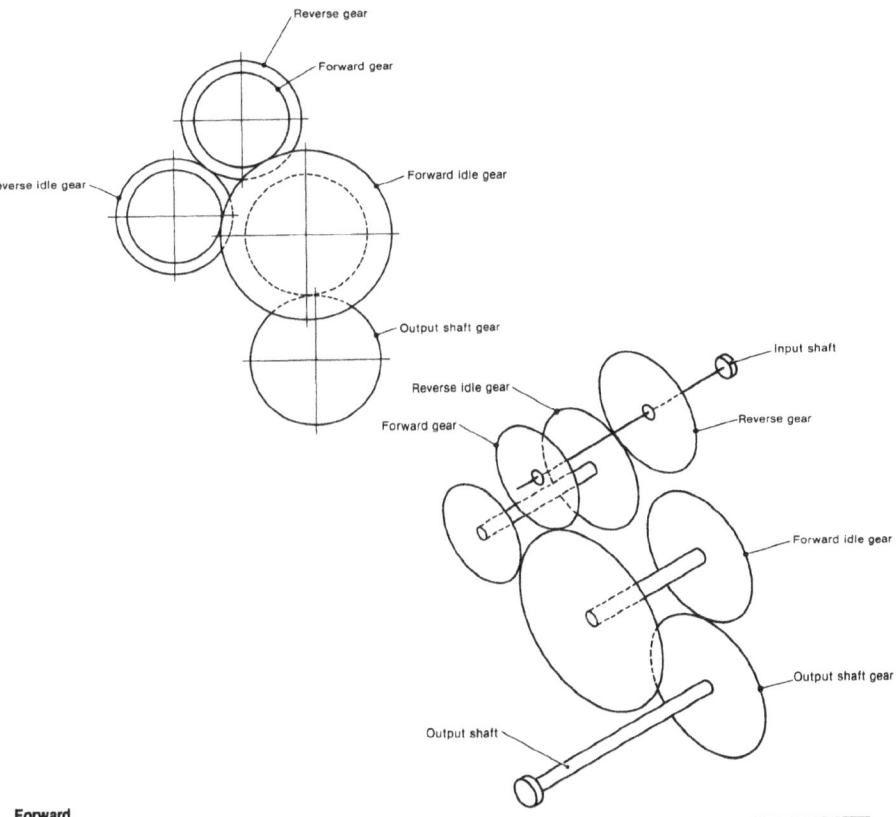

Forward

Model	Forward gear	Forward idle gear	Large gear	Reduction ratio
YSM8	Z = 20	Z = 35, 26	Z = 29	35/20 × 29/26 = 1.952
	Z = 19	Z = 36, 22	Z = 34	36/19 × 34/22 = 2.928
YSM12	Z = 24	Z = 42, 31	Z = 35	42/24 × 35/31 = 1.976
		Z = 42, 24	Z = 42	42/24 × 42/24 = 3.063

Reverse

Model	Reverse gear	Reverse idle gear	Forward idle gear	Large gear	Reduction ratio
YSM8	Z = 24	Z = 20—24	Z = 35—26	Z = 29	24/24 × 35/20 × 29/26 = 1.952
		Z = 19—24	Z = 36—22	Z = 34	24/24 × 36/19 × 34/22 = 2.928
YSM12	Z = 28	Z = 24—28	Z = 42—31	Z = 35	28/28 × 42/24 × 35/31 = 1.976
		Z = 24—28	Z = 42—24	Z = 42	28/28 × 42/24 × 42/24 = 3.063

Printed in Japan
A0A1001 8311

Chapter 9 Reduction and Reversing Gear
1. Construction

1-4 Clutch transmission mechanism

The reduction and reversing gears of this engine include a forward gear, reverse gear, output shaft gear and two idle gears (a forward idle gear and a reverse idle gear). In the idle gear, the gear wheel and pinion are constructed integrally with each other.

These gears are always in mesh and rotate both forward and backward.

(1) When moving forward:
There are two friction discs. The power is transmitted to the left friction disc, then from gear B to gear C (C_0 & C_1) and gear D to drive the propeller shaft.

(2) When moving astern:
The power is transmitted to the right friction disc, and in turn to gear A, gear E (E_0 & E_1), gear C (C_0 & C_1), and gear D to drive the propeller shaft.

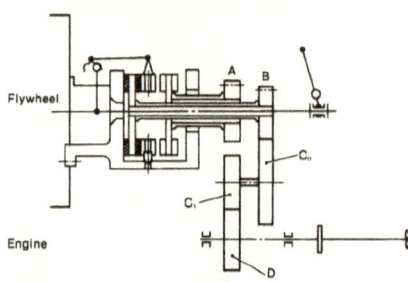

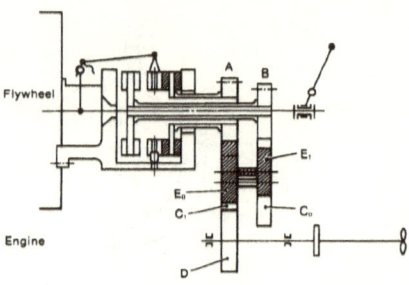

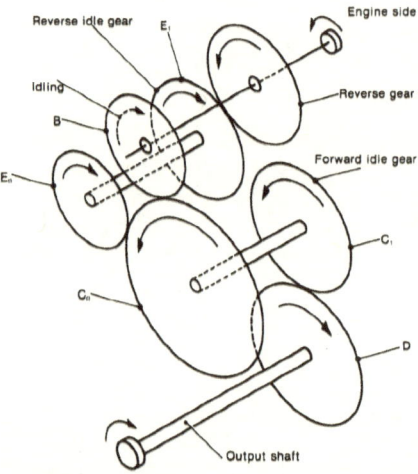

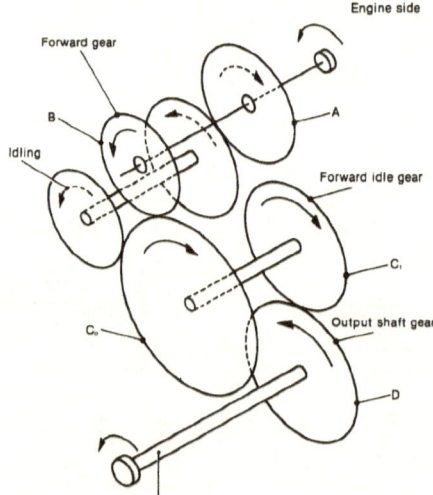

Thus, by operating a gear lever, the right and left friction discs are used as appropriate, depending upon the transmission mode of ahead or astern. All gears are constant meshed type, and the friction discs are normally turning in opposite directions except in their neutral position.

Chapter 9 Reduction and Reversing Gear
1. Construction

(3) When in neutral position:
The two friction discs are free from the friction plate, and gears A, B, C and D are all stationary even when the engine is running. A neutral positioning piece is furnished so as not to transmit power to between the friction plate and the friction discs. Therefore, "accompaniment" does not occur with the propeller shaft while the mechanism is in its neutral position.

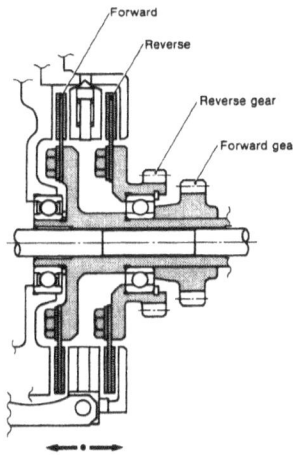

2. Installation

2-1 Clutch Case Alignment

When replacing parts of the fly-wheel housing or clutch case, carry out the following procedures for the clutch case alignment, which should also be applied in case of deviations in the alignment at the time of mechanical repair and servicing.

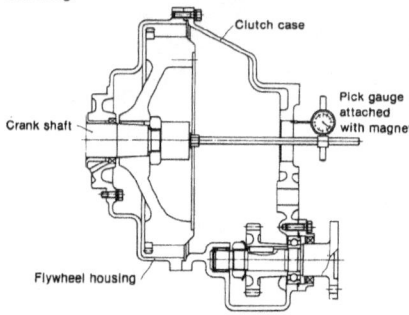

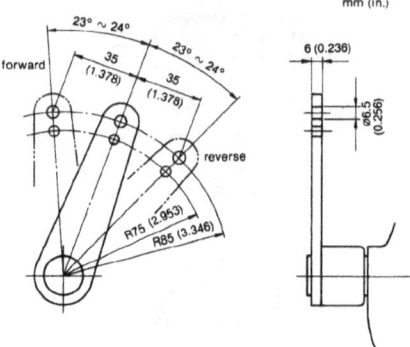

(1) Fix the clutch case temporarily to the fly-wheel housing.
(2) Attach the pick dial with a magnet to the end of the crank shaft and set the gauge.
(3) Rotate the crankshaft to read deflection of the gauge.
(4) Set the position of the clutch case so that the deflection of the gauge less than or equal to 0.2 mm.
(5) Set the knock pin to fix the position.

2-2 Operating lever

The reduction and reversing gears of this engine require little operating force, but can easily switch back and forth between forward and reverse.
Machine types YSM8-R and YSM12-R are constructed so that push-pull one-hand remote control can be employed, while machine types YSM8-Y and YSM12-Y can be equipped with a machine side operating unit and a simple link-type remote control unit.

(1) Configuration of operating lever for YSM8-R and YSM12-R

(2) Configuration of operating lever for YSM8-Y and YSM12-Y

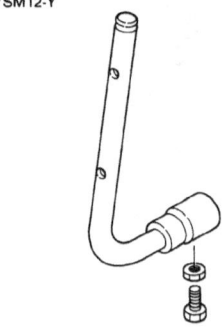

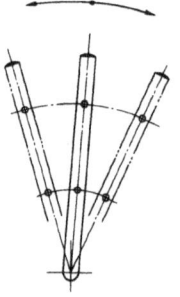
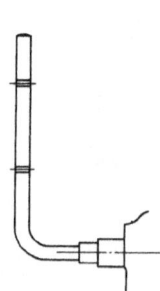

3. Handling the Reduction and Reversing Gears

3-1 Adjustments

3-1.1 Adjusting the adjusting screw for clutch neutral position

1. Remove the cap nut on the upper inclined surface of the clutch forward shaft gear box and loosen the clamp nut.
2. Operate the engine, and with the controlling lever in the neutral position, turn the neutral position adjusting screw clockwise or counterclockwise until the output shaft coupling stops rotating (about 1/2 or 1 full).
3. After making sure the output shaft coupling will not rotate forward or backward, tighten the clamp nut.
4. After tightening the clamp nut, securely tighten the cap nut.
5. Too much tightening may break the inside spring. Be very careful.

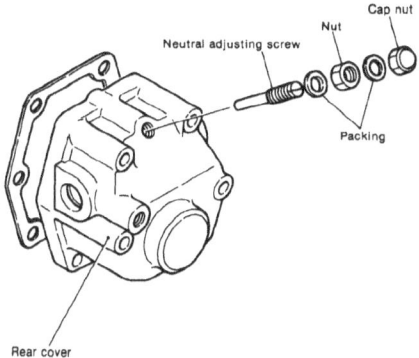

4. Inspection and Servicing

4-1 Condition of clutch housing
1. Check the clutch case for cracks using a test hammer and, if necessary, inspect by color-check. If cracks are noted, replace it with new one.
2. Check each bearing housing for burning damage. If any damage is detected, measure the inside diameter. If the inside diameter has reached the wear limit, replace the housing.

4-2 Condition of each bearing
1. Check each bearing for damage and rust. If a bearing is rusty or its balls, retainer, etc. are damaged, replace.
2. Smooth rotation
If the rotation of a bearing is uneven or produces noise, replace it with a new one.

4-3 Condition of each gear
1. Damaged tooth surface
Check the tooth surface of each gear for cracks, scratches and pitching. Replace when serious damage is found.
2. Bearing of tooth surface
Check the tooth surface of each gear for bearing.
If the bearing is less than 70% of the face width, find out why this has happened, and, if necessary, replace the gear. Neither the tooth top nor the tooth flank should have any bearing.
3. Check the fitted part of shafts or a key grooves for cracks and burning damage and replace, when needed.
4. Backlash of gear

mm (in.)

	YSM8	YSM12
	Standard value	
Forward gear and idler gear	0.12 ~ 0.2 (0.0047 ~ 0.0079)	
Reverse gear and idler gear		
Idler gear and large gear		

Replace the gear when gear noise becomes too loud.

4-4 Friction disk
1. Check the friction disk for cracks, burning damage and fracture, and repair any damage. Replace all discolored or seriously damaged friction disks.
2. Check the friction disk for wear.
If its thickness is less than the values listed below, replace.

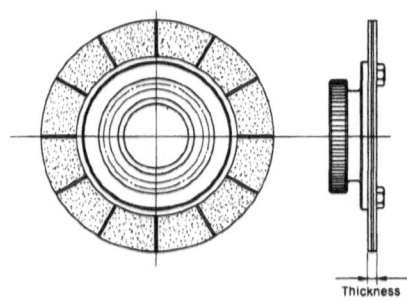

Thickness

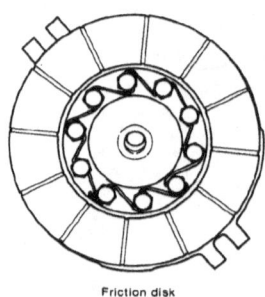

Friction disk

mm (in.)

	YSM8		YSM12	
	Standard value	Wear limit value	Standard value	Wear limit value
Thickness of friction disk	$6^{+0.3}_{0}$ (0.2362 ~ 0.2480)	4.5 (0.1772)	$6^{+0.3}_{0}$ (0.2362 ~ 0.2480)	4.5 (0.1772)

Chapter 9 Reduction and Reversing Gear
4. Inspection and Servicing

3. Replacing the friction disk
   1) Remove the clutch and take out the friction disk.
   2) After removing the binding wire, remove the bolt.
   3) After replacing the friction disk, tighten the bolt.
      kg·m (ft·lb)

Tightening torque	2.0 to 2.5 (14.26 ~ 18.07)

   4) By using a binding wire, bind the bolt in the direction in which the bolt is tightened.

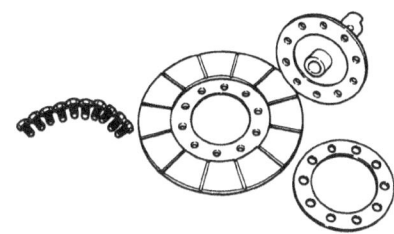

4-5 Friction disk and neutral position holding pawl.

1. Check the friction disk and neutral position holding pawl for damage and burning damage. If they are seriously damaged, replace.
2. Friction disk wear.

mm (in.)

Width of friction disk	YSM8		YSM12	
	Standard dimensions	Limit dimensions	Standard dimensions	Limit dimensions
	18 (0.7087)	17.8 (0.7008)	18 (0.7087)	17.8 (0.7008)

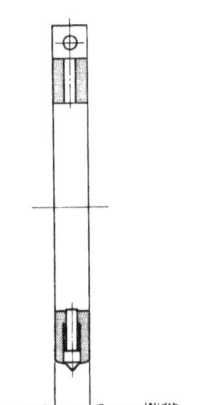
Width

3. Neutral position holding pawl.

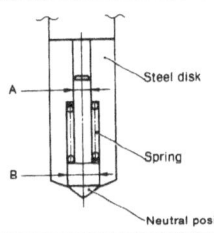

Steel disk
Spring
Neutral position holding pawl

mm (in.)

YSM8/YSM12	Standard dimensions	Clearance at assembly	Wear limit of component part
Outside diameter of pawl A	$6_{-0.15}^{-0.05}$ (0.2303 ~ 0.2343)	0.05 ~ 0.25 (0.0020 ~ 0.0098)	0.5 (0.0197)
Diameter of hole of disk	$6_{0}^{+0.1}$ (0.2362 ~ 0.2402)		
Outside diameter of pawl B	$9_{-0.15}^{-0.05}$ (0.3484 ~ 0.3524)		
Diameter of hole of disk	$9_{0}^{+0.1}$ (0.3543 ~ 0.3583)		

Check the pawl tip for wear

Chapter 9 Reduction and Reversing Gear
4. Inspection and Servicing

SM/YSM

4. Spring for neutral position holding pawl (for both YSM8 and YSM12)
Check the spring for breaks, corrosion, and permanent deformation.

mm (in.)

	Standard dimensions	Limit dimension
Free length of spring	23 mm (0.9055)	21 mm (0.8268)

4-6 Clutch housing A and clutch housing B

1. Check the friction surface of the clutch housing for cracks, damage, seizure, etc. Repair any damage. If the housing is cracked or seriously damaged, replace.
2. Wear of friction surface
After bolting clutch housing A and clutch housing B together, as shown in the diagram below, measure the wear and width of the friction surface.

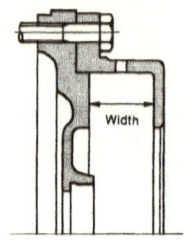

mm (in.)

	YSM8		YSM12	
	Standard dimension	Wear limit dimension	Standard dimension	Wear limit dimension
Friction surface and friction surface width	33.4 mm (1.3150)	35 (1.3780)	33.4 mm (1.3150)	35 (1.3780)

4-7 V-lever and spectacle link

1. Wear of V-lever underside
Check the V-lever's surface, where it comes into contact with the roller of the hold-down clamp, for damage and wear.

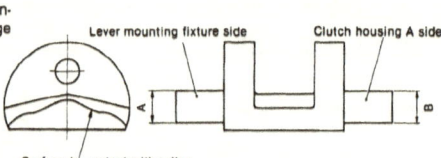

Note: R specifications differ from Y specifications in V-lever shape, but the two specifications are the same in shaft diameter.

2. Shaft diameter and clearance of V-lever

mm (in.)

	Standard dimensions	Clearance at assembly	Maximum allowable clearance limit
Shaft diameter A	$12 \begin{smallmatrix} -0.07 \\ -0.10 \end{smallmatrix}$ (0.4685 ~ 0.4697)	0.07 ~ 0.118 (0.0028 ~ 0.0046)	0.3 (0.0018)
Diameter of hole in lever mounting fixture	$12 \begin{smallmatrix} +0.018 \\ 0 \end{smallmatrix}$ (0.4724 ~ 0.4731)		
Shaft diameter B	$12 \begin{smallmatrix} -0.07 \\ -0.10 \end{smallmatrix}$ (0.4685 ~ 0.4697)	0.07 ~ 0.118 (0.0028 ~ 0.0046)	0.3 (0.0018)
Diameter of hole in clutch housing A	$12 \begin{smallmatrix} +0.018 \\ 0 \end{smallmatrix}$ (0.4724 ~ 0.4731)		

3. Spectacle link

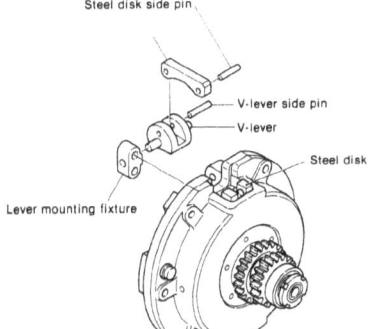
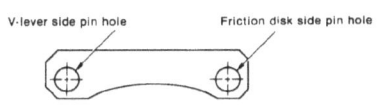

	mm (in.)
	Standard dimensions
Diameter of hole in V-lever	$8^{+0.020}_{+0.005}$ (0.3152 ~ 0.3157)
Diameter of pin hole in V-lever side (spectacle link)	$8^{+0.150}_{+0.115}$ (0.3195 ~ 0.3209)
Diameter of hole in friction disk side (spectacle link)	$8^{+0.015}_{0}$ (0.3150 ~ 0.3156)
Diameter of pin	$8^{+0.015}_{+0.006}$ (0.3152 ~ 0.3156)

4-8 Hold-down clamp

YSM8-R, YSM12-R

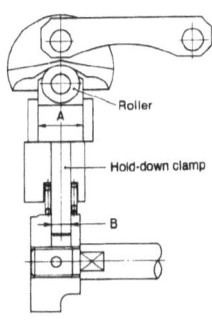

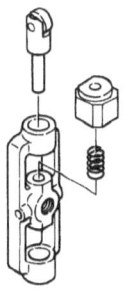

YSM8-Y, YSM12-Y

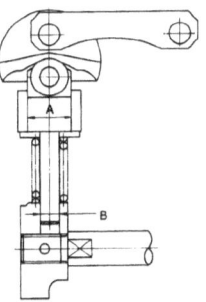

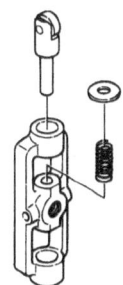

Chapter 9 Reduction and Reversing Gear
4. Inspection and Servicing
SM / YSM

1. **Hold-down clamp Roller**
   Check the roller surface for damage and wear. If it is seriously damaged or worn out, replace the roller. Make sure that the roller rotates smoothly.

mm (in.)

	YSM8-R YSM12-R	YSM8-Y YSM12-Y
	Standard dimensions	Wear limit dimension
Outside diameter of roller	15 (0.5906)	14.5 (0.5709)

2. **Clearance between roller and hold-down clamp case.**

mm (in.)

	Standard dimensions	Clearance at assembly	Wear limit
Shaft diameter of hold-down clamp A	18 (0.7087)	0.016 ~ 0.052 (0.0006 ~ 0.0020)	0.15 (0.0059)
Diameter of hole in hold-down clamp case A	18 (0.7087)		
Shaft diameter of hold-down clamp B	8 (0.3150)	0.013 ~ 0.043 (0.0005 ~ 0.0017)	0.15 (0.0059)
Diameter of hole in hold-down clamp case B	8 (0.3150)		

3. **Spring for hold-down clamp**
   Check the spring for breaks, corrosion, permanent deformations, etc.

mm (in.)

	YSM8-R, YSM12-R		YSM8-Y, YSM12-Y	
	Standard dimensions	Limit dimensions	Standard dimensions	Limit dimensions
Free length of spring for hold-down clamp	19 (0.7480)	17.5 (0.6890)	31 (1.2205)	29 (1.1417)

4-9 Forward shaft and sliding shaft (for both YSM8 and YSM12)

1. Clearance between forward shaft and sliding shaft

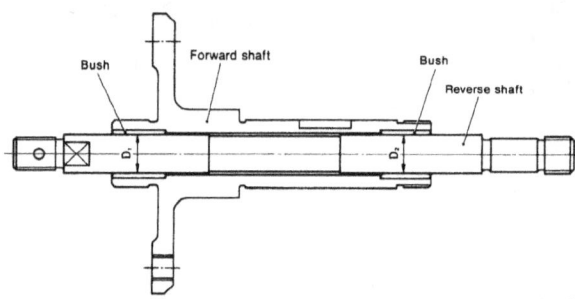

mm (in.)

	Standard dimensions	Clearance at assembly	Maximum allowable clearance
Outside diameter of sliding shaft D1	$15\,^{-0.10}_{-0.15}$ (0.5846 ~ 0.5866)	0.10 ~ 0.17 (0.0039 ~ 0.0067)	0.3 (0.0118)
Inside diameter of bush	$15\,^{+0.02}_{0}$ (0.5906 ~ 0.5913)		
Outside diameter of sliding shaft D2	$15\,^{-0.10}_{-0.15}$ (0.5846 ~ 0.5866)	0.10 ~ 0.17 (0.0039 ~ 0.0067)	0.3 (0.0118)
Inside diameter of bush	$15\,^{+0.02}_{0}$ (0.5906 ~ 0.5913)		

4-10 Lever fork

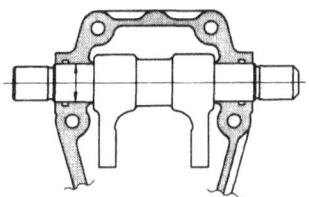

	Standard dimension	Clearance at assembly	Clearance at limit of use
Diameter of lever fork shaft	$20_{-0.050}^{\ 0}$ (0.7854 ~ 0.7874)	0.020 ~ 0.091 (0.0009 ~ 0.0036)	0.25 (0.0098)
Diameter of hole in rear lid	$20_{+0.020}^{+0.041}$ (0.7882 ~ 0.7890)		

mm (in.)

4-11 Shifter bush and shifter driving plate

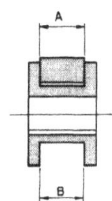 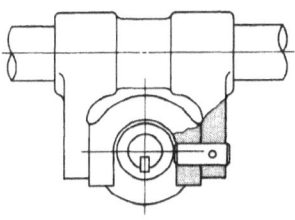

	Standard dimension	Clearance at assembly	Clearance at limit of use
Width of shifter bush	$16_{-0.050}^{-0.032}$ (0.6280 ~ 0.6287)	0.032 ~ 0.068 (0.0013 ~ 0.0027)	0.3 (0.0018)
Width of groove in shifter driving plate	$16_{\ 0}^{+0.018}$ (0.6299 ~ 0.6306)		

mm (in.)

4-12 Idle gear shaft (forward side and reverse side)

1. Check bearings for burning damage. If the damage is serious, replace the idle gear shaft.
2. Check the O ring for damage. If it is seriously damaged, replace the idle gear shaft.

4-13 Output shaft.

1. Check the key groove for cracking. If it is defective, replace the output shaft.
2. Check the bearing for burning damage and wear. If it is considerably damaged or worn, replace the bearing.
3. Check the oil seal section for wear. If it is considerably worn, replace the oil seal.
4. Check the oil seal. If it is defective, replace it.

5. Disassembling the Reduction and Reversing Gears

5-1 Disassembling the clutch

1. Remove split pin, slotted nut and shifter.

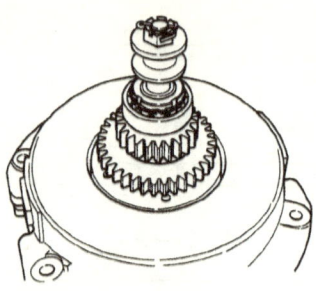

3. Extract the bearing

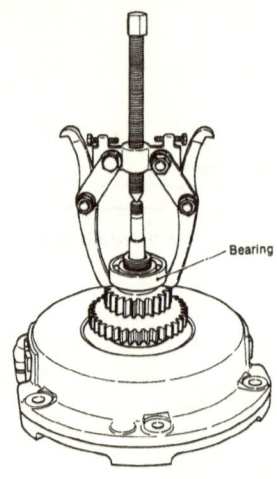

Bearing

2. By straightening the bent washer remove the lock nut.

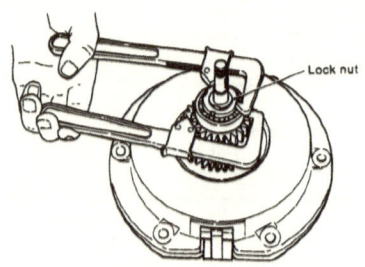

Lock nut

4. Remove the clamp bolts from clutch housings A and B.

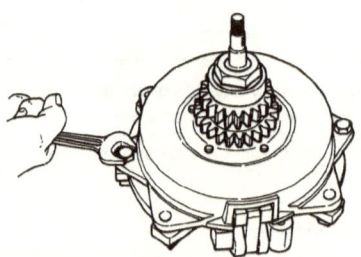

Chapter 9 Reduction and Reversing Gear
5. Disassembling the Reduction and Reversing Gears

5. Remove clutch housing B.
   This can be removed easily by prying open the gap between A and B.
   The positioning pawl and spring can jump out. Be careful. Each 4 pieces.

9. Component parts after disassembling

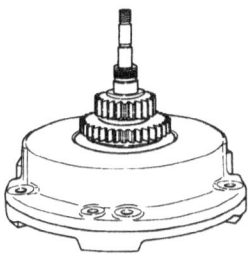
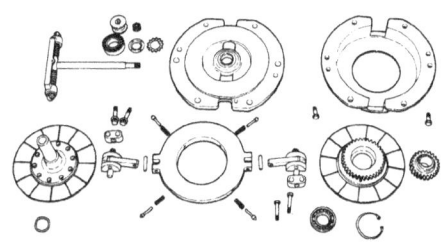

6. Remove the pin of the connecting spectacle link and the V-lever, pin, fixtures, housing A, and sliding shaft.

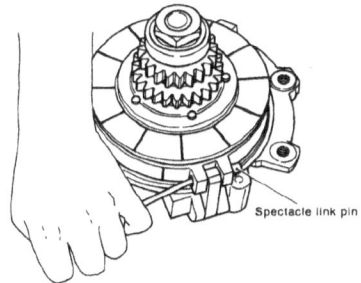

Spectacle link pin

7. Remove the forward gear, its feather key and circlip.
8. Remove the forward shaft and holding friction plate. Pull out the ball bearing at the same time.

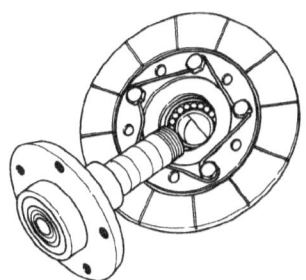

5-2 Disassembling the idle gear and output shaft

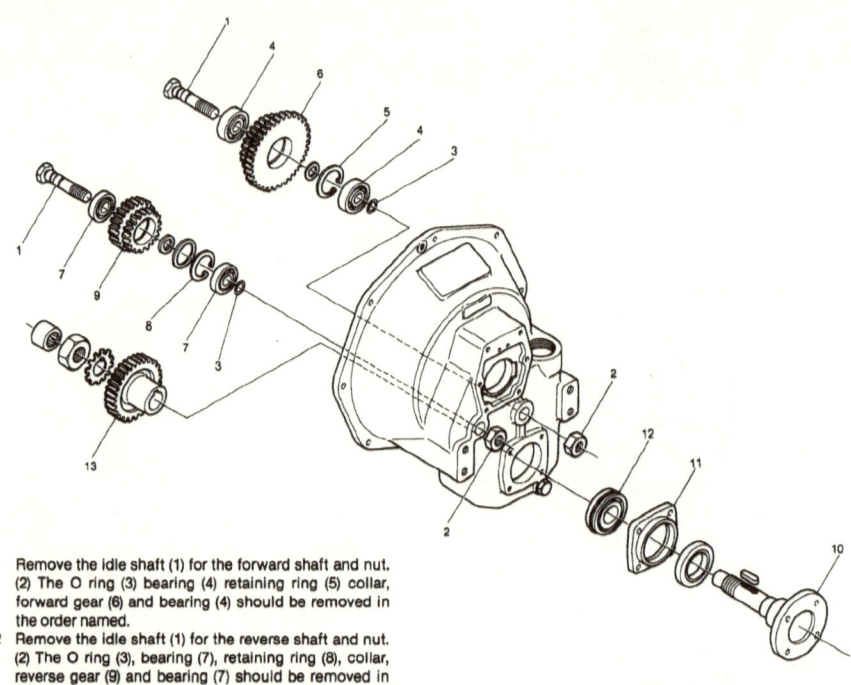

1. Remove the idle shaft (1) for the forward shaft and nut. (2) The O ring (3) bearing (4) retaining ring (5) collar, forward gear (6) and bearing (4) should be removed in the order named.
2. Remove the idle shaft (1) for the reverse shaft and nut. (2) The O ring (3), bearing (7), retaining ring (8), collar, reverse gear (9) and bearing (7) should be removed in the order named.
3. Extract the output shaft (10) by straightening its washer and loosening its clamp nut.
   The rear lid (11), bearing (12) and output gear (13) should be removed in the order named.

6. Reassembling the Reduction and Reversing Gears

Note: Rinse the component parts and reassemble them in the correct sequence.

6-1 Reassembling the idle gear and output shaft

1. Attach the output shaft.
   Be careful not to damage the oil seal.

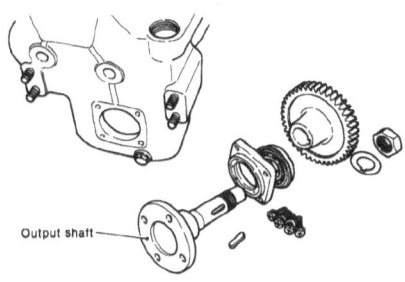
Output shaft

2. Attach the idle shaft for the reverse shaft along with its component parts.
   Reassemble the component parts by reversing the reassembly procedures.

Tightening torque	kg-m (ft-lb)
	8 to 10 (57.8 ~ 72.3)

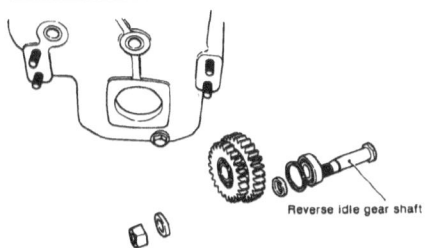
Reverse idle gear shaft

3. Attach the idle shaft for the forward shaft along with its component parts.
   Reassemble the component parts by reversing the disassembly procedures.

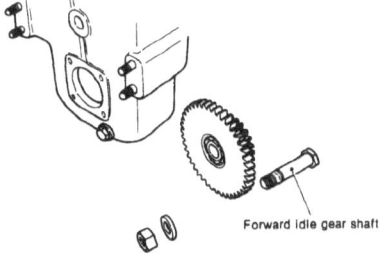
Forward idle gear shaft

6-2 Reassembling the clutch

1. Reassemble the forward shaft and the friction plate (reverse) with the holding friction plate placed in-between.
2. Insert the ball bearing and fit the circlip.
   The bearing No. should be visible from outside.
3. Put the sliding shaft and housing A back together, and attach them to the forward shaft.
   Do not fail to attach the neutral position holding spring.
4. Attach the V-lever, pin, fixture and connecting spectacle link pin.
   Arrange them so that the V-lever No. coincides with the friction plate housing No.

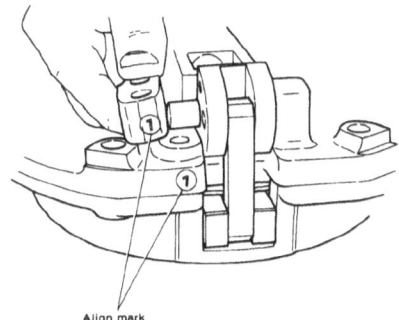
Align mark

Chapter 9 Reduction and Reversing Gear
6. Reassembling the Reduction and Reversing Gears

5. Fit the clutch housing B into place and tighten the clamp bolt.
   Align the mark on housing B with that on the V-lever.

   kg·m (ft-lb)

Tightening torque	2.3 to 2.7 (16.63 ~ 19.52)

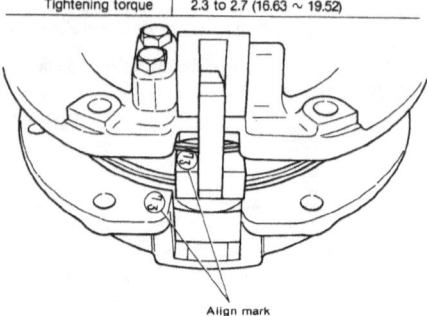

Align mark

6. Assemble the feather key, forward gear, ball bearing and bent washer, and tighten the lock nut.
   Place them inside the forward gear face with the longer flange.

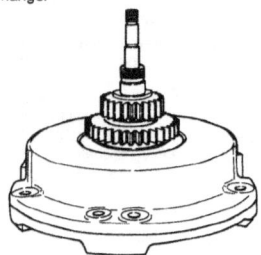

7. Mount the shifter, slotted groove and split pin.

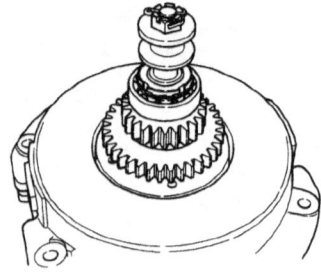

CHAPTER 10
REMOTE CONTROL SYSTEM

1. Composition 10-1
2. Construction 10-2

Chapter 10 Remote Control System
1. Composition

SM/YSM

1. Composition

	YSM8-R YSM12-R		YSM8-Y YSM12-Y
Speed control	(Option)	Morse one-handle MT	(Standard) Yanmar made
Clutch control		Bracket: Standard	—
Decompression control	(Standard) Yanmar made		—
Engine stop control	(Option) Yanmar made		—

2. Construction

2-1 YSM8-R, YSM-12R Remote control

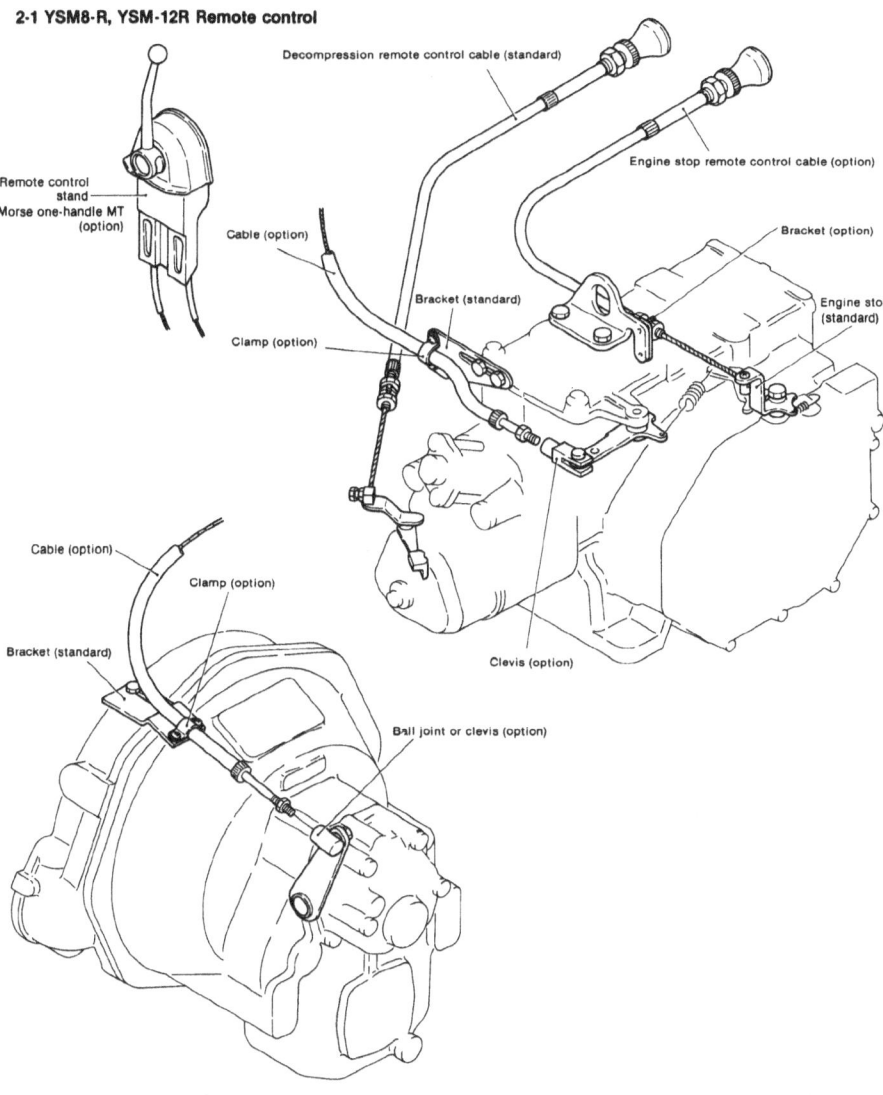

2-2 YSM8-Y, YSM-12Y Remote control

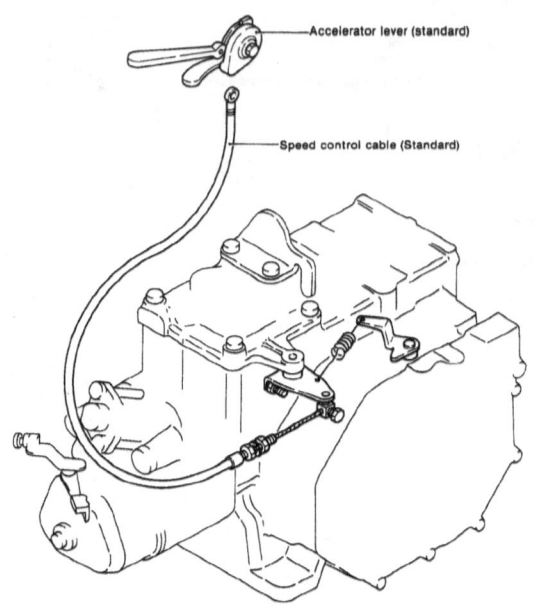

2-3 Action of the lever

1. Morse one-handle Remote Control Lever

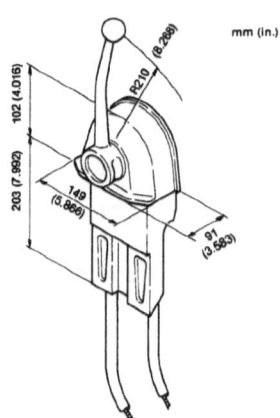

2. Regulator lever

(1) YSM8-R, YSM12-R

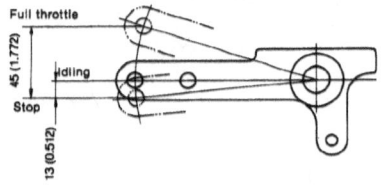

Chapter 10 Remote Control System
2. Construction

(2) YSM8-Y, YSM12-Y

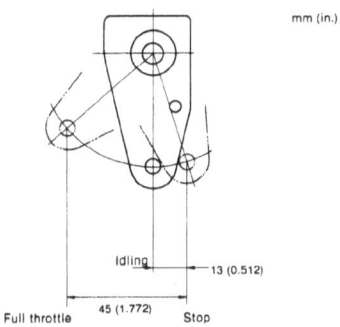

3. Clutch lever

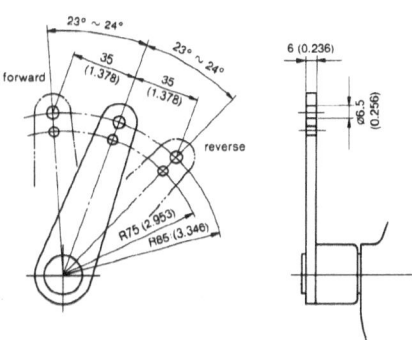

CHAPTER 11
ELECTRICAL SYSTEM

1. Composition 11-1
2. Battery 11-3
3. Starter Motor 11-6
4. Alternator 11-14
5. Alarm Circuit 11-22
6. Other Electric Equipment 11-25

Chapter 11 Electrical System
1. Composition _____ *SM/YSM*

1. Composition

1-1. Composition

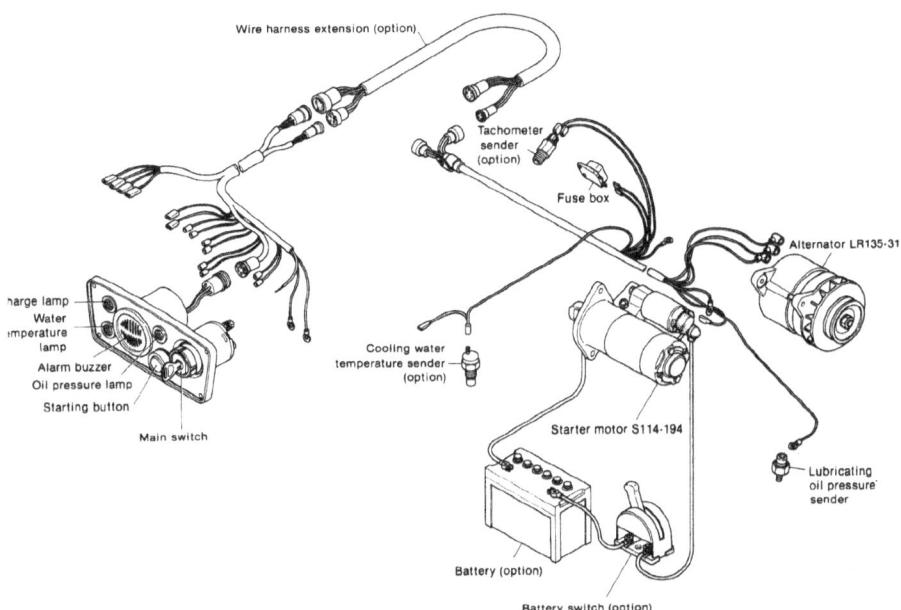

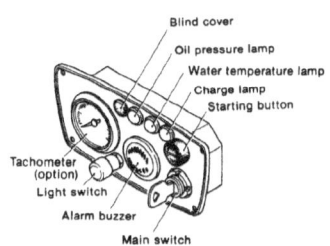

Chapter 11 Electrical System
1. Composition

1-2 Connection diagram for electric equipment

The electric equipment of the YSM models is broadly divided into 1) the starting devices, such as the starter, etc., and 2) charging devices, such as the alternator and 3) the various alarms, the connections of which are as shown in the diagram below.

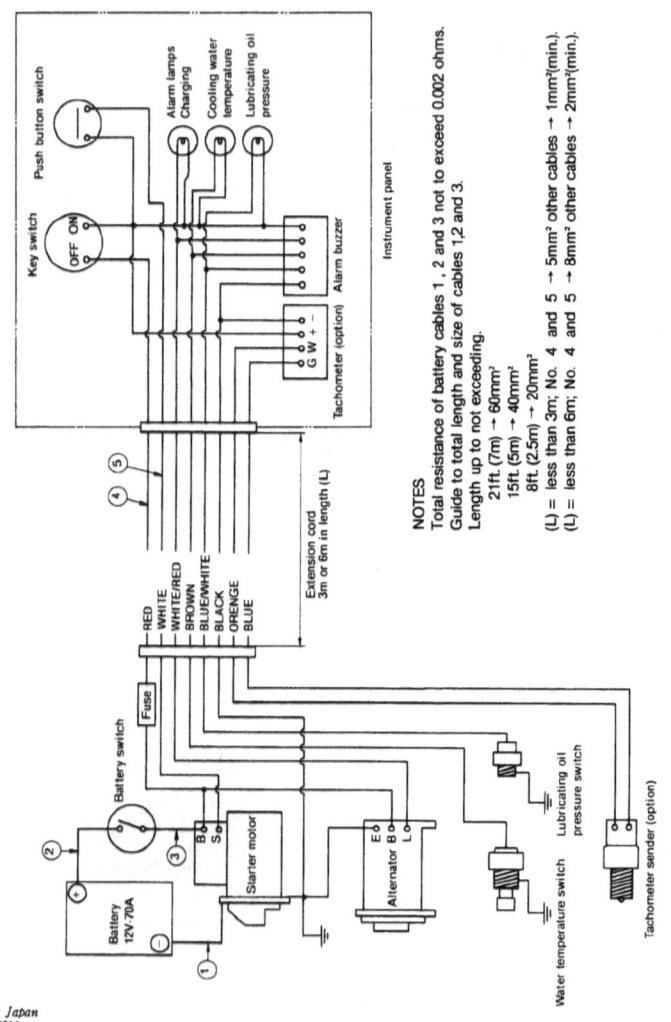

NOTES
Total resistance of battery cables 1, 2 and 3 not to exceed 0.002 ohms.
Guide to total length and size of cables 1,2 and 3.
Length up to not exceeding.
 21ft. (7m) → 60mm²
 15ft. (5m) → 40mm²
 8ft. (2.5m) → 20mm²
(L) = less than 3m; No. 4 and 5 → 5mm² other cables → 1mm²(min).
(L) = less than 6m; No. 4 and 5 → 8mm² other cables → 2mm²(min).

2. Battery

2-1 Construction

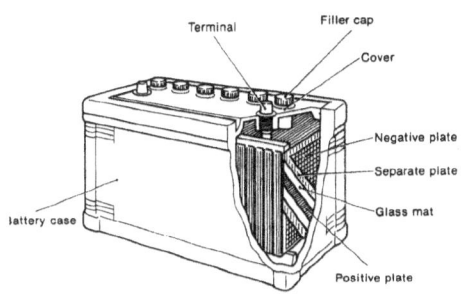

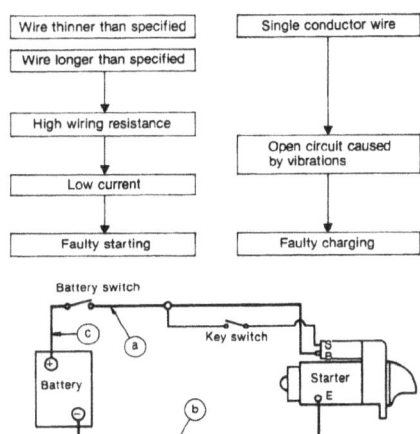

The battery utilizes chemical action to convert chemical energy to electrical energy. This engine uses a lead acid battery which stores a fixed amount of power that can be used when required. After use, the battery can be recharged and used again.
As shown in the figure, a nonconductive container is filled with dilute sulfuric acid electrolyte. Lead dioxide positive plates and lead dioxide negative plates separated by glass mats are stacked alternately in the electrolyte. The positive and negative plates are connected to their respective terminals.
Power is removed from the battery by connecting the load across these two terminals.
When the battery is discharging, an electric current flows from the positive plates to the negative plates. When the battery is being charged, electric current is passed through the battery in the opposite direction by an external power source.

2-2 Battery capacity and battery cables
2-2.1 Battery capacity
Since the battery has a minimum capacity of 12V, 70AH, it can be used for 100 ~ 150AH.

Minimum battery capacity	12V 70AH
Fully charged specific gravity	1,260

2-2.2 Battery cable
Wiring must be performed with the specified electric wire. Thick, short wiring should be used to connect the battery to the starter, (soft automotive low-voltage wire [AV wire]).
Using wire other than that specified may cause the following troubles:

The overall lengths of the wiring between the battery (+) terminal and the starter (B) terminal, and between the battery (−) terminal and the starter (E) terminal should be based on the following table.

Voltage system	Allowable wiring voltage drop	Conductor cross-section area	a + b + c allowable length
12V	0.2V or less/100A	20mm^3 (0.031in.^{2})	Up to 2.5 m (98.43in.)
		40mm^2 (0.062in.^{2})	Up to 5 m (196.86in.)

2-3 Inspection
The quality of the battery governs the starting performance of the engine. Therefore the battery must be routinely inspected to assure that it functions perfectly at all times.

2-3.1 Visual inspection
(1) Inspect the case for cracks, damage and electrolyte leakage.
(2) Inspect the battery holder for tightness, corrosion, and damage.
(3) Inspect the terminals for rusting and corrosion, and check the cables for damage.
(4) Inspect the caps for cracking, electrolyte leakage and clogged vent holes.
Correct any abnormal conditions found. Clean off rusted terminals with a wire brush before reconnecting the battery cable.

Chapter 11 Electrical System
2. Battery

2-3.2 Checking the electrolyte
(1) Electrolyte level

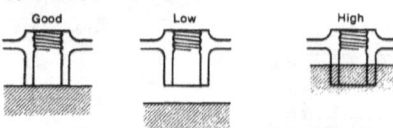
Good   Low   High

Check the electrolyte level every 7 to 10 days. The electrolyte must always be 10 ~ 20mm over the tops of the plates.

NOTES:
- The "LEVEL" line on a transparent plastic battery case indicates the height of the electrolyte.
- Always use distilled water to bring up the electrolyte level.
- When the electrolyte has leaked out, add dilute sulfuric acid with the same specific gravity as the electrolyte.

(2) Measuring the specific gravity of the electrolyte
1) Draw some of the electrolyte up into a hydrometer.

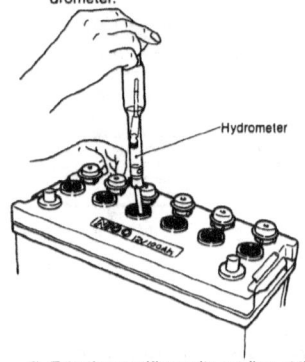
Hydrometer

2) Take the specific gravity reading at the top of the scale of the hydrometer.

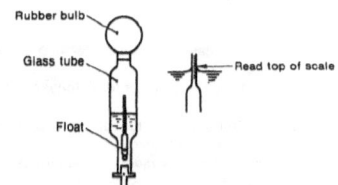
Rubber bulb
Glass tube
Read top of scale
Float

3) The battery is fully charged if the specific gravity is 1.260 at an electrolyte temperature of 20°C. The battery is discharged if the specific gravity is 1.200

(50%). If the specific gravity is below 1.200, recharge the battery.
4) If the difference in the specific gravity among the cells of the battery is ±0.01, the battery is OK.
5) Measure the temperature of the electrolyte.
Since the specific gravity changes with the temperature, 20°C is used as the reference temperature.
Reading the specific gravity at 20°C
$S_{20} = St + 0.0007 (t - 20)$
S_{20}: Specific gravity at the standard emperature of 20°C
St: Specific gravity of the electrolyte at t°C
0.0007: Specific gravity change per 1°C
t: Temperature of electrolyte

2-3.3 Voltage test
Using a battery tester, the amount of discharge can be determined by measuring the voltage drop which occurs while the battery is being discharged with a large current.

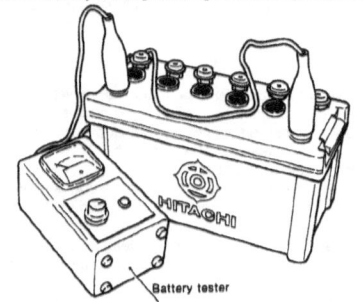
Battery tester

(1) Connect the tester to the battery.
12V battery tester
Adjust the current (A).
(2) Connect the (+) lead of the tester to the (+) battery terminal, and the (−) tester lead to the (−) battery terminal.
(3) Push the TEST button, wait 5 seconds, and then read the meter.
- Repeat the test twice to make sure that the meter indication remains the same.

2-3.4 Washing the battery
(1) Wash the outside of the battery with a brush while running cold or warm water over the battery. (Make sure that no water gets into the battery.)
(2) When the terminals or other metal parts are corroded due to exposure to electrolyte leakage, wash off all the acid.
(3) Check the vent holes of the caps and clean if clogged.
(4) After washing the battery, dry it with compressed air, connect the battery cable, and coat the terminals with grease. Since the grease acts as an insulator, do not coat the terminals before connecting the cables.

Chapter 11 Electrical System
2. Battery

2·4 Charging
2·4.1 Charging methods
There are two methods of charging a battery: normal and rapid.
Rapid charging should only be used in emergencies.
- Normal charging...Should be conducted at a current of 1/10 or less of the indicated battery capacity (10A or less for a 100AH battery).
- Rapid charging...Rapid charging is done over a short period of time at a current of 1/5 ~ 1/2 the indicated battery capacity (20A ~ 50A for a 100AH battery). However, since rapid charging causes the electrolyte temperature to rise too high, special care must be exercised.

2·4.2 Charging procedure
1. Check the specific gravity and adjust the electrolyte level.
2. Disconnect the battery cables.
3. Connect the red clip of the charger to the (+) battery terminal and connect the black clip to the (−) terminal.

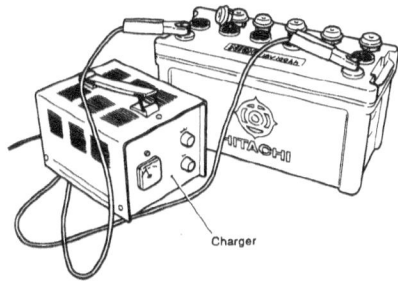
Charger

4. Set the current to 1/10 ~ 1/5 of the capacity indicated on the outside of the battery.
5. Periodically measure the specific gravity during charging to make sure that the specific gravity remains at a high fixed value. Also check whether gas is being generated.

2·4.3 Charging precautions
1. Remove the battery caps to vent the gas during charging.
2. While charging, ventilate the room and prohibit smoking, welding, etc.
3. The electrolyte temperature should not exceed 45°C during charging.
4. Since an alternator is used on this engine, when charging with a charger, always disconnect the battery (+) cable to prevent destruction of the diodes.
   (Before disconnecting the (+) battery cable, disconnect the (−) battery cable [ground side].)

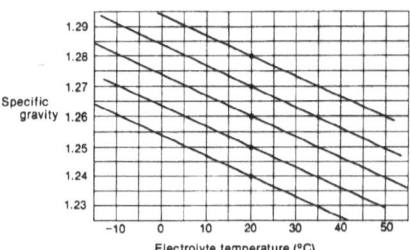
Electrolyte temperature and specific gravity

2·5 Battery storage precautions
The life of a battery depends considerably on how it is handled. Generally speaking, however, after about two years its performance will deteriorate, starting will become difficult, and the battery will not fully recover its original charge even after recharging. Then it must be replaced.
(1) Since the battery will self-discharge about 0.5%/day even when not in use, it must be charged 1 or 2 times a month when it is being stored.

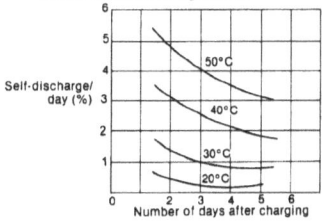

(2) If charging by the engine alternator is insufficient because of frequent starts and stops, the battery will rapidly lose power.
Charge the battery as soon as possible after it is used under these conditions.
(3) An easy-to-use battery charger that permits home charging is available from Yanmar. Take proper care of the battery by using the charger as a set with a hydrometer.
When the specific gravity has dropped to about 1.16 and the engine will not start, charge the battery up to a specific gravity of 1.26 (24 hours).
(4) Before putting the battery in storage for long periods, charge it for about 8 hours to prevent rapid aging.

Simple charger

3. Starter Motor

The starter motor is installed on the flywheel housing. When the starting button is pushed, the starter motor pinion flies out and engages the ring gear of the flywheel. Then the main contact is closed, current flows, and the engine is started.
After the engine starts, the pinion automatically returns to its initial position when the starting button is released. Once the engine starts, the starting button should be released immediately. Otherwise, the starter motor may be damaged or burned out.

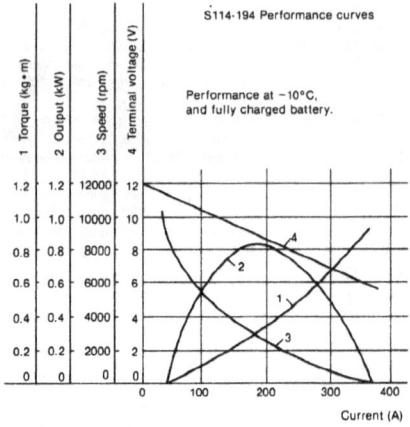

S114-194 Performance curves

Performance at −10°C, and fully charged battery.

3-1 Specifications and Performance.

Model		S114-194
Rating (sec)		30
Output (kw)		1.0
Clutch system		Overrunning
Engagement system		Magnetic shift
Pinion flyout voltage (V)		8 or less
No-load	Terminal voltage (V)	12
	Current (A)	60 or less
	Speed (rpm)	7000 or greater

3-2 Construction

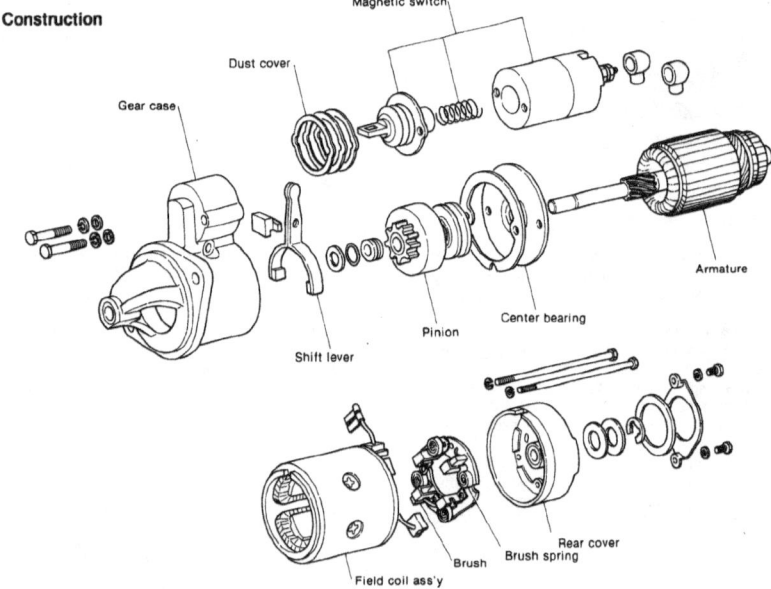

Chapter 11 Electrical System
3. Starter Motor

SM/YSM

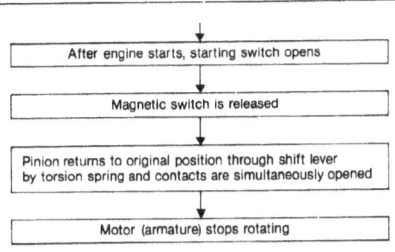

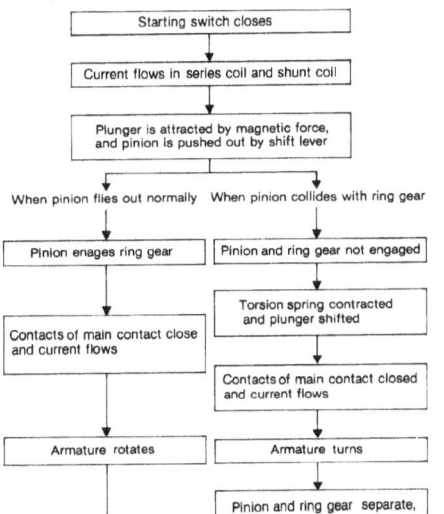

3-3 Operation

```
Starting switch closes
        ↓
Current flows in series coil and shunt coil
        ↓
Plunger is attracted by magnetic force,
and pinion is pushed out by shift lever
        ↓
   ┌────────────┴────────────┐
When pinion flies out normally   When pinion collides with ring gear
        ↓                              ↓
Pinion enages ring gear          Pinion and ring gear not engaged
        ↓                              ↓
                                Torsion spring contracted
                                and plunger shifted
        ↓                              ↓
Contacts of main contact close   Contacts of main contact closed
and current flows                and current flows
        ↓                              ↓
Armature rotates                 Armature turns
        ↓                              ↓
                                Pinion and ring gear separate,
                                pinion engages ring gear,
                                and ring gear rotates
Ring gear turns
```

↓
After engine starts, starting switch opens
↓
Magnetic switch is released
↓
Pinion returns to original position through shift lever
by torsion spring and contacts are simultaneously opened
↓
Motor (armature) stops rotating

3-4 Disassembly
3-4.1 Magnetic switch
1. Disconnect magnetic switch wiring.
2. Remove through bolt mounting magnetic switch.
3. Remove magnetic switch.

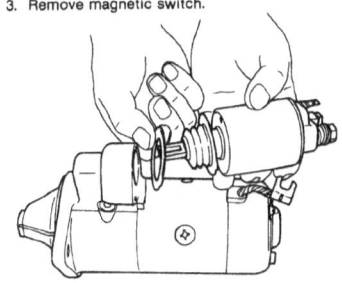

Chapter 11 Electrical System
3. Starter Motor

3-4.2 Rear cover
1. Remove dust cover.

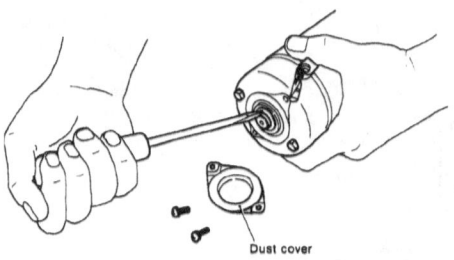

2. Remove E-ring, and remove thrust washer (be careful not to lose the washer and shim).
3. Remove the two through bolts holding the rear cover and the two screws holding the brush holder.
4. Remove rear cover.

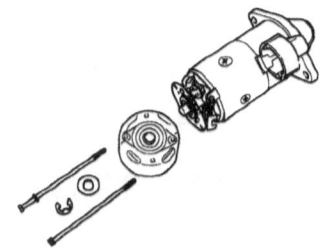

3-4.3 Brush holder
1. Float (−)brush from the commutator.
2. Remove (+)brush from the brush holder.
3. Remove brush holder.

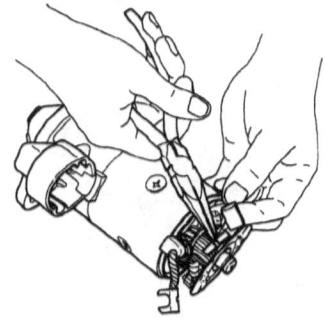

3-4.4 Yoke
1. Remove yoke. Pull it out slowly so that it does not strike against other parts.

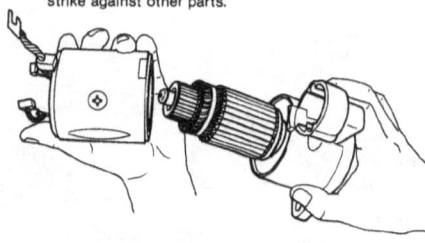

3-4.5 Armature
1. Slide pinion stopper to pinion side.

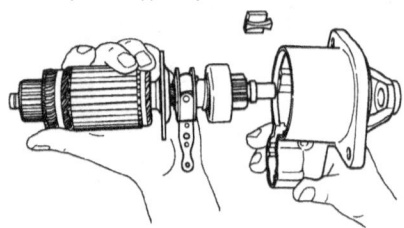

2. Remove the pinion stopper clip.

3-4.6 Pinion
1. Slide the pinion stopper to the pinion side.
2. Remove the pinion stopper clip.
3. Remove the pinion from the armature.

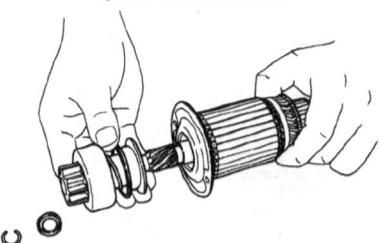

3-5 Inspection
3-5.1 Armature
(1) Commutator

Inspect the surface of the commutator. If corroded or pitted, sand with #500 ~ #600 sandpaper. If the commutator is severely pitted, grind it to within a surface roughness of at least 0.4 by turning it on a lathe. Replace the commutator if damage is irrepairable.

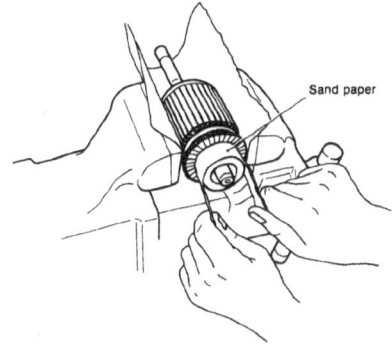

(2) Mica undercut

Check the mica undercut, correct with a hacksaw blade when the undercut is too shallow.

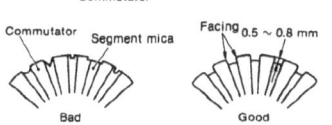

	Maintenance standard	Repair limit
Mica undercut	0.2 (0.0079)	0.5 ~ 0.8 (0.0197 ~ 0.0315)

mm (in.)

(3) Armature coil ground test

Using a tester, check for continuity between the commutator and the shaft (or armature core). Continuity indicates that these points are grounded and that the armature must be replaced.

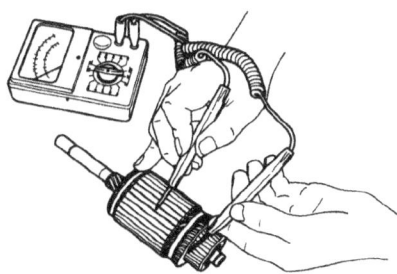

(4) Armature shaft

Check the bend of the shaft; replace the armature if the bend exceeds 0.08mm (0.0031in.).

3-5.2 Field coil
(1) Open test

Check for continuity between the terminals connecting the field coil brushes. Continuity indicates that the coil is open and that the coil must be replaced.

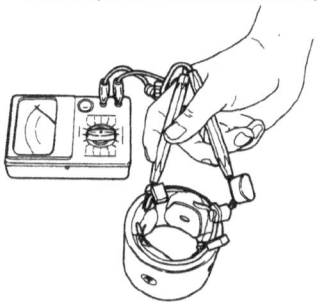

(2) Short test

Check for continuity between the yoke and any field coil terminal. Continuity indicates that the coil is shorted and that it must be replaced.

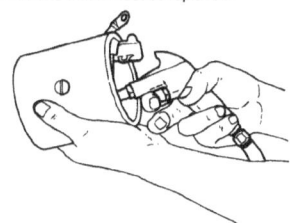

Chapter 11 Electrical System
3. Starter Motor

(3) Cleaning the inside of the yoke
If any carbon powder or rust has collected on the inside of the yoke, blow the yoke out with dry compressed air.
*Do not remove the field coil from the yoke.

3-5.3 Brush
The brushes are quickly worn down by the motor. When the brushes are defective, the output of the motor will drop.

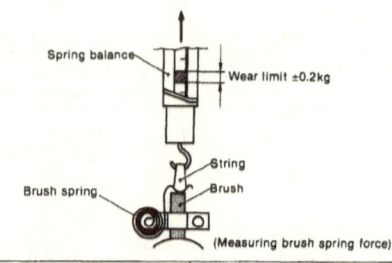

(Measuring brush spring force)

Standard spring load	1.6kg (3.527 lb)

(4) Brush holder ground test
Check for continuity between the insulated brush holder and the base of the brush holder assembly. Continuity indicates that these two points are grounded and that the holder must be replaced.

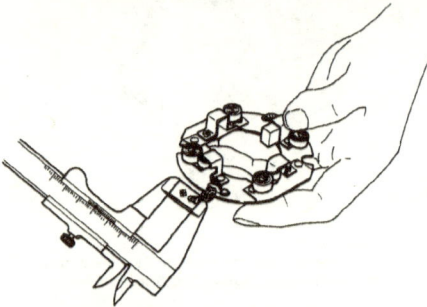

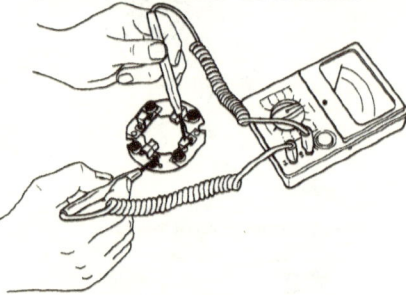

(1) Brush dimensions
Replace brushes which have been worn beyond the specified wear limit.

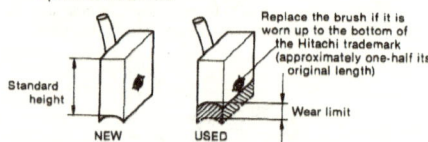

Replace the brush if it is worn up to the bottom of the Hitachi trademark (approximately one-half its original length)

mm (in.)

	S114-194
Brush standard height	16 (0.6299)
Wear limit	4 (0.1575)

(2) Brush appearance and movement in brush holder
If the outside of the brush is damaged, replace it. If the movement of the brushes in the brush holder is hampered because the holder is rusted, repair or replace the holder.

(3) Brush spring
Since the brush spring pushes the brush against the commutator while the motor is running, a weak or defective spring will cause excessive brush wear, resulting in sparking between the brush and the commutator during operation. Measure the spring force with a spring balance; replace the spring when the difference between the standard value and the measured value exceeds ±0.2kg.

3-5.4 Magnetic switch
(1) Shunt coil continuity test
Check for continuity between the S terminal and the magnetic switch body (metal part). Continuity indicates that the coil is open and that the switch must be replaced.

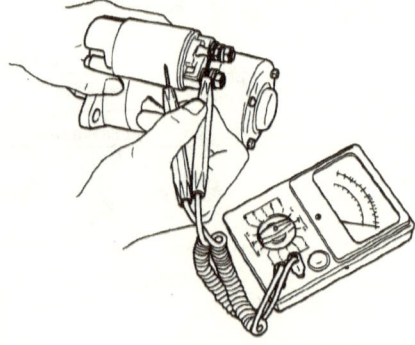

(2) Series coil continuity test
Check for continuity between the S terminal and M terminal. Continuity indicates that the coil is open and that it must be replaced.

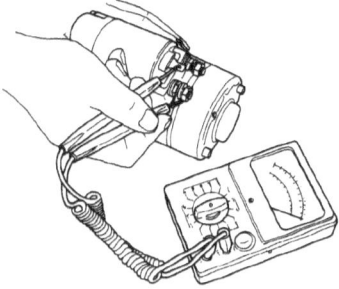

(3) Contactor contact test
Push the plunger with your finger and check for continuity between the M terminal and B terminal. Continuity indicates that the contact is faulty and that the contactor must be replaced.

3-5.5 Pinion
(1) Inspect the pinion teeth and replace the pinion if the teeth are excessively worn or damaged.
(2) Check if the pinion slides smoothly; replace the pinion if faulty.
(3) Inspect the springs and replace if faulty.
(4) Replace the clutch if it slips or seizes.

3-6 Reassembly precautions

Lubrication
Lubricate each bearing and spline (points indicated GREASE in the construction drawing) with high quality "Hitachi Electrical Equipment Grease A".
The following lubricants may be used in place of Hitachi Electrical Equipment Grease A.

| Magnetic switch plunger | Shell | Aeroshell No. 7 |
| Bearing and spline | Shell | Albania Grease No. 2 |

3-7 Adjusting the starting motor
When the pinion is pushed out by the magnetic switch, the distance from the pinion stopper to the pinion is termed the l dimension, the standard for which is as listed below.
mm (in.)

	S114-195
Dimension	0.3 ~ 1.5 (0.0118 ~ 0.0590)

Pressing the pinion

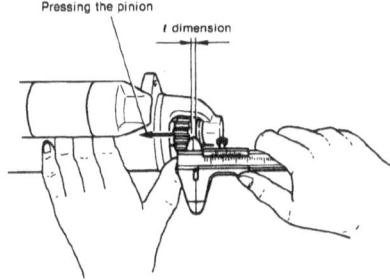

Measuring of l dimension

l dimension
Before measuring the l dimension, connect the ⊕ battery cable to terminal S and the ⊖ battery cable to the motor body. By attracting the plunger and by causing the shift lever to push out the pinion, measure the l dimension by pressing the pinion in the direction of the arrow to eliminate play, as shown in the diagram.
If the l dimension is outside the standard value, adjust it with an adjusting plate inserted in the section where the magnet switch is installed. The adjusting plate comes in two types; one is 0.5 mm (0.019 in.) thick and the other 0.8 mm (0.031 in.).

Adjusting plate

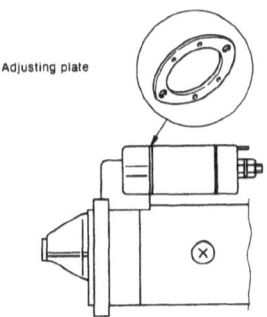

Chapter 11 Electrical System
3. Starter Motor

3-8 Handling the starting motor

3-8.1 Fitting the starting motor into place
The normal size of the gap between the pinion and the ring gear is 3 to 5 mm (0.118 ~ 0.197in.).
Be sure to tighten the wiring securely.

3-8.2 Precautions for starting the motor
(1) Pay attention to the charge condition of the battery. Undercharging makes it difficult to start the engine.
(2) After the motor has been started, immediately turn off the starting switch.
(3) If the engine will not start even though the starting switch has been turned on, turn it off and on for about 10 seconds.
(4) When re-turning on the starting switch, wait until the starting motor stops.
(5) During engine operation never turn on the starting switch.

3-9 Testing

3-9.1 No load test
Test procedure
(1) Connect the positive side of the ammeter (A) to the positive terminal of the battery, and connect the negative side of the ammeter to the B terminal of the starter.

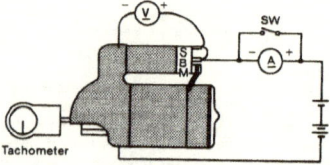

(2) Connect the negative terminal of the battery to the body of the starter.
(3) Connect the positive side of the voltmeter (V) to the B terminal of the starter, and connect the negative side of the voltmeter to the body of the starter.
(4) Attach the tachometer.
(5) Connect the B terminal of the starter to the S terminal of the magnetic switch.
- The magnetic switch should begin operating, and the speed, current, and voltage should be the prescribed values.
- A fully charged battery must be used.
- Since a large current flows when the starter is operated, close the protection circuit switch before initial operation, then open the switch and measure the current after the starter reaches a constant speed.

3-10 Standards for servicing the starting motor

mm (in.)

			S114-194
Brush	Standard strength of spring		1.6kg (3.52 lb.)
	Standard height/limit of reduction in dimension		16/4 (0.63/0.157)
Magnetic switch resistance at 20°C		Series coil/shunt coil	0.324/0.694 Ω
Commutator	Outside diameter	Standard outside diameter/ limit of reduction in size	33/2 (1.299/0.078)
	Difference between maximum and minimum diameters	Limit of correction/ Accuracy of correction	0.4/0.05 (0.015/0.002)
	Mica undercut	Limit of correction/ Accuracy of correction	0.2/0.5 ~ 0.8 (0.008/0.019 ~ 0.031)
Standard dimensions	Brush side bearing	Shaft diamer/Hole diameter	⌀0.492 $_{-0.002}^{-0.0013}$ ⌀0.492 $_{0}^{+0.0011}$
	Intermediate bearing	Shaft diamer/Hole diameter	⌀0.687 $_{-0.0008}^{+0.0008}$ ⌀0.693 $_{0}^{+0.001}$
	Pinion slide way	Shaft diamer/Hole diameter	⌀0.492 $_{-0.002}^{-0.0013}$ ⌀0.492 $_{0}^{+0.0011}$
	Pinion side bearing	Shaft diamer/Hole diameter	⌀0.492 $_{-0.002}^{-0.0013}$ ⌀0.492 $_{0}^{+0.0011}$

3-11 Various problems and there remedies

(1) Pinion fails to advance when the starting switch is closed

Problem	Cause	Corrective action
Wiring	Open or loose battery or switch terminal	Repair or retighten
Starting switch	Threaded part connected to pinion section of armature shaft is damaged, and the pinion does not move	Repair contacts, or replace switch
Starter motor	Threaded part connected to pinion section of armature shaft is damaged, and the pinion does not move	Replace
Magnetic switch	Plunger of magnetic switch malfunctioning or coil shorted	Repair or replace

(2) Pinion is engaged and motor rotates, but rotation is not transmitted to the engine

Problem	Cause	Corrective action
Starting motor	Overrunning clutch faulty	Replace

(3) Motor rotates at full power before pinion engages ring gear

Problem	Cause	Corrective action
Starter motor	Torsion spring permanently strained	Replace

(4) Pinion engages ring gear, but starter motor fails to rotate

Problem	Cause	Corrective action
Wiring	Wires connecting battery and magnetic switch open or wire connecting ground, magnetic switch and motor terminals loose	Repair, retighten, or replace wire
Starter motor	Pinion and ring gear engagement faulty Motor mounting faulty Brush worn or contacting brush spring faulty Commutator dirty Armature, field coil faulty Field coil and brush connection loose	Replace Remount Replace Repair Repair or replace Retighten
Magnetic switch	Contactor contact faulty Contactor contacts pitted	Replace Replace

(5) Motor fails to stop when starting switch is opened after engine starts

Problem	Cause	Corrective action
Starting switch	Switch faulty	Replace
Magnetic switch	Switch faulty	Replace

4. Alternator

The alternator serves to keep the battery constantly charged. It is installed on the cylinder block by a bracket, and is driven from the V-pulley at the end of the crankshaft by a V-belt.

The type of alternator used in this engine is ideal for high speed engines having a wide range of engine speeds. It contains diodes that convert AC to DC, and an IC regulator that keep the generated voltage constant even when the engine speed changes.

4-1 Specifications

Type	Alternator	LR135-31
	Regulator	TR1Z-28
Battery voltage		12V
Output current		35A/5000rpm
Polarity		2-wire system
Direction of rotation		CW as viewed from pulley side
Regulated voltage		14.3 ±0.3V
Speed at 13V		1000rpm or less
Weight		3.8kg (8.3776lb)

CW: Clockwise

4-2 Characteristics

LR135-31

Standard speed characteristic of 12V-35A Alternator with IC regulator.

—Cold
...Warm ("Warm" is the state of the engine reached after a temperature rise test is conducted at a constant 5000 rpm maximum output.)

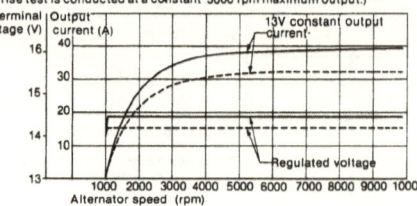

4-3 Construction

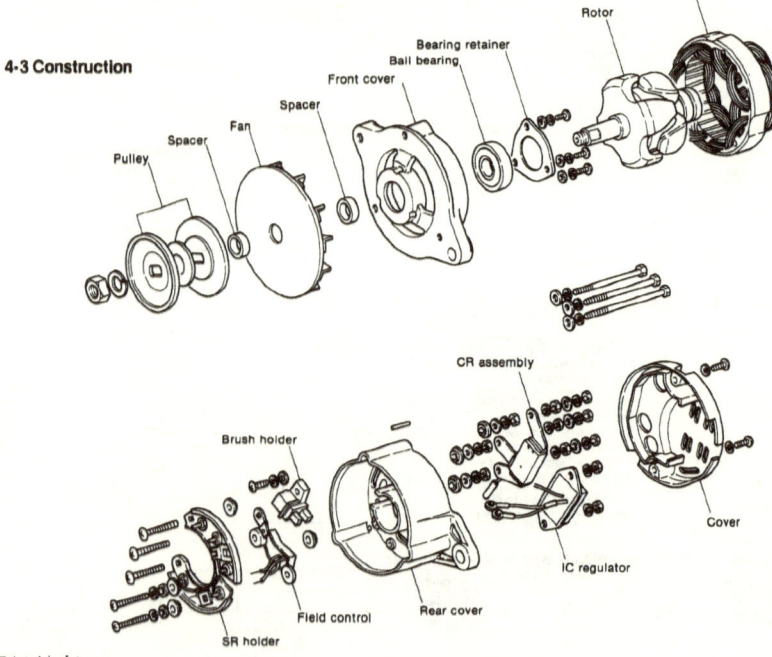

Chapter 11 Electrical System
4. Alternator

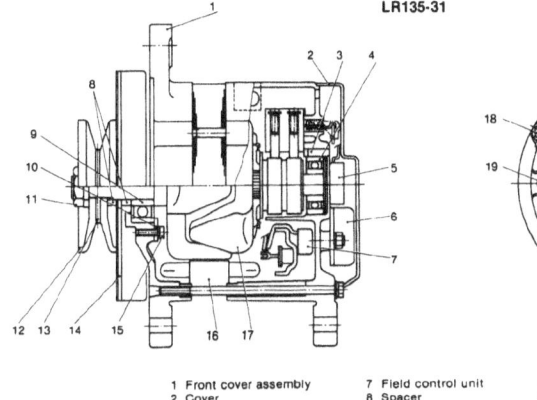

LR135-31

1 Front cover assembly
2 Cover
3 Pin (nylon resin)
4 Ball bearing
5 CR assembly
6 IC regulator
7 Field control unit
8 Spacer
9 Ball bearing
10 Bearing retainer
11 Pulley nut
12 Pulley
13 Pulley spacer
14 Fan
15 Screw
16 Stator assembly
17 Rotor assembly
18 Through bolt
19 Screw

4-4 Operation (LR135-31)
4-4.1 Circuit diagram

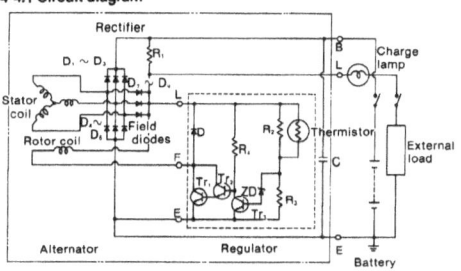

4-4.2 Description of operation
(1) Initial excitation

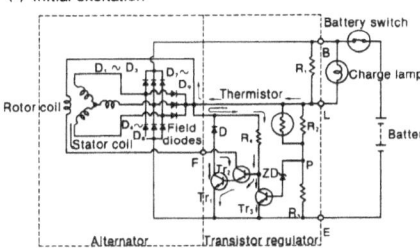

B: Generator output terminal   D: Transistor protection diode
L: Charge lamp terminal   ZD: Zener diode
E: Ground (battery (−)) terminal
$Tr_1 \sim Tr_3$: Transistor $D_1 \sim D_4$: Output rectification diodes
$R_1 \sim R_4$: Resistor
$D_5 \sim D_8$: ON/OFF operation of charge lamp and rotor coil current field supply diodes   C: Condenser

Basically, this circuit consists of an output Tr_1 transistor that turns the alternator rotor coil current on and off, a Tr_2 transistor that passes the base current to Tr_1, a Tr_3 control transistor that controls Tr_2, a zener diode ZD_1 and resistors R_1, R_2, R_3, and R_4, which pass on the current when the battery voltage reaches the regulated voltage, and a thermistor, as shown in the above figure.

When the battery switch is closed, current flows into Tr_2 and Tr_1, and the charge lamp lights up. At this time, the voltage at point P is lower than the zener voltage and current does not flow through the ZD (zener diode). Therefore, the base current does not flow through Tr_3, and Tr_3 is turned OFF.
The resistor R_1 is inserted in series with the charge lamp to prevent interruption of the rotor coil current if the charge lamp blows out, and to reduce the rise in speed (speed automatically adjusted) caused by the increase in the initial exciting current.

Chapter 11 Electrical System
4. Alternator
_____ SM/YSM

(2) Initial rotation

The alternator consists of field diodes (D7 ~ D9).
When the alternator is operated, generation begins.
When the speed of the alternator rises until its output voltage exceeds the battery terminal voltage, battery charging beings.

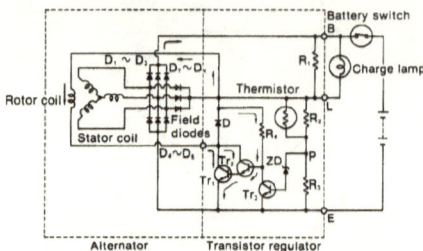

At this stage, the voltages at terminal B and terminal L are equal, and the charge lamp goes out to indicate that charging has begun. When charging begins, the Tr_2 base current, Tr_1 base current, and Tr_1 collector current (rotor coil current) are supplied from the alternator through D7 ~ D9 (field diodes). Since R_2 and R_3 are selected so that the voltage across P-E turns the ZD (zener diode) ON when the voltage across B-E exceeds the regulated voltage of the regulator, when the ZD (zener diode) is conducting, current flows through the path indicated above.

(3) Operation

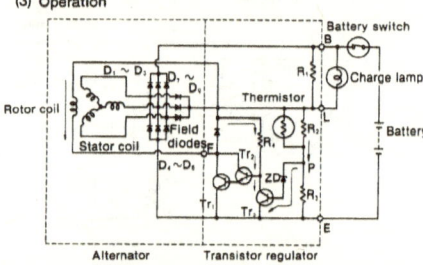

A Tr_3 collector-emitter voltage of at least 0.6V is necessary to allow the base current to flow through Tr_2 and Tr_1. But since the Tr_3 collector-emitter voltage is about 0.3V when Tr_3 is conducting, the Tr_2 and Tr_1 base current is interrupted, Tr_2 and Tr_1 are turned OFF, and current does not flow through the rotor coil.
When the rotor coil current is stopped, the alternator output voltage drops, the voltage across P-E applied to the ZD (zener diode) drops below the zener voltage, the zener diode is turned OFF, and the Tr_3 base current is interrupted.
As a result, Tr_3 is turned OFF, the base voltage of Tr_2 rises, and base current begins to flow through Tr_1.
This causes Tr_1 to conduct and the rotor coil current to begins to flow again.
As can be seen from the above description, when the output voltage of the generator is lower than the regulated voltage the Tr_1 output transistor conducts and rotor coil current flows. When the alternator output voltage is higher than the regulated voltage, control transistor Tr_3 conducts, output transistor Tr_1 is turned OFF, and the rotor coil current is interrupted.
The battery charging voltage is kept constant by turning the output transistor ON and OFF repeatedly in this manner.

4-5 Wiring (LR135-31)
(1) Wiring diagram

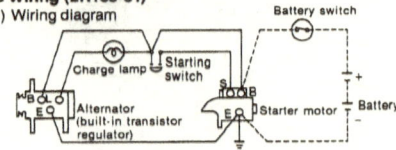

(2) Terminal connections
The alternator has the following terminals. Connect these terminals as indicated below.

Symbol	Terminal name	Connection to external wiring
B	Battery terminal	To battery (+) side
E	Ground terminal	To battery (−) side
L	Lamp (charge) terminal	To charge lamp terminal

The IC regulator terminals are as follows:

Symbol	Lead color
B	W (white)
E	B (black)
L	L (red)

4-6 Alternator handling precautions
(1) Pay attention to the polarity of the battery; be careful not to connect it in reverse polarity. If the battery is connected in reverse polarity, the battery will be shorted by the diode of the alternator, an overcurrrent will result, the diodes and transistor regulator will be destroyed, and the wiring harness will be burned.
(2) Connect the terminals correctly.
(3) When charging the battery from outside, such as during rapid charging, disconnect the alternator B terminal or the battery terminals.
(4) Do not short the terminals.
(5) Never test the alternator with a high voltage megger.

4·7 Alternator disassembly

Disassemble the alternator as follows.
The major points of disassembly are the removal of the cover, the separation of the front and rear sides, and detailed disassembly.

(1) Remove the cover attached to the rear cover, remove the through bolts, and disassemble into front and rear sides.

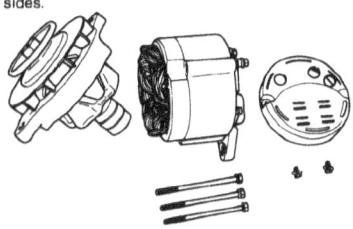

(2) Then when disassembling the front side pulley and fan, front cover and rotor, clamp the rotor in a vice through the copper plates and loosen the pulley nut, as shown in the figure.

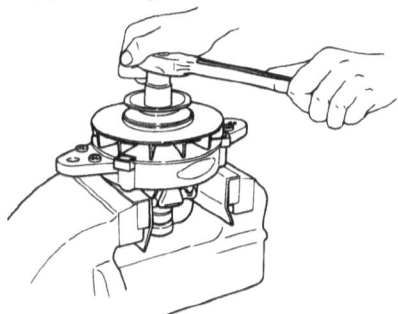

(3) When the fan and pulley have been removed, the rotor can be pulled from the front cover by hand.

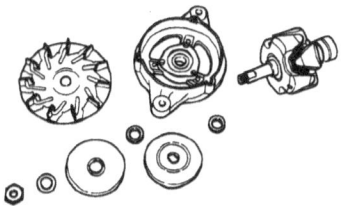

(4) Next, remove the bearing attached to the front cover. Loosen the bearing protector mounting bolts and pull the bearing by applying pressure to the bearing from the front cover.

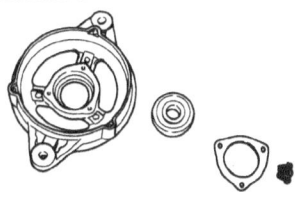

(5) Disassemble the rear side.
First, disconnect the resistor and IC regulator from the terminals.

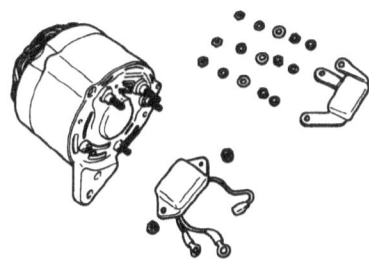

(6) Remove the bolts holding the SR holder and brush holder, remove the B.E.L. terminal nuts, and disassemble into the rear cover and stator (with SR holder).

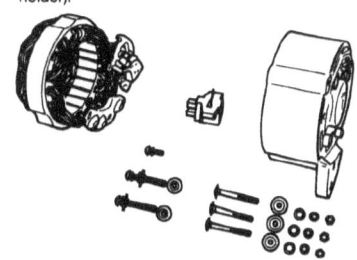

Chapter 11 Electrical System
4. Alternator

SM/YSM

(7) Melt the solder connecting the stator and the diode, and break it down to the stator, SR holder and auxiliary diode.

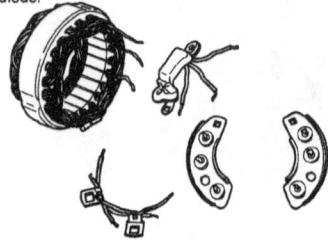

(8) Pull out the pin (nylon resin) inserted into the brush cover mounting section of the rear cover, and disassemble the rear cover.

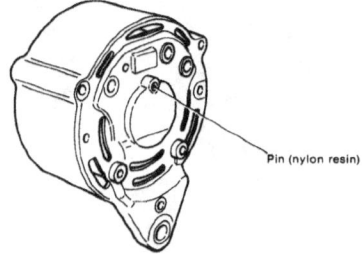

Pin (nylon resin)

(9) When (1)—(8) above are completed, the alternator is completely disassembled.

4-8 Inspection and adjustment
4-8.1 Diodes
(1) Diode short test

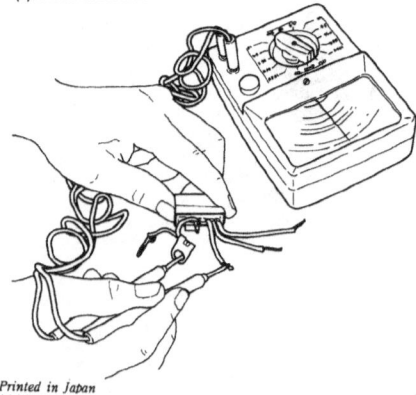

A set of 6 diodes and a set of 3 moulded diodes (field diodes) are used. The (+) diodes and (−) diodes of the six diode set conduct in opposite directions. (See the figure below.) Replace the diodes that conduct in both directions and the diodes that do not conduct in both directions.
Test for the continuity of each diode.

CAUTION: If a high voltage megger is used, a high voltage will be applied to the diode and the diode will be destroyed. Therefore, never test the diodes with a high voltage megger, etc.

(2) Replacement
1) Remove the cover.
2) Unsolder the diode assembly wiring. (CAUTION: Hold the diode with needle nose pliers so that the heat of the soldering iron is not transmitted to the diode.)
3) Remove the diode assembly mounting nut and bolt, and remove the diode ass'y.
Remove the nut and bolt holding the diode assembly in place, and then remove the diode assembly.

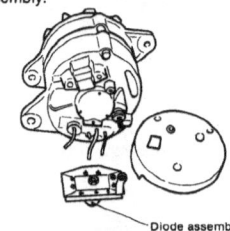

Diode assembly

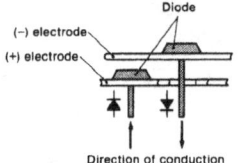

(−) electrode
(+) electrode
Diode
Direction of conduction

4-8.2 Rotor

(1) Slip ring wear
Because the slip rings wear very little, the diameter of the rings must be measured with a micrometer. Replace the rings (rotor assembly) when wear exceeds the maintenance standard by 1 mm.

mm (in.)

	Maintenance standard	Wear limit
Slip ring outside diameter	Ø31 (1.2205)	Ø30 (1.1811)

(2) Slip ring roughness
The slip ring should be smooth with no surface oil, etc. If the surface of the rings is rough, polish with #500 ~ #600 sandpaper, and if the surface is soiled, clean with a cloth dipped in alcohol.

(3) Rotor coil short test
Check the continuity between the rotor coil and slip ring with a tester. The resistance should be near the prescribed value.
If the resistance is extemely low, there is a layer short at the rotor coil; if the resistance is infinite, the coil is open. In either case, replace the rotor.

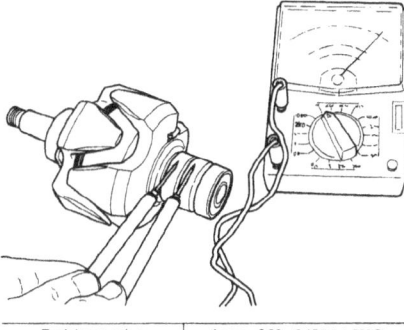

Resistance value:	Approx 3.83 ±0.15Ω (at 20°C)

(4) Rotor coil ground test
Check the rotor coil for grounding with a tester, or by checking the continuity between one slip ring and the rotor core or shaft.

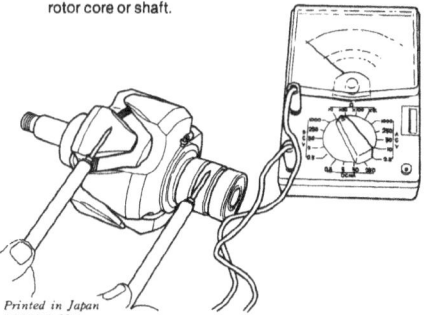

4-8.3 Stator coil

(1) Stator coil short test
Check the continuity between the terminals of the stator coil. Measure the resistance between the output terminals with a tester. The resistance should be near the prescribed value.
If the stator coil is open, indicated by infinite resistance, it must be replaced.

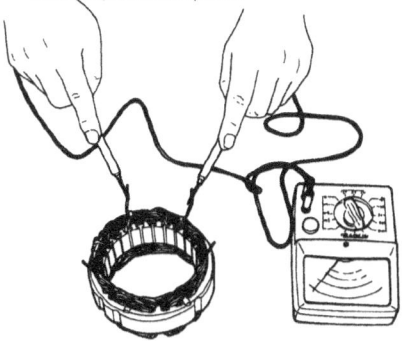

Resistance value	Approx 0.128Ω (at 20°C) 2-phase resistance

(2) Stator coil ground test
Check the continuity between one of the stator coil leads and the stator core.
The stator coil is good if the resistance is infinite. If the stator core is grounded, indicated by continuity, it must be replaced.

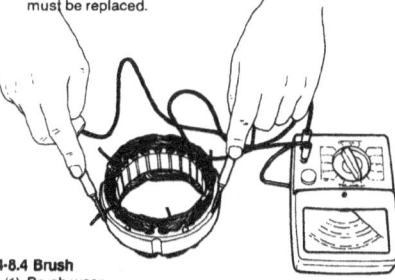

4-8.4 Brush

(1) Brush wear
Check the brush length.
The brush wears very little, but replace the brush if worn over the wear limit line printed on the brush.

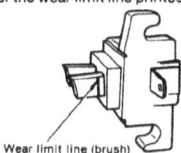

Wear limit line (brush)

Chapter 11 Electrical System
4. Alternator

	Maintenance standard	Wear limit
		mm(in.)
Brush length	14.5 (0.5709)	7.0 (0.2756)

(2) Brush spring pressure measurement
Measure the pressure with the brush protruding 2 mm from the brush holder, as shown in the figure. The spring is normal if the measured value is over 150 gr. Confirm that the brush moves smoothly in the holder.

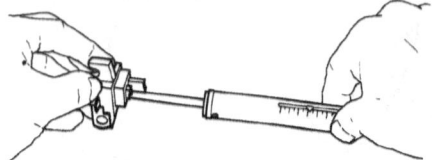

Brush spring strength	300 ±45g (0.562 ~ 0.761 lb.) (New brush)

4-9 Reassembly precautions
After inspection and servicing, reassemble the parts in the reverse order of disassembly, paying careful attention to the following items:
(1) When soldering the stator coil leads and diodes, hold them with needle nose pliers and solder quickly.
(2) Be sure that the insulation bushings, etc. are installed correctly when installing the terminal bolts and SR holder mounting screw.

4-10 Alternator performance test
4-10.1 Test equipment

Test equipment	Quantity	Specifications
Battery	1	12V
DC voltmeter	1	0 ~ 50V Range 0.5
DC ammeter	1	0 ~ 50A Range 1.0
Variable resistor	1	0 ~ 1Ω capacity:1 kW
Switch	2	Switch capacity: 40 A

4-10.2 Performance test circuit

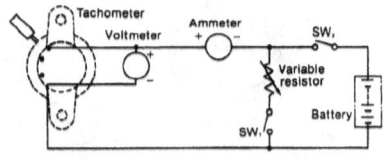

4-10.3 Performance test
(1) Speed measurement at 13 V (26 V rise speed)
 (a) Start the alternator slowly after opening SW1 and closing SW2.
 (b) After the alternator has reached a speed of approximately 500 rpm, open switch SW2.
 (c) Gradually increase the alternator speed while watching the voltmeter, and read the speed on the tachometer when the voltage reaches 13 V.
 (d) The speed at this time is 1,000 rpm or less, and is the 13 V rise speed.

(2) Output current measurement
 (a) Set the resistance of the variable resistor in the circuit in the figure to maximum, and drive the alternator after closing SW1 and SW2.
 (b) Increase the alternator speed to 5,000 rpm by adjusting the variable resistor, maintaining the voltage at 13 V.
 (c) Measure the deflection of the ammeter at this time.
 (d) An output current of 31 A is normal.
(3) Performance test precautions
 (a) Connect the alternator A terminal and battery (+) terminal, and the E terminal and battery (−) terminal with 2.5 m or less of wiring having a cross-sectional area of 8 mm² or more.
 (b) Check the wires for correct or loose connection.

Chapter 11 Electrical System
4. Alternator
_____ SM/YSM

4-11 Alternator troubleshooting and repair
(1) Failure to charge

Problem	Cause	Corrective action
Wiring, current	Open, shorted, or disconnected	Repair or replace
Alternator	Open, grounded, or shorted coil Terminal insulator missing Diode faulty	Replace Repair Replace
Transistor regulator	Transistor regulator faulty	Replace regulator

(2) Battery charge insufficient and discharge occurs easily

Problem	Cause	Corrective action
Wiring	Wiring shorted or loose, wiring thickness or length unsuitable	Repair or replace Replace
Generator	Rotor coil layer short Stator coil layer short; One phase of stator coil open Slip ring dirty V-belt loose Brush contact faulty Diode faulty	Replace Replace Clean or polish Retighten Repair Replace

(3) Battery overcharged

Problem	Cause	Corrective action
Battery	Electrolyte low or unsuitable	Add distilled water Adjust specific weight Replace
Transistor regulator	Regulator transistor shorted	Replace regulator.

(4) Current charge unstable.

Problem	Cause	Corrective action
Wiring	Wiring shorted at a break in the covering due to hull vibration or intermittent contact at break	Repair or replace
Alternator	Layer short Balance spring damaged Slip ring dirty Coil open	Replace Replace Replace Repair or replace

5. Alarm Circuit

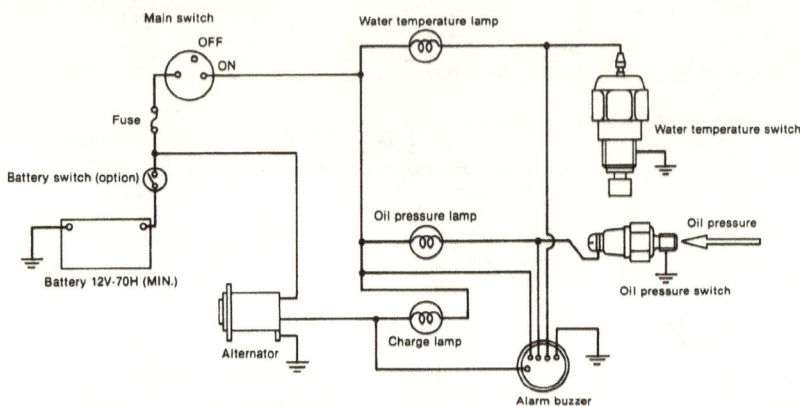

Connection diagram of alarm circuit

In order to indicate whether or not the lubricating oil is being fed to each engine section properly during engine operation, and whether or not the temperature of cooling water is normal, alarm lamps have been provided in the operating room and their switches have been arranged on the engine side of the room. If any abnormal condition is noted, the proper lamp will come on and also a buzzer will sound to give warning.

5-1 Oil pressure alarm

If the engine oil pressure is below 0.2 ± 0.1 kg/cm², with the main switch in the ON position, the contacts of the oil pressure switch are closed by a spring, and the lamp is illuminated through lamp → oil pressure switch → ground circuit system. If the oil pressure is normal, the switch contacts are opened by the lubricating oil pressure and the lamp remains off.

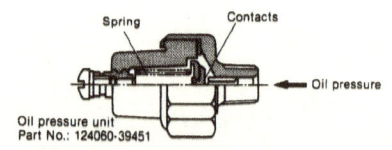

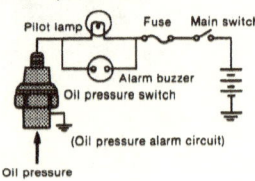

(Oil pressure alarm circuit)

Oil pressure unit
Part No.: 124060-39451

Oil pressure unit specifications

Rated voltage	12 V
Operating pressure	0.2 ± 0.1 kg/cm² (1.422 ~ 4.266 lb/in.²)
Lamp capacity:	3W

Chapter 11 Electrical System
5. Alarm Circuit

SM/YSM

Inspection

Problem	Inspection item	Inspection method	Corrective action
Lamp not illuminated when main switch set to ON	1. Fuse blown out	Visual inspection	Replace fuse (20A)
	2. Oil pressure lamp blown out	(1) Visual inspection	Replace lamp
		(2) Lamp not illuminated even when main switch set to ON position and terminals of oil pressure switch grounded	
	3. Operation of oil pressure switch	Lamp illuminates when checked as described in (2) above	Replace oil pressure switch
Lamp not extinguished while engine running	1. Oil level low	Stop engine and check oil level with dipstick	Add oil
	2. Oil pressure low	Measure oil pressure	Repair bearing wear and adjust regulator valve
	3. Oil pressure faulty	Switch faulty if abnormal at (1) and (2) above	Replace oil pressure switch
	4. Wiring between lamp and oil pressure switch faulty	Cut the wiring between the lamp and switch and wire with separate wire	Repair wiring harness

5-2 Cooling water temperature alarm

A water temperature lamp and water temperature gauge, backed up by an alarm in the instrument panel, are used to monitor the temperature of the engine cooling water. A high thermal expansion material is set on the end of the water temperature unit. When the cooling water temperature reaches a specified high temperature, the contacts are closed, and an alarm lamp and buzzer are activated at the instrument panel.

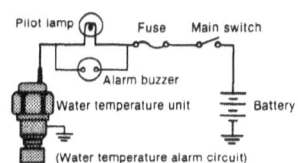

(Water temperature alarm circuit)

Water temperature switch

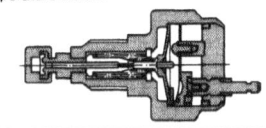

Operating temperature		Current capacity
ON	OFF	
60 ±2°	56 ±2°	DC12V, 7A

Pilot lamp: 12 V, 3 W
Alarm buzzer: 12 V, 1 W

Water temperature unit
Part No.: 46150-004530

The parts of the alarm circuit which must be checked are the open pilot bulb, fuse, and wiring. To check, disconnect the wiring at the water temperature unit side and ground the cord—the pilot lamp is normal if the pilot lamp illuminates. Moreover, be sure to check the operating temperature of the unit after replacing.

5-3 Alarm buzzer

The alarm buzzer sounds when the engine oil pressure, cooling water temperature, or charging becomes abnormal. The trouble source is indicated by illumination of the appropriate alarm lamp simultaneously with the sounding of the buzzer.

Type	WI1-02
Voltage	10 ~ 15V
Current drain	100mmA
Sound level	75dB(A) at 1m
Weight	0.2 kg

Part No.: 124271-91350

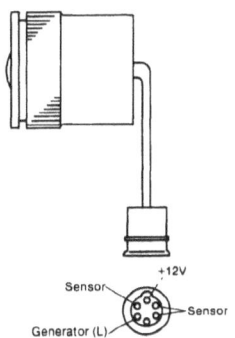

Chapter 11 Electrical System
5. Alarm Circuit

_____ SM/YSM

Normal operation is as follows:

	Alarm buzzer	Charge lamp	Oil pressure lamp	Water temperature lamp
Main switch ON, engine stopped	Alarm	Illuminated	Illuminated	Extinguished
Main switch ON, engine running	No alarm	Extinguished	Extinguished	Extinguished
Key switch OFF, engine stopped	No alarm	Extinguished	Extinguished	Extinguished

5-4 Charge lamp

If the voltage generated by the alternator exceeds that of the battery terminal during engine operation, charging of battery takes place and the charge lamp goes out. If any abnormal condition develops in the charging circuit during engine operation, the lamp will go on and an alarm buzzer will sound.

Inspection

Problem	Inspection item	Inspection method	Remedy
Lamp not illuminated when main switch set to ON	1. Fuse is blown.	Visual inspection (20A fuse)	Replace 20A fuse.
	2. Charge lamp is burnt out.	1. Visual inspection 2. Turn ON key switch, remove L terminal cord of alternator, and ground the cord. Lamp will not come on.	Replace lamp.
	3. Regulator operation.	Inspection according to procedures given in (2) causes lamp to come on.	Replace regulator within alternator.
Lamp not extinguished while engine running.	1. Alternator operation.	(1) By turning ON the key switch, make sure of the battery voltage across the F terminal cord of the alternator and earthing conductor. (2) The no-load voltage developed by the alternator is low. (same procedures as those for measuring 13V, [see page]).	When the voltage is 0, check for fuse and battery capacity. Refer to the sections on the inspection and servicing of the alternator.

6. Other Electric Equipment

6-1 Fuse

The fuse is installed in order to protect the circuit of each electric device from overloading. If it is blown during engine operation, install a new fuse with a rated capacity after thoroughly checking each circuit for abnormal signs.

Outside dimensions (mm)	Tubular fuse for motorcars	
	Diameter of socket	$\varnothing 6.5 ^{+0}_{-0.2}$
	Length	30 ± 8
	Capacity	20A

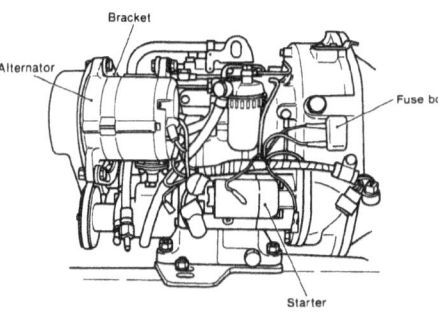

Note: Be sure to use 20A fuses.

6-2 Instrument panel

Chapter 11 Electrical System
6. Other Electric Equipments ——————————————————————————— *SM/YSM*

6-3 Tachometer

A tachometer that monitors ring gear speed and converts it to frequency to operate the meter is optional.

(1) Operating circuit

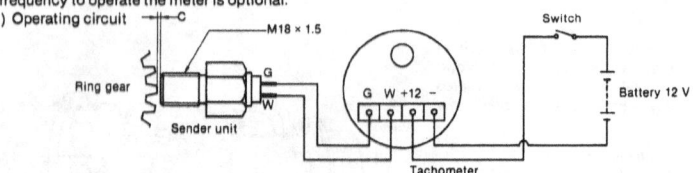

	Sender unit	Tachometer	
		YSM8-R	YSM12-R
Yanmar No.	124070-91160	124070-91100	104571-91100
VDO (West Germany) Part No.	340.804/007/007	430.230/019/001	430.230/019/002

(2) Sender unit sensitivity limits

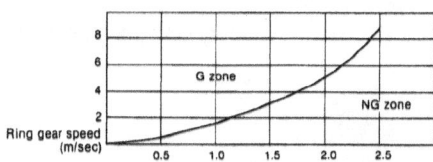

	YSM8-R	YSM12-R
No. of ring gear teeth	114	126
Module	2.54	2.54
Tachometer frequency	6,650 Hz	7,350 Hz

CHAPTER 12
INSTALLATION AND FITTING

1. Propeller and Stern Arrangement 12-1
2. Engine Installation 12-2
3. Stern Equipment..................................12-10
4. Interior Piping and Wiring.........................12-14
5. Front Power Take-Off.............................12-19

1. Propeller and Stern Arrangement

1-1 Propeller and shaft diameter

Model	Reduction ratio	Output (HP/rpm)	Propeller shaft (rpm)	Propeller, 3-blade	
				Dia.(in.)	Pitch(in.)
YSM8	1.95	5/2200	1127	14	9
		6/2600	1332	13	8-1/2
		7/3200	1639	12	7-1/2
YSM8G	2.93	5/2200	751	18	12
		6/2600	888	16-1/2	11
		7/3200	1093	15	10
YSM12	1.98	8/2200	1113	15	10
		9/2600	1316	14	9
		10/3000	1518	13	8-1/2
YSM12G	3.06	8/2200	718	19	15
		9/2600	849	18	13
		10/3000	980	17	12

1-2 Propeller shaft coupling

(1) Standard (for YSM8-Y, YSM12-Y)

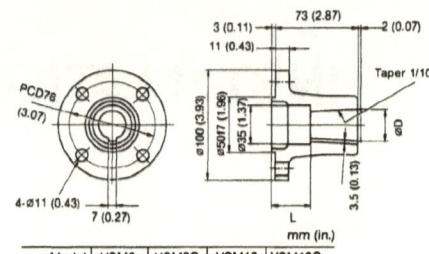

mm (in.)

Model	YSM8	YSM8G	YSM12	YSM12G
ØD	22(0.86)	25(0.98)	25(0.98)	28(1.10)
L	43(1.69)	34(1.33)	34(1.33)	34(1.33)

(2) Option (for all model)

mm (in.)

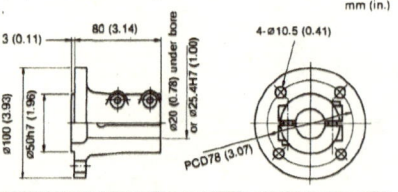

1-3 Propeller shaft and stern tube.

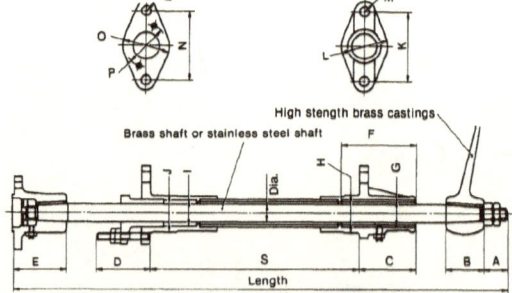

High stength brass castings
Brass shaft or stainless steel shaft

mm

MODEL	Dia.	Length	S (standard)	A	B	C	D	E	F	G	H	I	J	K	L	M·Q	N	O	P
YSM8	22	1800	400	32	52	65	57	54	88	35	46	35	46	90	60	2-14ø Holes, 1/2" Coach screw	90	60	54
YSM8G YSM12	25	2000	500	32	52	75	76	73	100	38	50	38	50	100	65	2-14ø Holes, 1/2" Coach screw	100	65	62
YSM12G	28	2400	600	40	60	80	75	73	110	41	56	41	56	110	75	2-18ø Holes, 5/8" Coach screw	110	75	70

2. Engine Installation

2-1 Engine room
The overall layout of the engine room is planned for easy inspection, servicing and handling of the engine, front power take-off and auxiliary machinery.
Do not overlook the position and space of the fuel tank, battery and Kingston cock and their related piping, wiring and remote control cables in the engine room layout. Thoroughly study all the equipment and apparatuses to be installed, and consult the shipyard and make a paper plan to provide optimum engine room space.
The engine room conditions required to handle the engine will be covered below.
(1) Ventilation inside engine room
Since an increase in the engine room temperature causes a reduction in the intake air volume and thus a drop in engine output, ventilation inside the engine room must be ample.
(2) Space must be sufficient to move the propeller shaft flange face toward the stern when disassembling the clutch, changing the gear, etc.

2-2 Engine bed
(1) Although the installation angle of the engine differs with the hull shape and engine installation position, it must be 8° or less when the vessel is cruising. If the tilt exceeds 8°, the output will decrease, the exhaust gas will color without the speed rising, vessel speed will fall or the parts will wear abnormally, and oil consumption will increase.

(2) Engine bed shall be designed so that there is no contact between the bottom of the engine and the hull.

• YSM8

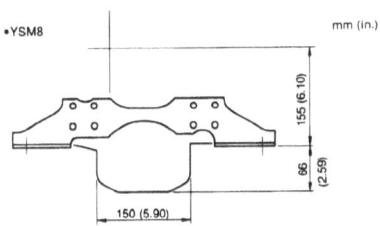

mm (in.)

• YSM12

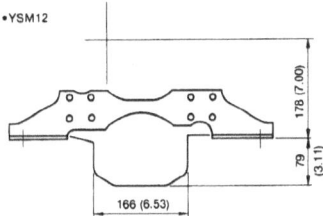

(3) Sufficient space must be available for easy setting of the wrench to the reamer bolt on the propeller shaft joint.
(4) The bed must be constructed so that a wrench can be set at the bottom of the engine base to retighten the engine mounting bolts.
(5) Make the bed such that the propeller shaft and engine drive shaft are in a straight line.

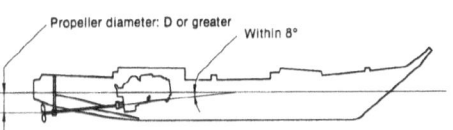

Chapter 12 Installation and Fitting
2. Engine Installation

2-3 Engine installation angle

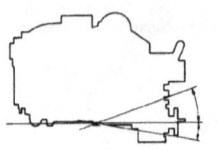 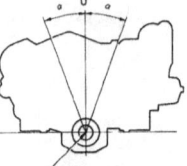

Propeller shaft center

Degree	Inclination under operation		Allowable installation angle (max.)
	Constant	Peak	Degree
α	25	35	—
β	20	35	15
γ	10	15	5

Chapter 12 Installation and Fitting
2. Engine Installation ──────────────────────────────── *SM/YSM*

2-4 Dimensions

(1) YSM8-R

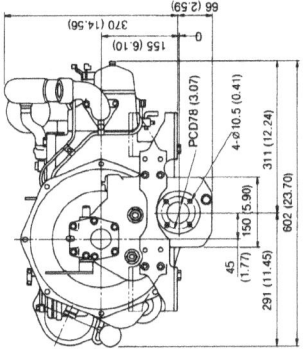
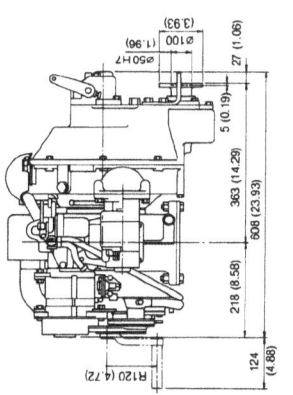
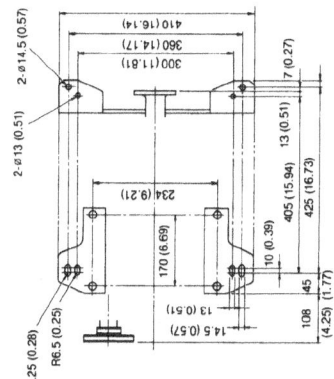
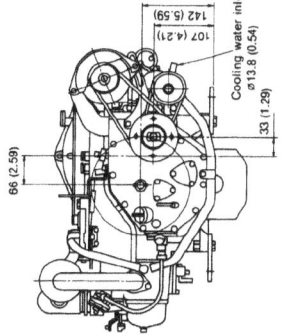

Chapter 12 Installation and Fitting
2. Engine Installation ———————————————————————————————————— SM/YSM

(2) YSM12-R

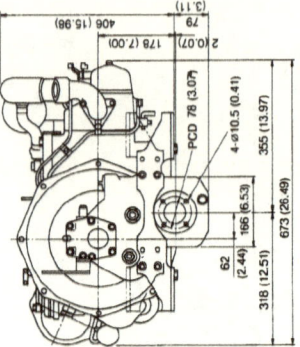

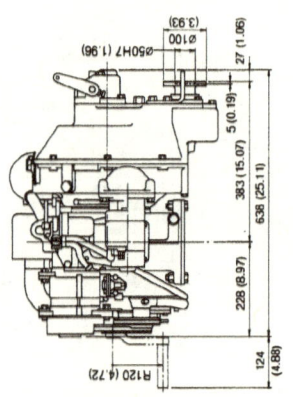
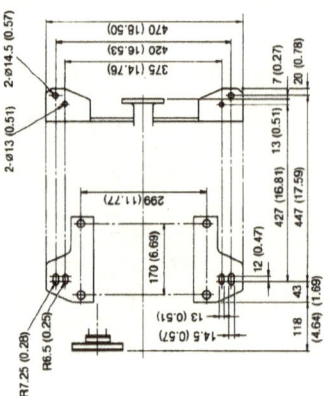

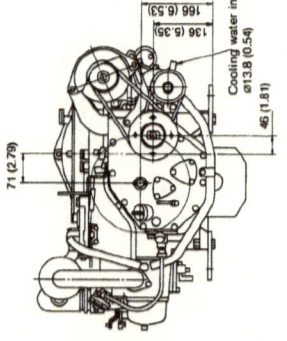

Chapter 12 Installation and Fitting
2. Engine Installation

SM/YSM

(3) YSM8-Y

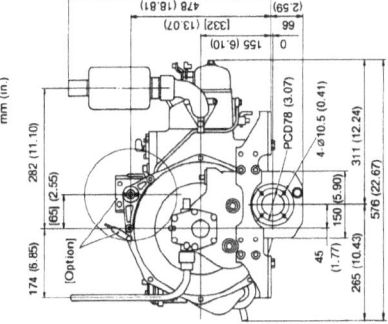
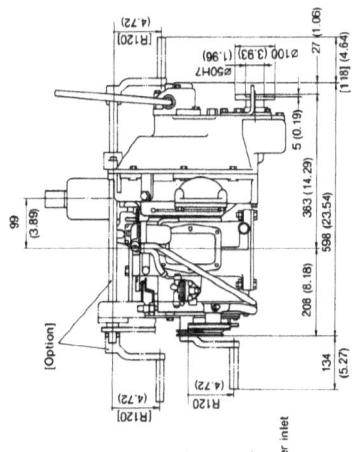
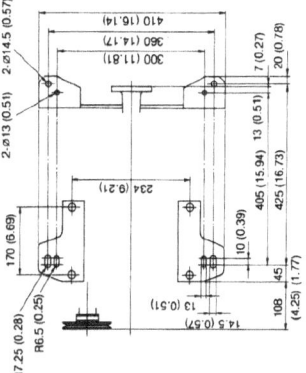
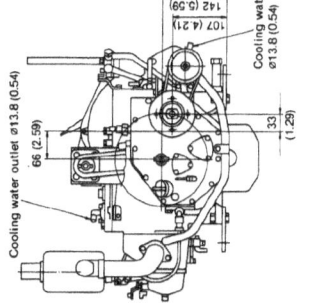

Chapter 12 Installation and Fitting
2. Engine Installation

(4) YSM12-Y

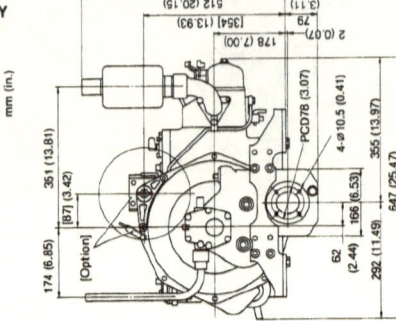
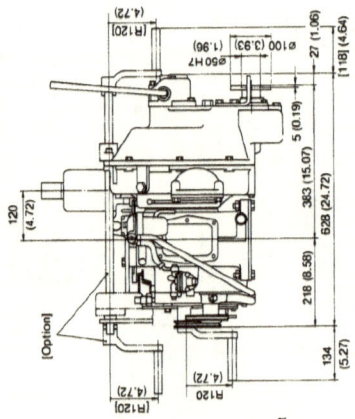
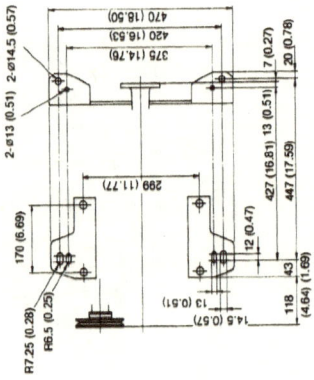
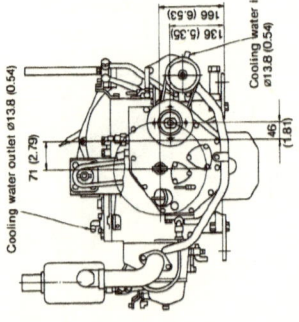

Chapter 12 Installation and Fitting
2. Engine Installation

SM/YSM

2-5 Engine installation method
2-5.1 Fixed installation

2-5.2 Flexible mounting

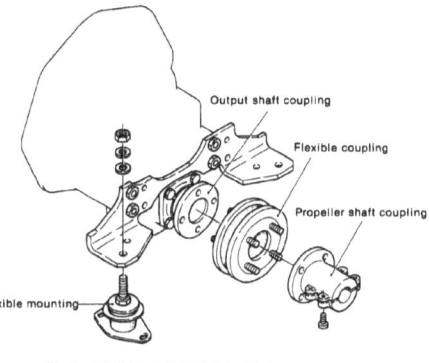

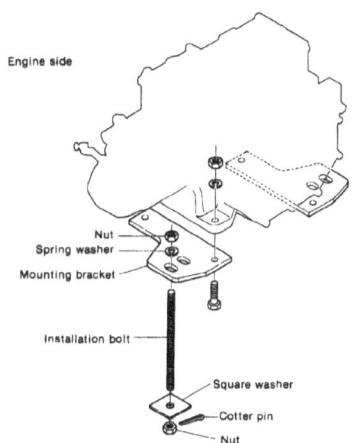

(1) Ajustable type flexible mounting

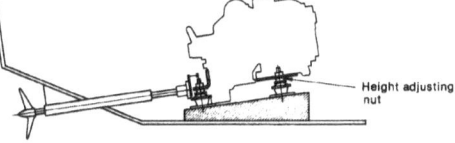

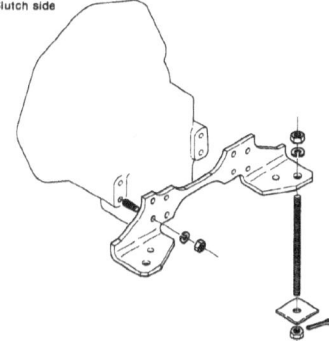

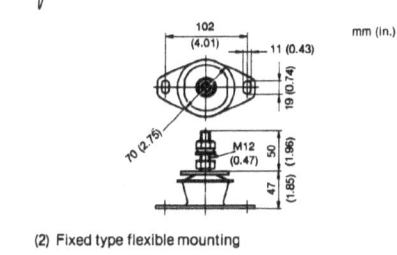

(2) Fixed type flexible mounting

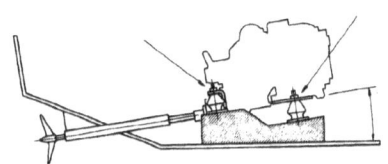

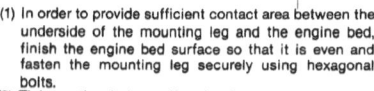

(1) In order to provide sufficient contact area between the underside of the mounting leg and the engine bed, finish the engine bed surface so that it is even and fasten the mounting leg securely using hexagonal bolts.
(2) Tighten the bolts uniformly. Do not unevenly or excessively tighten bolts that are not centered.
(3) Adjust the shim on the underside of the mounting leg so that the propeller shaft is coupled with the thrust shaft in a straight line.

Printed in Japan
A0A1001 8311

Chapter 12 Installation and Fitting
2. Engine Installation
SM/YSM

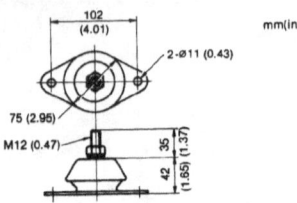

Before installing the propeller shaft in the engine (intermediate shaft when there is an intermediate shaft), make sure that the couplings of both shafts are centered. When the center of the engine is too high, adjust by cutting the engine bed, and when the engine is too high, adjust by inserting plates.

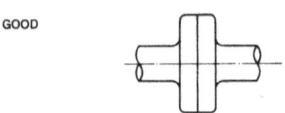

(3) Flexible coupling
When the engine is installed with flexible mountings a flexible coupling must always be used at the propeller shaft coupling.
NOTE: Install only after the drive shaft coupling and propeller shaft coupling have been centered.

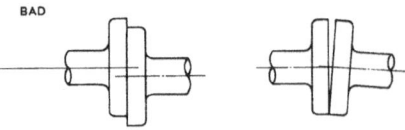

(a) Install a dial gauge on the propeller shaft coupling and measure the circumference versus drive shaft coupling center run-out (at four equally spaced points around the circumference).
(b) Then lock the drive shaft, turn the propeller shaft and dial gauge, and measure the outside periphery of the drive shaft and adjust to the value measured at (a) above.

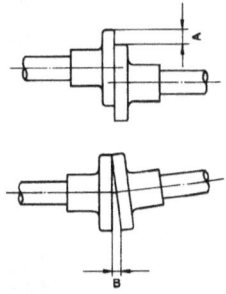

2-6 Centering
2-6.1 Coupling mating face measurement

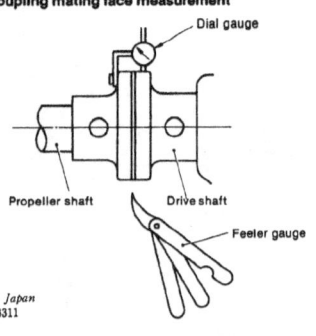

Coupling misalignment A	0.05 mm or less (0.002in.)
Coupling face run-out B	0.2 mm or less (0.0079in.)

2-6.2 After launching the vessel, check whether the drive shaft and propeller shaft are aligned.

3. Stern Equipment

3-1 Stern tube installation

The bearing at the point at which the stern equipment passes through the hull is called the stern tube. The propeller shaft is supported by inserting lignumvitae (wood), cutless bearing (rubber) and other support materials. The propeller shaft is inserted into the stern tube and the bow end is connected to the intermediate shaft or drive shaft, while the propeller shaft is installed in the stern end taper.

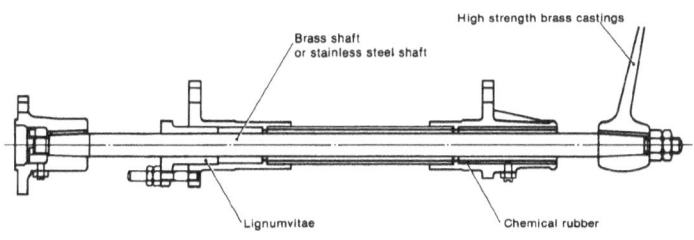

(a) Initial drilling
Bore a 30 ~ 40 mm diameter temporary hole smaller than the stern tube through the hull as shown in the drawing

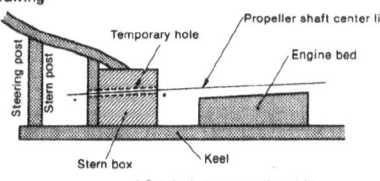

* Set the hole center, than drill

(b) Passing the centering line through the temporary hole
Pass the centering line through the temporary hole and fasten one end to the steering post and the other end to the engine room wall as shown below (The line should be tight.)

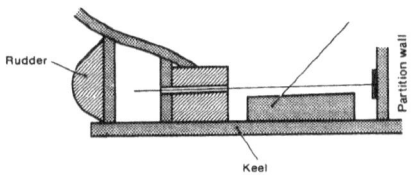

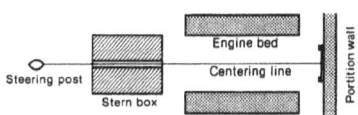

Make a parallel-cross frame (below) and attach it to the engine room wall. Then insert plate A, which carries the centering line, so that it is movable in all directions to allow correction of the line's position.
Fasten the line as illustrated in below [b] for easy removal. The empty hole in plate A (after the line is removed) permits pencil marking-off or center peep.

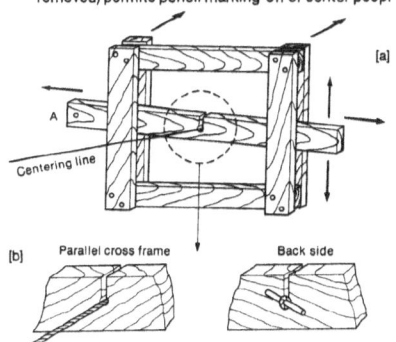

Chapter 12 Installation and Fitting
3. Stern Equipment
SM/YSM

(c) Centering
Measure the dimensions between various points and the centering line and set the temporary position of the engine in accordance with the dimensions given in the drawing.
  (1) Measure the dimension between the centering line and the top of the engine bed to determine the installation level and height of the crankshaft center line, then measure the clipping margins of the engine bed.
  (2) Measure the dimensions between the centering line and the inside surface of the engine bed.
  (3) At the flywheel and clutch, measure the dimensions between the centering line and the ship's bottom to check that the clutch case, engine oil pan, and flywheel clear the ship's bottom or sleepers.
  (4) Then temporarily fix the centering line adjusting plate A.

NOTE 1: Since centering based on the stern tube hole is performed on land, ample engine bed chipping allowances under the center line must be provided to allow for possible distortion after launching.
NOTE 2: If the flywheel, oil pan or clutch case touch the ship's bottom or any sleeper, raise the shaft center. However, in this case, the engine installation angle must be no more than 8°.
NOTE 3: The engine should be installed on as horizontal a plane as possible. Remember, propeller efficiency is highest when the engine is horizontal.

(d) Final drilling
After temporary centering, mark off one stern tube hole on each side of the stern box based on the centering line, and then bore holes that exactly fit the stern tube (no play).

(e) Stern tube installation
  (1) Remove the centering line, but either leave the frame of parallel crosses or mark off its center position on the front wall of the engine room
  (2) Insert the stern tube, check for interference, and temporarily tighten.
  (3) Centering for stern tube installation
    (a) Prepare a wooden block having a center hole covered with a thin tin plate.
    Hammer the block into the propeller side of the stern tube, obtain the center point with a compass and then make a small hole at this point with a nail or the line. Pass one end of the centering line through the hole and fasten the other end to the empty hole in plate A (3-1 (b)).

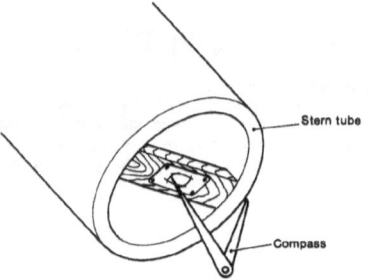

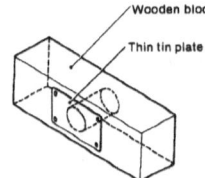

NOTE 1: The center deflection of the stern tube is 3 ~ 4 times greater at the front of the engine bed. Therefore, sufficient care must be exercised.
NOTE 2: If the stern tube holes are so large that stern tube play is excessive, tighten the stern tube to the correct position and mark that position so that the tube can be replaced correctly.
Check that the centering line is at the center of the stern tube at the inside flange. If not, center by moving either the stern tube or the centering line.
    (b) When centering the propeller side of the stern tube, the use of a centering jig with various outside diameters that fit the stern tube (below) will prove very convenient.

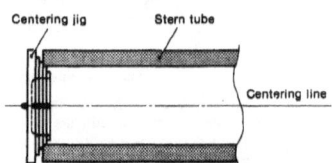

A tapered jig can be made for an infinite variety of stern tube inside diameters.

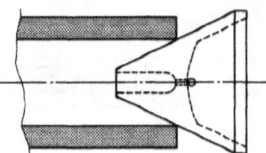

Chapter 12 Installation and Fitting
3. Stern Equipment

(4) Fitting of stern tube tightening surface
Pay careful attention to the rectangularity between the stern tube and stern tube tightening surface of the stern box when fitting.

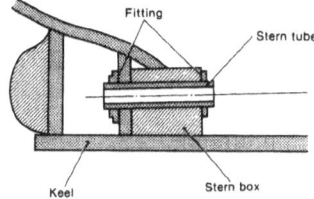

NOTE: If the stern tube and stern tube tightening surface of the stern box are not exactly rectangular, the stern tube will bend when tightened, causing overheating, seizing, abnormal lignumvitae wear and other troubles.

(5) Attaching the stern tube

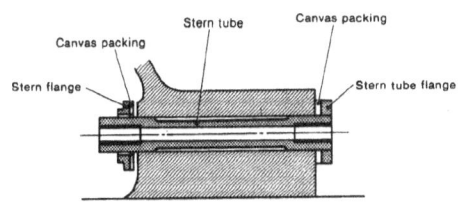

(a) Paint the outside of the stern tube with rust-preventive paint.
(b) Paint the stern tube flange and the surface of the stern box with white paint, and attach the canvas packings.
(c) Install the stern tube.
(d) Paint the outside of the stern post and the stern tube flange with white paint, and install the canvas packing and the stern flange.
Also paint the screw holes with white paint and tighten the screws.
(e) Attach the clamp for the stern tube chemical rubber tube and install the fastening wire.
(f) Drive in the coach screws to lock the inside and outside stern tube flanges and lock the stern flange nuts.

3-2 Propeller shaft installation
After fitting the stern tube packing gland to the propeller shaft, fit the propeller shaft to the stern tube by hand. Before fitting the propeller shaft to the stern tube, clean the interior of the stern tube and coat the lignumvitae with grease. When suspending the propeller shaft with a rope when inserting the shaft, the rope must not contact the rubber coil directly. Since propeller shaft insertion is performed at the narrowest part of the hull, be careful not to damage the brass coil and rubber coil. After inserting the propeller shaft, check the clearance between the stern tube and shaft while turning the shaft.

Insert the waterproof packing at the stern tube packing gland. Use braided string boiled in grease as the packing. Do not use a long coil, but rings cut one at a time, such as piston rings. When inserting the packing, the notches must alternate.

Tighten the packing uniformly while measuring the distance from the stern tube face to the gland face so that the packing gland is not tightened unevenly.

3-3 Propeller installation

(1) First, remove the shaft key, coat the shaft with red lead or bearing blue, fit the propeller shaft, and mark the position of the propeller on the brass coil. Then check the propeller shaft and propeller hole contact—if the contact is poor, correct. Poor contact and play during use will damage the key and key groove. After repairing, install the propeller and mark its position on the brass coil.

Then remove the propeller, insert the key on the shaft and fit and tighten the propeller. However, before this, check whether the marks made after repair match. If they do not, the key is touching and must be removed and cut.

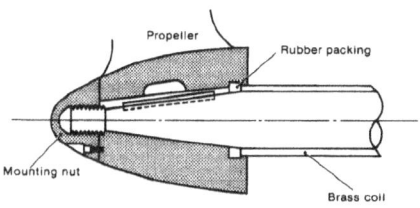

(2) Measuring the dimensions of the waterproofing rubber between the propeller shaft and propeller.

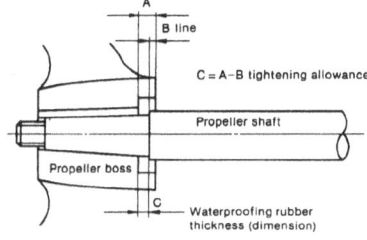

Chapter 12 Installation and Fitting
3. Stern Equipment

Insert the propeller onto the propeller shaft and mark the end of the propeller on the brass coil. The difference between the A dimension and B dimension in the figure is the waterproof rubber dimension, but a slight tightening allowance must be made.

(3) Propeller position

With the propeller installed, the ship's full speed will not be obtained if the spacing between the propeller and hull is not equal to, or greater than, the value given in the figure.

The position of the propeller section shaft center must be at least the diameter of the propeller from the surface of the water with the ship fully loaded.

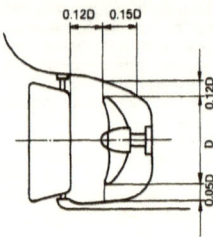

4. Interior Piping and Wiring

4-1 Exhaust pipe
4-1.1 Exhaust silencer installation

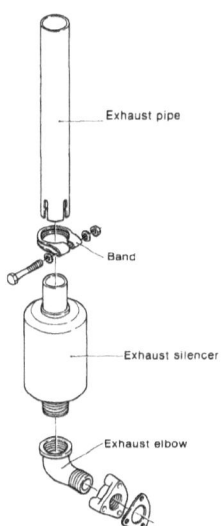

(2) Precautions
1) Always use an exhaust elbow when the direction of the exhaust must be changed.
2) Clamp the pipe to the hull at suitable positions.
3) Decide the exhaust silencer installation position according to the structure of the hull, but since the silencer reaches a high temperature, it should protrude past the cabin.
4) When piping the exhaust, the prevention of heat damage and fire must be considered because the exhaust is hot. Always cover the surface of the exhaust pipe with a rug.
5) Take measures to prevent rain from entering the exhaust pipe when the ship is moored.
6) Avoid long piping. When the piping must be long and the change of direction large, use large diameter pipe.

4-1.2 Mixing elbow installation
(1) Installation method and dimensions

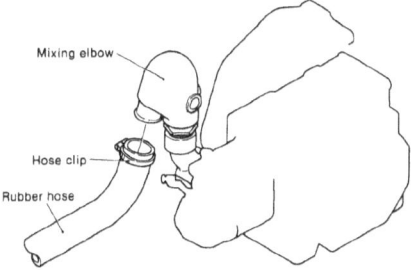

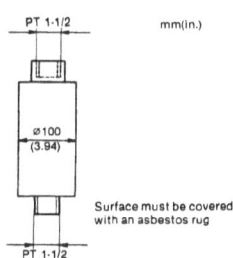

- Rubber hose connection dimensions

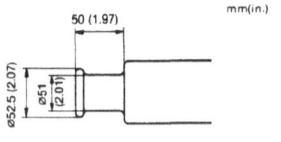

Rubber hose
Inside diameter: 50.8 mm
Outside diameter: 63 ~ 70 mm
Hose clip: 65 ~ 70 mm

(1) Installation method and dimensions
- Install the exhaust silencer either directly to the exhaust elbow installed on the exhaust manifold or on the exhaust pipe.
- When the silencer is installed in the exhaust pipe, use an exhaust pipe socket.
- In the case of a horizontal exhaust, use a horizontal exhaust elbow.

Chapter 12 Installation and Fitting
4. Interior Piping and Wiring _____ *SM/YSM*

When the outlet port of the cooling water is above the waterline (when C is greater than 200 mm):

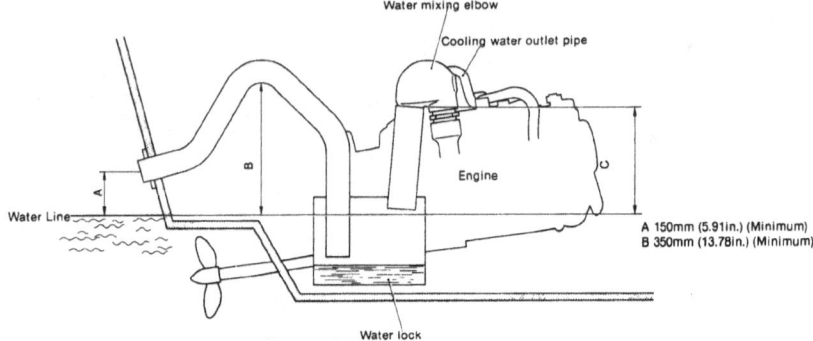

A 150mm (5.91in.) (Minimum)
B 350mm (13.78in.) (Minimum)

When the cooling water outlet port is below the waterline (when C is smaller than 200 mm):

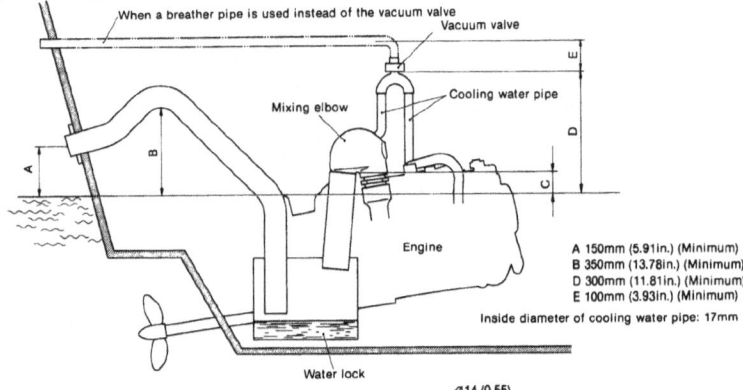

A 150mm (5.91in.) (Minimum)
B 350mm (13.78in.) (Minimum)
D 300mm (11.81in.) (Minimum)
E 100mm (3.93in.) (Minimum)

Inside diameter of cooling water pipe: 17mm

4-2 Cooling water pipe
4-2.1 Kingston cock (R-type:option)
(1) Installation
- Determine the position of the Kingston cock by the position of the cooling water pipe and the direction of the cooling water pump inlet joint.
- Finish the contact face of the Kingston cock hole drilled in the ship's bottom by grinding.
- Install the cock using canvas on the outside of the hull and canvas or rubber packing on the inside.

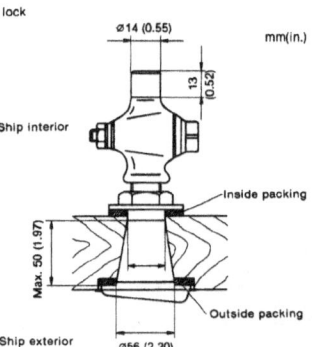

12-15

Chapter 12 Installation and Fitting
4. Interior Piping and Wiring

_____ SM/YSM

(2) Scoop strainer
The inlet section should have a double bottom to prevent troubles stemming from a lack of cooling water caused by the sucking in of vinyl sheets etc., at the Kingston cock inlet port. Install the strainer so that the large area of the scoop strainer faces away from the direction of the ship's forward movement, as shown in the figure.

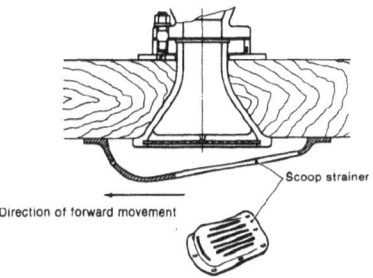

(3) Piping
- Use rubber hose for piping from the Kingston cock to the cooling water pump.
  Rubber hose size: Inside diameter x outside diameter x length = 13 × 20 × ℓ (mm)
  Hose clip size: ⌀22 mm

- The piping must be as straight as possible and bends must not be severe—diameter must be 100 mm or greater.

(4) When two Kingston cocks are used
When one of the Kingston cocks becomes clogged, operation can be switched to the other while the clogged cock is being cleaned, even during operation. In this case, use a 3-way cock for switching.

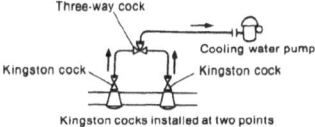

Kingston cocks installed at two points

4-2.2 Cooling water outlet pipe
(1) When a mixing elbow is installed, refer to the exhaust rubber hose piping section.

(2) When the mixing elbow is not used, connect a rubber hose to the cooling water outlet fixture so that the cooling water is purged directly from the ship.

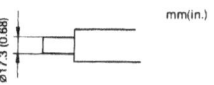

outlet fixture

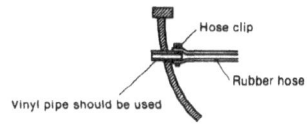

Rubber hose size: Inside diameter × outside diameter × length = 17 × 24 × ℓ (mm) Hose clip: 2pcs.

4-2.3 Bilge pipe piping precautions

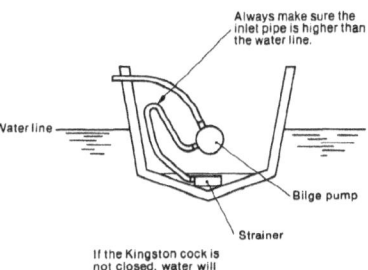

If the Kingston cock is not closed, water will enter from the cock.

4-3 Fuel tank and fuel piping
4-3.1 Fuel tank
(1) Clean the interior of the fuel tank with light oil and install the tank in the hull.
(2) The fuel tank must be positioned so that fuel is easy to add, fuel level is easy to check, and draining is easy. Moreover, take engine maintenance and inspection into consideration when deciding fuel tank position.
(3) A fuel pump is installed as standard, but the fuel tank should be installed at the highest possible point as near the engine as possible.

(4) Fuel tank (option) details

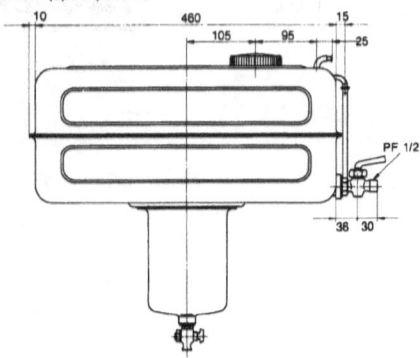
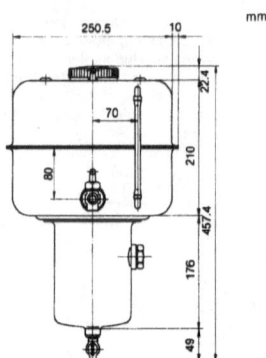

4-3.2 Fuel piping
(1) The hose must be as straight as possible. Minimum bend diameter: 50mm
(2) Be careful that the fuel piping does not touch the exhaust pipe or other hot parts.
(3) Fuel pipe (option) details.

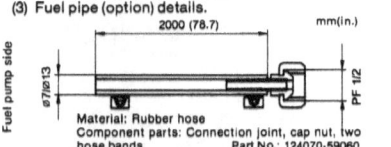

4-4 Electrical system
4-4.1 Battery installation and wiring
(1) Select a battery position which meets electrical wiring requirements.
   The battery must be positioned for easy checking of the electrolyte level.
(2) Install the battery on the battery mounting frame.
(3) Connect the wiring securely so that there is no voltage drop, and cover the terminals for protection.
(4) Select battery cables (battery—starter ground, battery—battery switch, battery switch—starter) having a total resistance of less than 0.002Ω.

4-4.2 Instrument panel
(1) Mounting dimensions

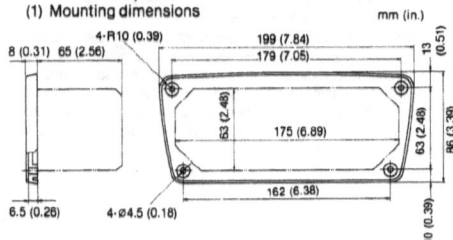

Drill the mounting holes and bolt holes in accordance with the instrument panel mounting diagram.
(2) Installation location and dimensions
The instrument panel should be installed in the cabin, but if it is installed outside, pay careful attention to the following points.
1) Install in a location where there is no danger of the panel being splashed by sea water.
2) When the instrument panel is installed where it may be splashed by sea water, install it in a recessed position or install a cover.

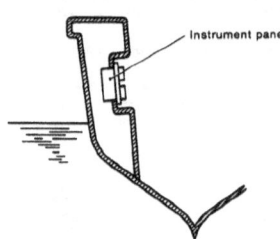
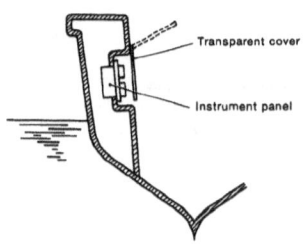

Chapter 12 Installation and Fitting
4. Interior Piping and Wiring

3) Installation angle
The instrument panel must be installed at an angle of between 45° and 90° to prevent indicating errors.

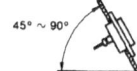

4-5 Remote control
4-5.1 Remote control stand installation dimensions
(1) Morse one-handle remote control (MT)

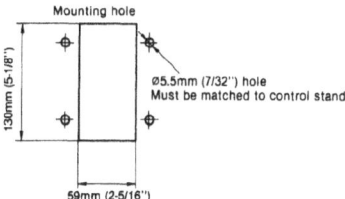

(2) Engine stop remote control, decompression remote control

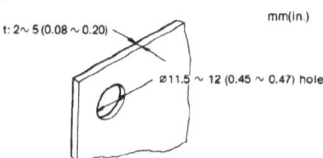

Common to both stop remote control and decompression remote control

4-5.2 Remote control cable precautions
The remote control push-pull cable must be as straight as possible. Numerous bends will increase the operating load and shorten the life of the cable.

5. Front Power Take-Off

Power to drive the deck machinery and small generator, pump, compressor, etc. can be taken from the front of the engine.
Power take-off capacity, drive system selection and the quality of installation centering have a considerable effect on the engine, and care must be exercised.

5-1 Front power take-off details
A crankshaft V-pulley is used as the front power take-off coupling.

5-3 Front power take-off general precautions
(1) With belt drive, the belt tension must be adjusted so that an excessive load is not applied to the drive shaft. Regardless of the horsepower rating taken out, make the diameter of the pulley on the working machine side as large as possible and set the number of engine rotations to high-speed. (Use of the engine for hours at a low speed gives rise to hunting, etc. If the diameter of the pulley is large, the V-belt is becomes more durable.

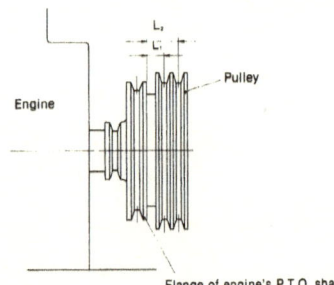

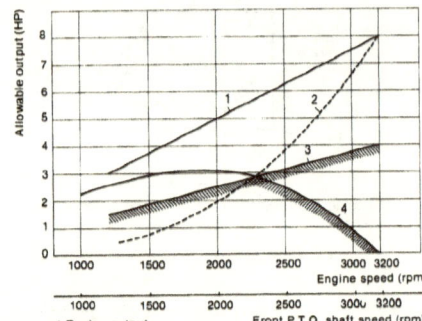

YSM8

1 Engine output
2 Propeller power
3 Front P.T.O. output at propeller not driven
4 Front P.T.O. output at propeller driven

5-2 Front drive system
Power is transmitted sideways via V-belt without the use of outside bearings.

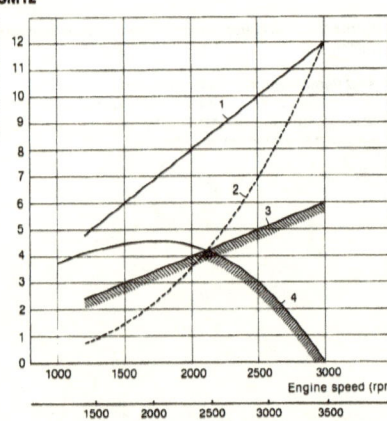

Caution: Dimension of L1: less than 20mm
Dimension of L2: less than 40mm

YSM12

1 Engine output
2 Propeller power
3 Front P.T.O. output at propeller not driven
4 Front P.T.O. output at propeller driven

CHAPTER 13
OPERATING INSTRUCTIONS

1. Fuel Oil and Lubricating Oil 13-1
2. Engine Operating Instructions......................13-8
3. Troubleshooting and Repair........................13-12

Chapter 13 Operating Instructions
1. Fuel Oil and Lubricating Oil

1. Fuel Oil and Lubricating Oil

Selection of and proper attention to fuel and lubricating oils have a substantial effect on engine performance, and are vital factors governing engine life.

The use of low quality fuel and lubricating oils will lead to various engine troubles. Yanmar diesel engines will display satisfactory performance and ample reliability if the fuel and lubricating oil recommended by Yanmar are used correctly. For the engine to have long-term high performance, sufficient knowledge of the properties of the fuel and lubricating oils and their selection, management and usage is necessary.

1-1 Fuel
1-1.1 Properties of fuel
Numerous kinds of fuels are used with diesel engines, and the properties and composition of each differ somewhat according to the manufacturer.
Moreover, the various national standards are introduced here for reference purposes.

1-1.2 Recommended fuels

Manufacturer	Brand name
Caltex	Caltex Diesel Oil
Shell	Shell Diesoline or local equivalent
Mobil	Mobil Diesel Oil
Esso	Esso Diesel Oil
British Petroleum	BP Diesel Oil

1-1.3 Fuel selection precautions
Pay careful attention to the following when selecting the fuel.
(1) Must have a suitable specific gravity
Fuel having a specific gravity of 0.88 ~ 0.94 at 15°C is suitable as diesel engine fuel. Specific gravity has no relation to spontaneous combustibility, but does give an idea of viscosity and combustibility or mixing of impurities.
Generally, the higher the specific gravity, the higher the viscosity and the poorer the combustibility.
(2) Must have a suitable viscosity
When the viscosity is too high, the fuel flow will be poor, operation of the pump and nozzle will be inferior, atomization will be faulty and fuel combustion will be incomplete.
If the viscosity is too low, the plunger, nozzle, etc. will wear rapidly because of insufficient lubrication. Generally, however, the higher the viscosity, the lower the quality of the fuel.
(3) Cetane value must be high.
The most important indicator of fuel's combustibility is its cetane value (also represented by cetane index or diesel index), The cetane value is particularly important for fuels used in high-speed engines. The relationship between the cetane value, startability and firing delay is shown in the below figure. Firing delay becomes smaller and starting characteristics better as the cetane value becomes higher.

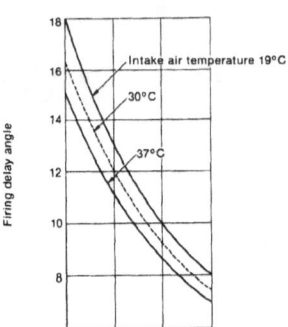

Relationship between cetane value and firing delay

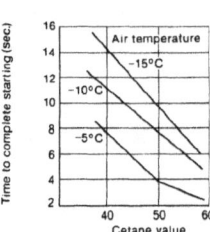

Cetane value and starting characteristic

The use of a fuel with an unsuitable cetane value will cause the following troubles:
1) Difficult starting.
2) Poor operation.
3) High combustion pressure and diesel knock.
4) Lower output and engine damage because of overheating caused by knocking.
5) Sticking of nozzles and exhaust valves.
6) Severe smoking, carbon build-up inside the engine, and oil contamination.
7) Deterioriation of the oil and excessive wear in the piston rings, ring grooves, and cylinder liner.
(4) The level of impurities must be low
1) Sulfur
With proper combustion sulfur in the fuel turns to nitrous acid gas (SO_2) and sulfuric anhydride (SO_3). When combustion is imperfect, it becomes sulfuric acid containing water that corrodes and wears the cylinder liners, pistons, exhaust valve and exhaust pipe.

Chapter 13 Operating Instructions
1. Fuel Oil and Lubricating Oil

SM/YSM

Properties and compositions of fuel of various national standards

National standard Properties and components		Japan JIS-K-2204-1965		U.S.A. ASTM-D975-74	U.K. BS-2689-70	
		Class No.1 light oil	Class No.2 light oil	No. 2D Diesel oil	Class A1	Class A2
Specific gravity	15/4°C	—	—	—	—	—
Kinetic viscosity	30°C cst	2.7 or more	2.5 or more	(~ 5.2)	(~ 7.5)	(~ 7.5)
	37.8°C (100°F) cst	(2.3 or more)	(2.2 or more)	2.0~4.3	1.6 ~ 6.0	1.6 ~ 6.0
Reaction		Neutral	Neutral	—	—	—
Flash point	°C	50 or more	50 or more	51.7 or more	55 or more	55 or more
Flow point	°C	−5 or less	−10 or less	−12 or less	—	—
Residual carbon	Weight %	(10% residual oil) 0.15 or less	(10% residual oil) 0.15 or less	0.35 or less	0.2 or less	0.2 or less
Moisture	Volume %	—	—	—	0.05 or less	0.05 or less
Ash	Weight %	—	—	0.01 or less	0.01 or less	0.01 or less
Sulfur	Weight %	1.2 or less	1.2 or less	0.5 or less	0.5 or less	1.0 or less
Cetane valve		50 or more	45 or more	40 or more	50 or more	45 or more
Sludge or sedimentation	%	—	—	0.05 or less	0.01 or less	0.01 or less
Distillation properties, temperatures at 90% distillation	°C	350 or below	350 or below	282.21 ~ 338	357 or below	357 or below

Printed in Japan
A0A1001 8311

Chapter 13 Operating Instructions
1. Fuel Oil and Lubricating Oil _____ **SM/YSM**

2) Water content
   A high water content causes sludge, resulting in lower output, imperfect combustion and trouble in the fuel injection system.
3) Carbon content
   If the carbon content is high, carbon will remain inside the combustion chamber, causing accelerated cylinder liner and piston wear and corrosion of the pistons and exhaust valves.
4) Residual carbon (coke content)
   Coke becomes a carbide that sticks to the end of the nozzle, causing faulty injection. In addition, unburned carbon will build up on the pistons and liners, causing piston ring wear and sticking.

1-1.4 Simple methods of identifying fuel properties
(1) Fuel that is extremely odorous and smoky contains a large amount of volatile components and impurities.
(2) Fuel that emits little smoke when used in a lamp is of good quality.
(3) Fuel that emits a crackling sound when soaked in paper and ignited contains a high water content.
(4) If a transparent film of diesel oil is squeezed between two pieces of glass, the water content and impurities can be determined.
(5) If the fuel contains resin or carbon black particles and impurities will appear when fuel and sulfuric acid are mixed in equal parts.
(6) Discoloration of litmus test paper indicates the presence of acids.

1-1.5 Troubles caused by bad fuel
(1) Clogging of exhaust valve
   In addition to faulty compression, incomplete combustion, and high fuel consumption, a clogged exhaust valve will cause fuel to be mixed in the exhaust, leading to corrosion of the exhaust valve seat.
(2) Clogging of piston ring grooves
   Clogged piston ring grooves will cause accelerated cylinder liner and piston wear due to sticking rings, fuel gas blowback, faulty lubrication, incomplete combustion, high fuel consumption, contaminated lubricating oil, and combustion gas blowback.
(3) Clogged or corroded injection valve hole
   This will cause incomplete combustion and piston and liner wear, fuel injection mechanism wear, corrosion, and groove wear and corrosion.
(4) Sediment inside crankcase
   Since sediment in the crankcase is often mistakenly judged as coming from the lubricating oil, care must be taken in determining its true origin.

1-1.6 Relationship between fuel properties and engine performance

Fuel property	Starting characteristic	Lubrication characteristic	Smoke generation	Exhaust odor	Output	Fuel consumption	Clogging of combustion chamber
Firing Cetane value	Directly related— Starting characteristic improves as cetane value increases	Directly related— Lubrication improves as cetane value rises	Closely related— Smoke increases as cetane value decreases	Directly related— Decreased by increasing cetane value	Irrelevant	Related	Related— Decreased by reducing cetane value
Volatility 90% end point	No clear relationship	Related— Becomes poor when volatility is poor	Directly related— Increases as volatility decreases	No direct relationship	Irrelevant	Irrelevant	Related— Increases as volatility decreases
Viscosity	No clear relationship	Some relationship— Becomes poor when viscosity increases	Related— Increases as viscosity increases	No independent relationship	Irrelevant	Irrelevant	Related— Increases with viscosity
Specific gravity	Irrelevant	Irrelevant	Related— Increases as specific gravity increases	No independent relationship	Directly related— Associated with calorific value	Related— Associated with calorific value	Related— Depends on properties of engine
10% residual carbon	Irrelevant	Irrelevant	Related— Improves as residual carbon decreases	No independent relationship	Irrelevant	Irrelevant	Related— Decreases as residual carbon decreases
Sulfur				No independent relationship			
Flash point				No independent relationship			

Chapter 13 Operating Instructions
1. Fuel Oil and Lubricating Oil
SM/YSM

1-1.7 Fuel handling precautions
(1) Fill the fuel tank after work to prevent condensation of water in the tank.
(2) Always use a tank inlet strainer. Water mixed in the fuel can be removed by removing the strainer quickly.
(3) Remove the plug at the bottom of the fuel tank and drain out the water and sediment after every 100 hours of operation, and when servicing the pump and nozzle.
(4) Do not use fuel in the bottom of the fuel tank because it contains large amounts of dirt and water.

1-2 Lubricating oil
Selection of the lubricating oil is extremely important with a diesel engine. The use of unsuitable lubricating oil will cause sticking of the piston rings, accelerated wear and seizing of the piston and cylinder liner, rapid wear of the bearings and other moving parts, and reduced engine durability. Since this engine is a high-speed engine, always follow the lubricating oil replacement interval.

1-2.1 Action of the lubricating oil
(1) Lubricating action: Builds a film of oil on each moving part reduce wear and its accompanying damage.
(2) Cooling action: Removes heat generated at moving parts by carrying it away with the lubricating oil flow.
(3) Sealing action: Maintains the air tightness of the pistons and cylinders by the oil film on the piston rings.
(4) Cleaning action: Carries away carbon produced at the cylinders as well as dust that has entered from the outside.
(5) Rustproofing action: Prevents corrosion by coating metal surfaces with a thin film of oil.

Various additives are added to the lubricating oil to assure that adequate performance is assured under the high-speed, high-load and other severe operating conditions met by modern diesel engines. While these additives differ with each manufacturer, commonly used additives include:
(1) Flow point reduction additive
(2) Viscosity index improvement additive
(3) Oxidation prevention additive
(4) Cleaning dispersent
(5) Lubrication additive
(6) Anticorrosion additive
(7) Bubble elimination additive
(8) Alkali neutralizer

1-2.2 Required lubricating oil conditions
(1) Must be of suitable viscosity
If the viscosity is too low, the oil film will be too thin and the lubricating action insufficient. If the viscosity is too high, the friction resistance will be increased and starting will become especially difficult.
(2) Viscosity change with temperature must be small. While the lube oil temperature goes from low at starting to high during operation, the viscosity change by temperature should be small. That is, the viscosity index should be high at all temperatures.
(3) Must have good lubricating capability
That is, it must coat metal surfaces as a thin film. In other words, the lubricating oil must coat the metal surfaces so that metal-to-metal contact caused by breaking of the oil film at the top dead center and bottom dead center piston position does not occur, or that the oil film is not broken by collision, even at the bearings.
(4) Mixability with water must be low
Since water can mix with the oil because of the presence of cooling water in the engine, the emulsification of water and oil, which causes the oil to lose its lubricating properties, must be prevented.
(5) Must be neutral and difficult to oxidize
Since acids and alkalis corrode metal, the lubricating oil must be neutral. Moreover, since even a neutral oil will be oxidized easily by contact with the combustion gas, the oil must be stable with few oxidizing elements.
(6) Must withstand high heat and must evaporate or combust with difficulty
Oil must have a high flash point. If it is evaporated by heat or is not burned completely, carbon will be produced. This carbon is toxic.
(7) Must not contain any water or dirt and must have a low sulfur and coke content

1-2.3 Classification by viscosity

SAE No.	−17.8°C (6°F)		98.9°C (210°F)		Applicable temperature range (outside temperature)
	Saybolt universal viscosity (sec)	Dynamic viscosity (cst)	Saybolt universal viscosity (sec)	Dynamic viscosity (cst)	
5W	Under 4,000	Under 869	—	—	20°C or less
10W	6,000 ~ 12,000	1,303 ~ 2,606	—	—	
20W	12,000 ~ 48,000	2,606 ~ 10,423	—	—	
20	—	—	45 ~ 58	5.73 ~ 9.62	20°C ~ 35°C
30	—	—	58 ~ 70	9.62 ~ 12.93	
40	—	—	70 ~ 85	12.93 ~ 16.77	35°C or greater
50	—	—	85 ~ 110	16.77 ~ 22.68	

Chapter 13 Operating Instructions
1. Fuel Oil and Lubricating Oil

Since only the 98.9°C viscosity is stipulated for S.A.E. No. 20 ~ 50 oil in the table, and only the −17.8°C viscosity is stipulated for S.A.E. No. 5W ~ 20W oil, they are not guaranteed at other temperatures. On the other hand, S.A.E. No.10W viscosity is stipulated and oil having the viscosity equal to that of S.A.E. No.30 even at 98.9°C is called S.A.E. No.10W—30, or multigrade oil. Multigrade oil comprises S.A.E. No. 5W—20, 10W—30, and 20W—40. In arctic regions, oil from S.A.E. No. 20W to 10W—30 can be used.

1-2.4 SAE service classification and API service classification

SAE new classification (1970)	API service classification (1960)
CA	DG
CB·CC	DM
CD	DS

(1) DG grade: Used when deposits and engine wear must be controlled when the engine is normally operated at a light load using low sulfur fuel.
(2) DM grade: Used when the generation of deposits and wear caused by sulfur in the fuel is possible under severe conditions.
(3) DS grade: Used under extemely severe operating conditions or when excessive wear or deposits are caused by the fuel.

Classification	Engine service (API)
CA	Light duty diesel engine service: Mild, moderate operation diesel engine service with high-performance fuel, and mild gasoline engine service. The oil designed for this service was mainly used in the 1940s and 50s. This oil is for high performance fuel use and has bearing corrosion and high temperature deposit prevention characteristics.
CB	Moderate duty diesel engine service: Mild, moderate operation diesel engine service using low performance fuel requiring bearing corrosion and high temperature deposit prevention characteristics. Includes mild gasoline engine service. Oil designed for this service was introduced in 1949. The oil is used with high sulfur fuels and has bearing corrosion and high temperature deposit prevention characteristics.
CC	Moderate duty diesel engine service and gasoline engine service: Applicable to low supercharged diesel engines for moderate to severe duty. The oil designed for this service was introduced in 1961 and is widely used in trucks and agricultural equipment, construction machinery, farm tractors, etc. The oil features high deposit prevention characteristics in low supercharged diesel engines, and rust, corrosion and low temperature sludge prevention characteristics in gasoline engines.
CD	Severe duty diesel engine service: Applicable to high-speed, high-output high supercharged diesel engines which are subjected to considerable wear and deposits. This oil was introduced in 1955, and is used as a wide property-range fuel in high supercharged engines. It also has bearing corrosion and high temperature deposit prevention characteristics.

1-2.5 Fuel oil
SAE new classification CB grade or CC grade fuel having suitable viscosity for the atmospheric temperature must be used in this engine.

Chapter 13 Operating Instructions
1. Fuel Oil and Lubricating Oil

1-2.6 Recommended lubricating oils

Supplier	Brand Name	SAE No.			
		Below 10°C	10~20°C	20~35°C	Over 35°C
SHELL	Shell Rotella Oil	10W, 20/20W	20/20W	30 40	50
	Shell Talona Oil	10W	20	30 40	50
	Shell Rimula Oil	20/20W	20/20W	30 40	—
CALTEX	RPM Delo Marine Oil	10W	20	30 40	50
	RPM Delo Multi-Service Oil	20/20W, 10W	20	30	50
MOBIL	Delvac Special	10W	20	30	—
	Delvac 20W—40	20W—40	20W—40	—	—
	Delvac 1100 Series	10W, 20/20W	20/20W	30 40	50
	Delvac 1200 Series	10W, 20/20W	20/20W	30 40	50
ESSO	Estor HD	10W	20	30 40	—
	Esso Lube HD	—	20	30 40	50
	Standard Diesel Oil	10W	20	30 40	50
B.P. (British Petroleum)	B.P. Energol ICMB B.P. Energol DS-3	20W	20W	40	50

1-2.7 Engine oil replacement and handling

(1) Necessity of replacement

Since the engine oil is exposed to high temperatures during use and is mixed with air at high temperatures, it will oxidize and its properties will gradually change. In addition, its lubricating capabilities will be lost through contamination and dilution by water, impurities, and the fuel. Emulsification and sludge are produced by heat and mixing when the lubricating oil contains water and impurities, causing its viscosity to increase. Moreover, if the carbon in the cylinders enters the crankcase, the oil will turn pure black and the change in its properties can be seen at a glance. The continued use of deteriorated oil will not only cause wear and corrosion of moving parts, but will ultimately cause the bearings and cylinders to seize. Therefore, deteriorated oil must be replaced.

(2) Replacement period

Although the engine oil change interval differs with the engine operating conditions and the quality of the lubricating oil and fuel used, the oil interval should be change as follows when CB grade oil is used in a new engine:

1st time .... After approximately 20 hours of use
2nd time........ After approximately 30 hours of use
From 3rd time ... After every 100 hours of use

Drain the old oil completely and replace it with new oil while the engine is still warm.

CAUTION: Never mix different brands of lubricating oil.

1-2.8 Feeding the lubricating oil

Although the crank chamber is not connected with the clutch case, the same lubricating oil is employed for both.

(1) Remove the oilers on the clutch case and the head cover. Be sure to add lubricating oil to the upper mark on the dipstick, the amount of oil should not be below the lower mark on the dipstick, nor should too much oil be added.

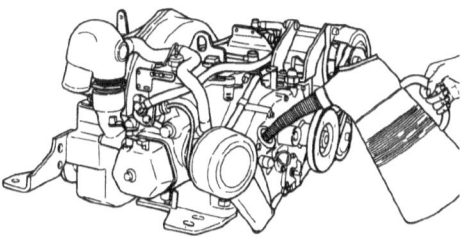

Engine

Chapter 13 Operating Instructions
1. Fuel Oil and Lubricating Oil

SM/YSM

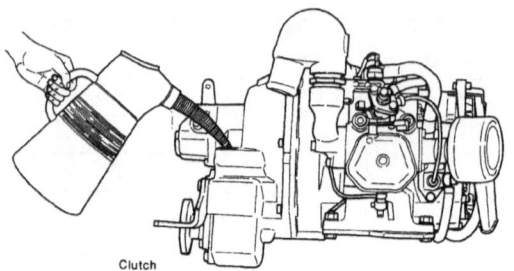
Clutch

(2) Since it takes sometime for the oil to flow completely into the clutch case and oil pan, wait for 2 ~ 3 minutes after filling before checking the oil levels. Moreover, check the oil while the ship is afloat.

1-2.9 Oil capacity
Lubricating oil capacity at an engine mounting angle (rake) of 8° is given below.

liter

	YSM 8	YSM 12
Crankcase total/effective	1.9/0.8	3.0/1.0
Clutch case total/effective	0.7/0.2	0.7/0.2

* Check the crankcase oil level by completely inserting the dipstick. Check the clutch case oil level without screwing in the cap.
The oil levels must be between the upper and lower limit marks on both dipsticks.

2. Engine Operating Instructions

2-1 Preparations before starting
2-1.1 Fueling up
(1) Check the fuel level in the fuel tank and add fuel if necessary.
Fuel consumption for 10 hour/day operation is given below.

YSM8	7HP/3200 rpm	Approx. 18ℓ
YSM12	10HP/3000 rpm	Approx. 26ℓ

(2) Remove water and dirt collected in the bottom of the tank using the fuel tank drain cock.
(3) Add clean fuel to the tank.
Since dirt and water sink to the bottom of the fuel drum, do not turn the drum upside down and do not pump the fuel from the bottom of the drum.

2-1.2 Adding lubricating oil
(1) Check the oil level with the dipstick, and add oil, if necessary, to bring the level up to the to mark of the dipstick.
The level must neither be too low nor too high.
(2) The crankcase and clutch case are separated.
Check both and add oil separately.
(3) Since the crankcase oil flows into the crankcase through the camshaft and valve chambers, wait 2 ~ 3 minutes before checking its level.

2-1.3 Lubricating each part
(1) Lubricate each pin of the remote control lever.

2-1.4 Checking fuel priming and injection
(1) Operate the priming lever of the fuel pump.
(2) Set the regulator handle to the full speed position and check for injection sound by turning the engine over several times.
(3) If there is no fuel injection sound, bleed the air from the fuel system.

2-1.5 Bleeding the fuel system
Since the presence of air in the fuel system anywhere between the fuel tank and the injection valve will cause faulty fuel injection, always bleed the air from the system when the fuel system is disassembled and reassembled.

Bleeding the fuel system
(1) Open the fuel tank cock.
(2) Bleed the air from the fuel filter.
Loosen the air bleeding plug at the top of the fuel filter body and operate the manual handle of the fuel pump until no more bubbles appear in the fuel flowing from the filter.
Then install and tighten the air bleeding plug.

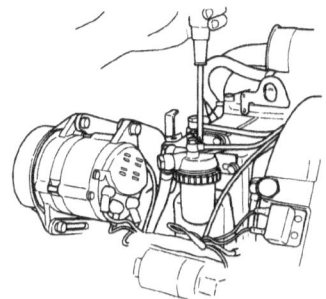

(3) Bleeding the air from the fuel pump
By loosening the pipe joint bolt on the fuel pump side, bleed the air from the fuel pump.

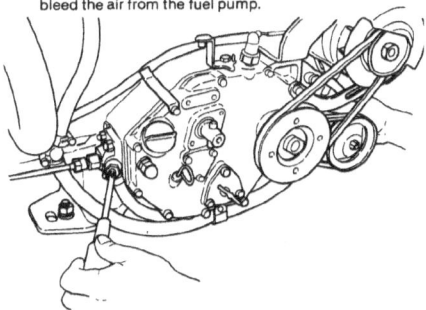

(4) Bleed the air from the fuel return pipe.
Loosen the connector bolt of the fuel return pipe installed on the fuel injection valve, and bleed the air by operating the priming lever.
(5) Bleed the air from the fuel injection pipe.
Loosen the nipple on the fuel injection valve side, set the regulator handle to the operating position and the decompression lever to the decompression position, and crank the engine. When no more bubbles appear in the fuel flowing from the end of the injection pipe, retighten the nipple.
(6) Check injection.
After bleeding the air, set the regulator handle to the operating position, set the decompression lever to the decompression position, and crank the engine. When fuel is being injected from the injection valve, an injection sound will be heard and you can feel resistance if you place your hand on the fuel injection pipe. This check must not be performed more than two or three times since overchecking will flood the combustion

Chapter 13 Operating Instruction
2. Engine Operating Instruction

chamber with fuel, and faulty combustion will occur at starting.

2-1.6 Checking for abnormal sounds by cranking
(1) Set the regulator handle to the STOP position, release the compression of the engine by setting the decompression lever, and crank the engine about 10 times to check for abnormal sounds.
(2) Crank the engine with the starting handle or starter motor.
(Always turn the engine in the proper direction of rotation.)

2-1.7 Checking the cooling system
(1) Open the Kingston cock.
(2) Check for bending and cross-sectional deformation of the cooling water inlet pipe.
(3) Set all water drain cocks to the CLOSED position.

2-1.8 Checking the remote control system
(1) Check that the remote control handle operates correctly.
(2) Check that the engine stop remote control operates smoothly.

2-1.9 Checking the electrical system
(1) Check the battery electrolyte level and add distilled water if low.
(2) Turn the battery switch on, set the main switch to the ON position, and check if the oil pressure lamp and charge lamp are illuminated and if the alarm buzzer sounds when the engine is stopped.
(The charge lamp should be on while the engine is stopped and should be off while the engine is running.)

2-1.10 Checking appearance and exterior
(1) Check for loose or missing bolts and nuts.
(2) Check for loose or disconnected piping and hoses.
(3) Check that there are no tools or other articles near rotating parts or on the engine.

2-2 Starting and warm-up
2-2.1 Electric Starting
(1) Starting procedure
Pull the neutral knob and set the control lever to the MEDIUM SPEED position.

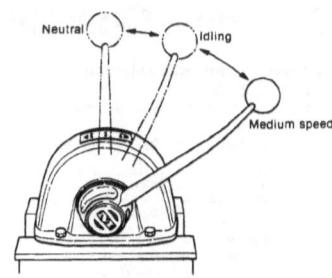

(2) Set the main switch to the ON position.
The alarm buzzer will sound.
(3) Push the starting button to start the engine.
Release the start button after the engine has started.
(4) When the engine has started, the alarm lamps and buzzer will go off.
If the lamps or buzzer stay on, immediately stop the engine and check for trouble.

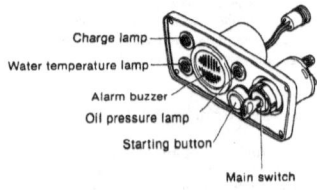

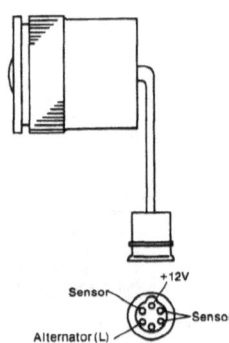

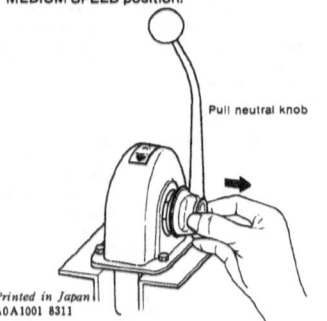

Pull neutral knob

Chapter 13 Operating Instruction
2. Engine Operating Instruction
_____ SM/YSM

(5) Starting in cold weather
1) Pull the neutral knob, and set the control lever to the HIGH SPEED position.

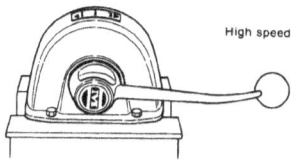
High speed

2) Set the decompression handle to the DECOMPRESSION position.
3) Set the main switch to the ON position and start the engine by pushing the starting button. After the engine has started, return the control lever to the MEDIUM SPEED position.
*When the control lever is set to the HIGH SPEED position, injection timing is automatically delayed to facilitate starting.
CAUTION: When the engine is started with the control lever in the HIGH SPEED position, the starting button must be released immediately and the control lever must be returned to the idling position after the engine has started.
If the starting button is not released, the starter motor will overrun, causing it to be damaged or burnt out.

2-2.2 Manual starting (for YSM 8-Y and YSM 12-Y)
To start the engine manually, turn the starting handle by hand so that the crankshaft rotates about 10 turns. When the crankshaft has gathered momentum, set the decompression handle to the operation position.
Although the starting handle momentarily offers some resistance, keep going. The engine will ignite and you will hear if rotate.

2-2.3 After starting
(1) Warm-up operation
The engine must not be suddenly operated at full load immediately after starting. Warm up the engine for about 5 minutes after starting by running the engine at about half speed, and begin full load operation only after the temperature of each part has risen to a uniform value. Neglecting to warm up the engine will result in:
1) Seizing of the piston and liner due to sudden neat expansion of the piston.
2) Burning of piston rings and seizing of bearings/bushings because of insufficient lubrication.
3) Faulty intake and exhaust valve seat contact and shortening of the life of each part due to sudden heating.
  Warm-up time (no-load operation)
  1,000 ~ 1,200 rpm 3 minutes
  1,600 ~ 1,800 rpm 2 minutes
CAUTION: Do not run the engine at full speed for 50 hours after installation to assure proper break-in.

(2) Checking after starting
Check the following with the clutch in the NEUTRAL position:
1) Meters and lamps on the instrument panel
 • Check that all alarm lamps are off (1,000 rpm or higher).
 • Alarm buzzer must be off.
2) Cooling water discharge state
(Check that the cooling water temperature reaches 45 ~ 55°C before beginning operation.)
3) Check for abnormal sounds and heating.
4) Check for oil and water leakage from piping.

2-3 Operation
If warm-up operation is normal, engage the clutch and begin normal operation. Check the following during operation and stop the engine and take suitable corrective action if there are any abnormalities.

2-3.1 Checks during operation
(1) Oil pressure
Check that the lubricating oil pressure and operating oil pressure lamps are off.
Lubricating oil pressure during operation: 2.5 ~ 3.5 kg/cm²
(2) Cooling water
Periodically check whether water is being discharged from the cooling water outlet pipe.
If the cooling water is being discharged intermittently or if only a small amount of water is being discharged during high speed operation, immediately stop the engine and check if air is being sucked into the cooling system, the impeller of the water pump is abnormal, or the water pipes and Kingston cock are clogged.
Cooling water temperature during operation: 45 ~ 55°C.
Check that the water temperature alarm lamp is off.
(3) Fuel
Check the fuel level in the fuel tank and add fuel before the tank becomes too low. If the fuel level is low, air will enter the fuel injection system and the engine will stop.
(4) Charging
Check that the charge lamp is off.
If the charge lamp is still on even when the engine is run at 1,000 rpm or above, the charging system is faulty and the battery is not being charged.
(5) Temperature of each part
At full power operation, the surface temperature of each engine part is about 50 ~ 60°C and hot to the touch. If engine temperature is too high, the oil will be used up, the propeller shaft will not be centered, or other troubles may occur.
(6) Leakage and abnormalities
Check for water leakage, oil leakage, gas leakage, loose bolts, abnormal sounds, abnormal heating, and vibration.
(7) Exhaust color
Black exhaust smoke indicates that the engine is being overloaded and that the lives of the intake and ex-

13-10

Chapter 13 Operating Instruction
2. Engine Operating Instruction
SM/YSM

haust valves, piston rings, cylinder liners, and injection nozzle will be shortened. Do not run the engine for long periods when it is overlouded.
(8) Abnormal sounds, abnormal heating
When abnormal sounds or abnormal heating occur during operation, immediately stop the engine and check for trouble.

2-3.2 Operating precautions
(1) Always set the battery switch and main switch to the ON position during operation.
(2) Do not touch the starting button during operation. Operation of the starter motor pinion will damage the gears.
(3) Since the ship will resonate and vibrate at a certain speed, depending on the structure of the hull, do not operate it at that speed.
(4) Always set the clutch to the neutral position and wait for the propeller to stop rotating before raising the propeller shaft (if hoisting type stern gears are installed).
(5) Do not suddenly apply a full load to the engine or operate it at full load for long periods.

2-4 Stopping

2-4.1 Stopping procedure
(1) Before stopping, put the clutch in NEUTRAL and run the engine at approximately 1,000 rpm for about 5 minutes.
(2) Before stopping, temporarily raise the speed to the rated speed to blow out residue in the cylinders. Then stop the engine by pulling the engine stop lever to cut the fuel.

2-4.2 Stopping precautions
(1) Do not stop the engine with the decompression lever. If the engine is stopped with the decompression lever, fuel will remain in the combustion chamber and abnormal combustion will occur when the engine is started again, perhaps damaging the engine.
(2) If the engine is stopped immediately after full-load operation, the temperature of each part will rise suddenly, leading to trouble.

2-4.3 Inspection and procedures after stopping
(1) Always close the Kingston cock after the engine is stopped.
Water may enter because of a faulty water pump, etc.
(2) In cold weather, the cooling water should always be drained after engine use to prevent freezing. There are water drain cocks on the cylinders and the exhaust manifold. (Drain the water after the engine has cooled.)
(3) Check for oil leakage and water leakage, and repair as required.
(4) Check for loose bolts and nuts, and repair as required.

2-5 Storage when moored for an extended period
(1) Securely close engine room windows and doors so that rain and snow cannot enter.
Also plug the exhaust outlet since water that enters the cylinder from the exhaust pipe will be compressed when the engine is started, causing serious trouble.
(2) The ship may also sink because of water leakage at the stern tube stuffing box packing. This can be prevented by tightening the packing.
(3) Change the lubricating oil before cranking the engine.
(4) Wipe off each part and coat with oil to prevent rusting of the engine exterior.
(5) Coat the regulator handle stand and each link with a thin film of lube oil or grease.
(6) Run the engine once a week to lubricate each part. This will prevent rusting of the bearings, pistons, and cylinder liners.

2-6 Emergency stop
(1) Loosen the fuel valve high-pressure pipe to release the fuel.
(2) Pull the decompression lever (decompression mechanism) so that compression is not applied to the combustion chamber.
(3) Block the air intake port so that air does not enter the combustion chamber.

3. Troubleshooting and Repair

If trouble occurs in the engine, the engine must be immediately stopped or run at low speed until the cause of the trouble is located.
If even extremely small troubles are not detected and corrected early, they can lead to serious trouble and even disaster. Detecting and correcting troubles quickly is extremely important.

3-1 Troubles and corrective action at starting

Trouble	Cause	Corrective action
Engine fails to start	(1) Battery not charged (2) Starter motor faulty (3) Moving parts seized (4) Lubricating oil viscosity too high	1) Recharge battery 2) Disassemble and repair starter motor 3) Inspect and repair 4) Replace with lubricating oil of suitable viscosity
Starter motor rotates, but engine fails to start	(1) Fuel not injected, or injection faulty	1) Prime and bleed air from fuel lines 2) Inject fuel through injection valve and replace needle if required 3) Clean fuel filter 4) Check operation of fuel pump, plunger, plunger spring, and delivery valve, and replace if required 5) The remote control system or governor is faulty, so check if fuel is cut off, and adjust if required 6) Adjust fuel limitter
	(2) Fuel injection timing incorrect	1) Check if alignment mark of timing gear is aligned
	(3) Compression pressure low	1) Lap valves when air tightness of intake and exhaust valve is poor 2) Replace cylinder head packing if gas is leaking 3) Clean or replace piston rings when sticking occurs 4) Replace cylinder liner if worn 5) Readjust the valve timing
	(4) Drop in compression ratio	1) Replace piston pin bearing and crank pin bearing if worn 2) Replace piston rings if worn

Chapter 13 Operating Instruction
3. Troubleshooting and Repair

3-2 Troubles and corrective action during operation

Trouble	Cause	Corrective action
Engine stops suddenly	(1) Overload (2) Fuel tank empty (3) No fuel injection due to air in fuel system (4) Piston, bearing, or other moving parts seized	1) Lighten the load 2) Add fuel 3) Bleed air 　　Inspect fuel system 4) Inspect and repair or replace the parts
Speed decreases unexpectedly	(1) Governor maladjusted (2) Overload (3) Piston seized (4) Bearing seized (5) Fuel filter clogged (6) Fuel injection pump or injection valve sticking Dirt in fuel pump delivery valve (7) Air in fuel system (8) Water in fuel	1) Adjust 2) Lighten the load (Check propeller system and power take-off system) 3) Stop the engine, and repair or replace 4) Stop the engine, and repair or replace 5) Clean the fuel filter 6) Stop the engine, and repair or replace 7) Prime and bleed air 8) Drain the fuel tank and fuel filter 　　Add fuel if insufficient
Exhaust color is bad	(1) Load is unsuitable (2) Fuel injection timing is off (3) Fuel is unsuitable. (4) Injection valve faulty (5) Intake and exhaust valve adjustment faulty (6) Intake and exhaust valves leaking. (7) Injection limitter maladjusted (8) Injection pressure too low (9) Precombustion chamber melted	1) Adjust the load (Check propeller system and power take-off system) 2) Adjust injection timing 3) Change the fuel type 4) Test injection and replace valve if required 5) Adjust valve head clearance 6) Lap or grind valves 7) Adjust 8) Set injection pressure to 160 kg/cm^2 with shims 9) Replace the precombustion chamber...Perform item (1) above
Full load operation impossible	(1) Fuel filter clogged (2) Fuel pump plunger worn	1) Check and replace filter element 2) Replace plunger and barrel as a set
Engine knocks	(1) Bearing clearance too large (2) Connecting rod bolt loose (3) Flywheel bolt, coupling bolt loose (4) Injection timing faulty (5) Too much fuel injected because of faulty fuel pump or injection valve	1) Inspect, and repair or replace parts 2) Check and retighten 3) Check and retighten or replace bolt as required 4) Check and adjust 5) Check fuel injection pump and injection valve and replace if required

Chapter 13 Operating Instruction
3. Troubleshooting and Repair ──────────────────────────────── *SM/YSM*

3-2 Troubles and corrective action during operation

Trouble	Cause	Corrective action
Engine oil pressure low	(1) Lubricating oil leakage (2) Bearing, crankpin bearing clearance too large (3) Oil filter clogged (4) Oil pump rotor clearance too large (5) Oil temperature high; cooling water flow insufficient (6) Lubricating oil viscosity low (7) Excessive gas leaking into crankcase	1) Check engine interior and exterior piping, replenish oil 2) Check clearance, and replace bearing if necessary 3) Check and replace filter element 4) Check and replace if necessary 5) Check oil pump, and replace if necessary 6) Replace with oil having a high viscosity index 7) Check pistons, piston ring, and cylinder liners and replace if necessary
Lubricating oil temperature too high	(1) Cooling water flow insufficient (2) Excessive gas leaking in to crankcase (3) Overload	1) Check water pump 2) Check piston rings and cylinder liners 3) Lighten the load
Cooling water temperature high	(1) Air sucked in with cooling water (2) Cooling water flow insufficient (3) Cooling system dirty (4) Thermostat faulty	1) Check water pump inlet side pipe connections 2) Check water pump 3) Flush cooling system with cleaner 4) Replace thermostat
Propeller shaft rotates even when clutch is in neutral position	(1) Neutral position adjustment faulty (2) Friction plate seized	1) Reset neutral position adjusting bolt 2) Check and repair
Ahead, neutral, astern switching faulty	(1) Clutch face seized (2) Moving parts, lever system malfunctioning (3) Remote control system malfunctioning	1) Replace 2) Readjust 3) Repair or replace.
Abnormal heating	(1) Clutch slipping because of overload operation (2) Bearing damaged (3) Excessive oil (4) Oil deteriorated	1) Reduce load 2) Replace. 3) Check oil level and adjust to prescribed level 4) Replace oil
Abnormal sound	(1) Gear backlash excessive or too small	1) Replace

Note: As for electrical equipment refer to chapter 11 "Electrical System".

CHAPTER 14
DISASSEMBLY AND REASSEMBLY

1. Disassembly and Reassembly Precautions 14-1
2. Disassembly and Reassembly Tools 14-2
3. Other 14-11
4. Disassembly 14-12
5. Reassembly 14-16
6. Tightening Torque 14-21
7. Packing Supptement and Adhesives 14-22

DISASSEMBLY AND REASSEMBLY

This chapter covers the most efficient method of disassembling and reassembling the engine. Some parts may not have to be removed, depending on the maintenance and inspection objective. In this case, removal is unnecessary and disassembling in accordance with this section is not required.

However, if you follow the disassembly and reassembly procedures, adjustment methods, and precautions described in this chapter, you should be able to prevent subsequent troubles and a loss in engine performance after reassembly. The engine must be test-run to confirm that the engine is functioning properly and delivering full performance.

Since this chapter does not cover detailed disassembly and reassembly procedures for each part, refer to pertinent chapters for details.

1. Disassembly and Reassembly Precautions

(1) Record the parts that require replacement, and replace them with new parts during reassembly.
Be careful not to reassemble with the old parts.

(2) Do not forget adhesives and packing agents for sealing during reassembly.
Packing of the specified quality and packing agents matched to the packing material must be used.

(3) The prescribed tightening torque must be observed when tightening bolts and nuts. Moreover, since the strength of the bolts and nuts depends on their material, be sure to use the correct bolts and nuts at their proper places.

Special bolts, nuts .... Head cover, rod bolts, flywheel, etc.
Strong bolts .... Bolts marked (7) (JIS.7T)
Common bolts, nuts ... Unmarked (JIS.4T)

In addition, check the disassembly and reassembly precautions for each engine model.

Chapter 14 Disassembly and Reassembly
2. Disassembly and Reassembly Tools

SM/YSM

2. Disassembly and Reassembly Tools

The following tools are necessary when disassembling and reassembling the engine. These tools must be used according to disassembly process and location.

2-1 General handtools

Name of tool	Shape	Remarks
Spanner		10 × 13
Spanner		17 × 19
Spanner		22 × 24
Screwdriver for + (cross recessed head) screws		
Screwdriver for − (Philips head) screws		
Steel hammer		
Copper hammer		

Chapter 14 Disassembly and Reassembly
2. Disassembly and Reassembly Tools

SM/YSM

Name of tool	Shape	Remarks
Mallet		
Nipper		
Plier		
Offset wrench		1 set
Box spanner		1 set

Chapter 14 Disassembly and Reassembly
2. Disassembly and Reassembly Tools

Name of tool	Shape	Remarks
Scraper		
Lead rod		
File		1 set
Rod spanner for hexagon socket head screws		5 mm

Chapter 14 Disassembly and Reassembly
2. Disassembly and Reassembly Tools

SM/YSM

2-2 Special handtools

Name of hand tool	Shape and size	Application
Flywheel extractor (made to special order)	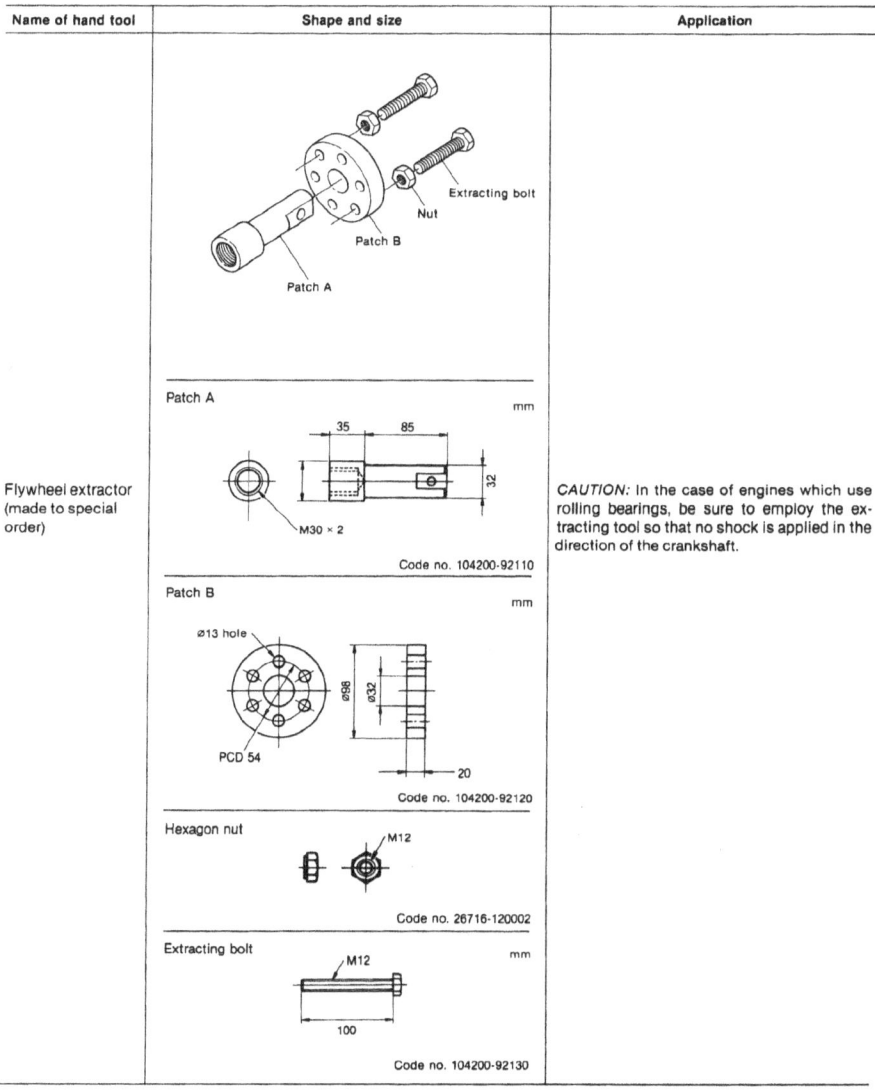 Patch A — Code no. 104200-92110 (M30 × 2, 35, 85, 32) Patch B — Code no. 104200-92120 (ø13 hole, ø58, ø32, PCD 54, 20) Hexagon nut — M12 — Code no. 26716-120002 Extracting bolt — M12, 100 — Code no. 104200-92130	*CAUTION:* In the case of engines which use rolling bearings, be sure to employ the extracting tool so that no shock is applied in the direction of the crankshaft.

14-5

Chapter 14 Disassembly and Reassembly
2. Disassembly and Reassembly Tools

SM/YSM

Name of hand tool	Shape and size	Application
End nut spanner (made to special order)	mm 	Model	Size	Code No.	 |---|---|---| | YSM8 | 47 | 104211~92100 | | YSM12 | 57 | 104511~92100 |	
Liner extractor (made to special order)	Lower fixture, Nut, Extracting bolt, Upper fixture, Lock nut Upper fixture mm | Model	Size A	Size B	Size C	Code No. | |---|---|---|---|---| | YSM8 | 59 | 85 | ⌀18 | 103338~92020 | | YSM12 | 43 | 74 | ⌀18 | 172200~92020 | Lower fixture mm | Model	Size D	Size E	Size F	Code No. | |---|---|---|---|---| | YSM8 | ⌀18 | ⌀84.5 | ⌀94 | 101400~92010 | | YSM12 | ⌀18 | ⌀74.5 | ⌀84 | 101300~92010 |	Liner extractor Cylinder liner puller tool Upper fixture Lower fixture

Chapter 14 Disassembly and Reassembly
2. Disassembly and Reassembly Tools

———————— SM/YSM

Name of hand tool	Shape and size	Application
Liner extractor (made to special order)	Extracting bolt — M16 × 2.0, 380 mm, Code no. 103338-92030 Hexagon nut — M16 × 2.0, Code no. 26716-160002 M16 × 2.0, Code no. 26756-160002	
Piston pin extractor (commercially available product)	Dimensions: 20, A, B, C (mm) | Model | A | B | C | Code No. | |---|---|---|---|---| | YSM8 | $\varnothing 22^{\ 0}_{-0.5}$ | $\varnothing 12^{\ 0}_{-0.5}$ | 85 | | | YSM12 | $\varnothing 27^{\ 0}_{-0.5}$ | $\varnothing 17.5^{\ 0}_{-0.5}$ | 95 | |	

Printed in Japan
A0A1001 8311

Chapter 14 Disassembly and Reassembly
2. Disassembly and Reassembly Tools

— SM/YSM

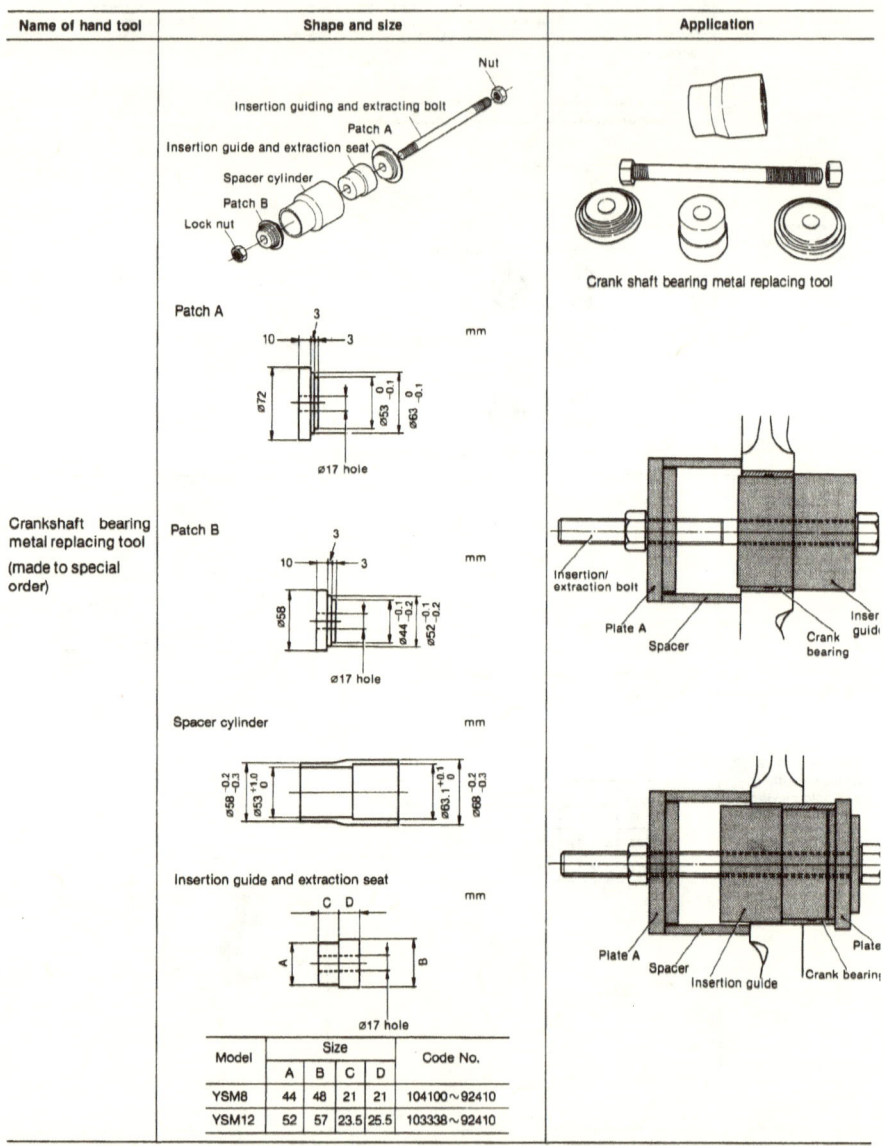

Name of hand tool	Shape and size	Application
Crankshaft bearing metal replacing tool (made to special order)	(see figures)	Crank shaft bearing metal replacing tool

Model	Size			Code No.
	A	B	C	D	
YSM8	44	48	21	21	104100~92410
YSM12	52	57	23.5	25.5	103338~92410

Chapter 14 Disassembly and Reassembly
2. Disassembly and Reassembly Tools

SM/YSM

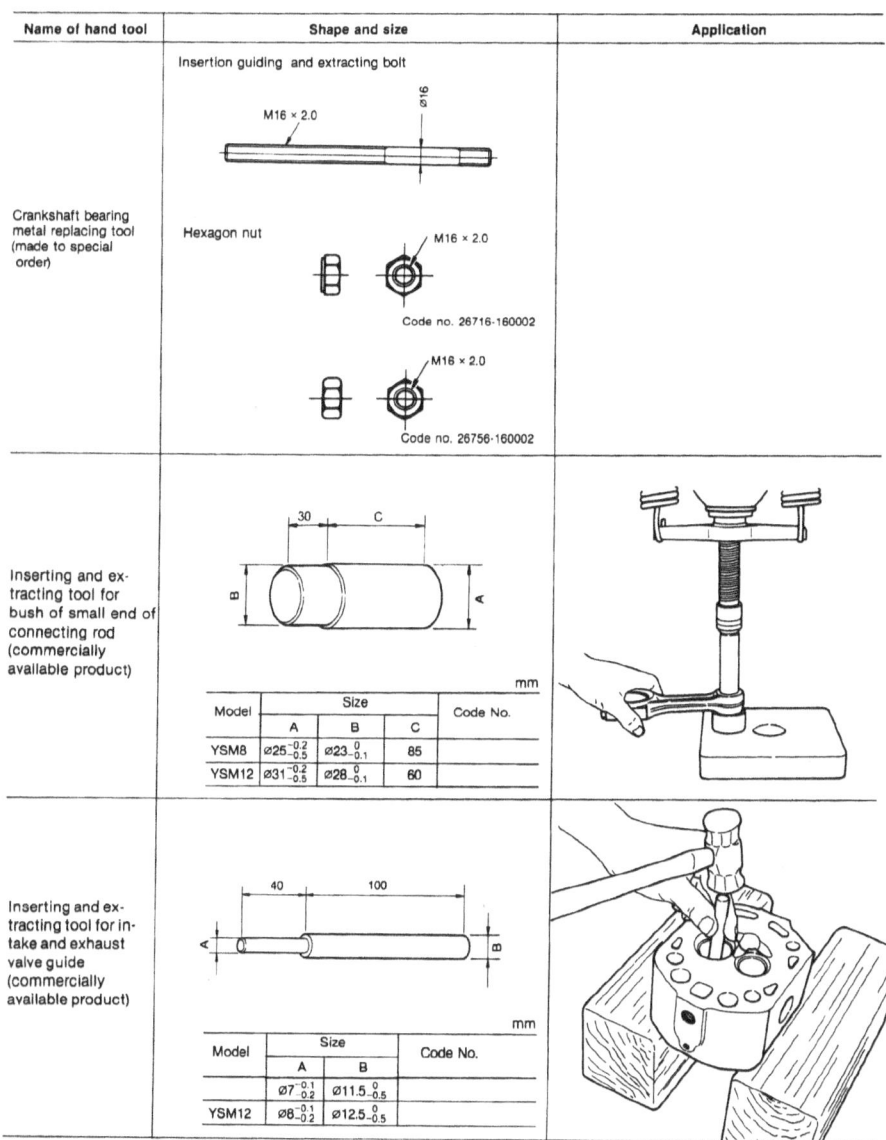

Name of hand tool	Shape and size	Application
Crankshaft bearing metal replacing tool (made to special order)	Insertion guiding and extracting bolt — M16 × 2.0, ⌀16. Hexagon nut — M16 × 2.0, Code no. 26716-160002; M16 × 2.0, Code no. 26756-160002	
Inserting and extracting tool for bush of small end of connecting rod (commercially available product)	Dimensions: 30, C, A, B (mm) Model / Size A / B / C / Code No. YSM8 / ⌀25$_{-0.5}^{-0.2}$ / ⌀23$_{-0.1}^{0}$ / 85 YSM12 / ⌀31$_{-0.5}^{-0.2}$ / ⌀28$_{-0.1}^{0}$ / 60	
Inserting and extracting tool for intake and exhaust valve guide (commercially available product)	Dimensions: 40, 100, A, B (mm) Model / Size A / B / Code No. ⌀7$_{-0.2}^{-0.1}$ / ⌀11.5$_{-0.5}^{0}$ YSM12 / ⌀8$_{-0.2}^{-0.1}$ / ⌀12.5$_{-0.5}^{0}$	

2-3 Measuring instruments

Nomenclature		Accuracy and range
Vernier calipers		1/20 mm, 0 ~ 150 mm,
Micrometer		1/100 mm, 0 ~ 25 mm, 25 ~ 50 mm, 50 ~ 75 mm, 75 ~ 100 mm,
Cylinder gauge		1/100 mm, 18 ~ 35 mm, 35 ~ 60 mm, 50 ~ 100 mm,
Thickness gauge		0.05 ~ 2 mm,
Torque wrench		0 ~ 13 kg-m.
Nozzle tester		0 ~ 500 kg/cm^2.

3. Other

Supplementary packing agent

Type	Use
"Three Bond 3B8-005"	White. Since "Three Bond 3B8-005" is a nonorganic solvent, is does not penetrate asbestos sheets made principally of or completely of asbestos. Always use it with grey asbestos sheet packing for complete oiltightness. When "Three Bond 3B8-005" is difficult to obtain, use silicone nonsolvent type "Three Bond No. 50."
"Three Bond No. 50"	Grey. Silicone nonsolvent type liquid packing. Semidry type packing agent coated on mating faces to prevent oil and gas leakage. Does not penetrate asbestos sheet and assures complete oiltightness.
"Three Bond No. 1"	Reddish brown. Paste type wet viscous liquid packing. Ideal for mating faces which are removed but reinstalled. Particularly used to prevent water leakage and to prevent seizing of bolts and nuts.

The surface to be coated must be thoroughly cleaned with thinner or benzene and completely dry. Moreover, coating must be thin and uniform.

Products of Three Bond Co., Ltd.

Paint

Color spray

Metallic Ecole Silver is used entirely on this engine.

Wipe off the surface to be painted with thinner or benzene, shake the spray can well, push the button at the top of the can and spray the paint onto the surface from a distance of 30 ~ 40 cm.

Paint

Type
White paint
(Mixed oil paint)

Usage point
Cylinder liner insertion hole

Use
Paint parts that contact the cylinder body when inserting the cylinder liner to prevent rusting and water leakage.

Yanmar cleaner

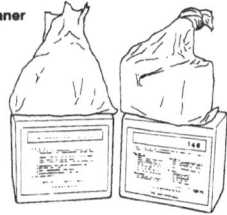

Cooling passage cleaner is made by adding one part "Unicon 146" to about 16 parts water (specific gravity ratio). To use, drain the water from the cooling system, fill the system with cleaner, allowing it to stand overnight (10 ~ 15 hours). Then drain out the cleaner, fill the system with water, and operate the engine for at least one hour.

NEJI LOCK SUPER 203M: a locking agent for screws

For coating on screws and bolts to prevent loosening, rusting, and leaking. To use, wipe off all oil and water on the threads of studs, coat the threads with screw lock, tighten the stud bolt, and allow to stand until the screw lock hardens. Use screw lock on the oil intake pipe threads, oil pressure switch threads, fuel injection timing shim faces, and front axle bracket mounting bolts.

Chapter 14 Disassembly and Reassembly
4. Disassembly

4. Disassembly

NOTE: When disassembling this machine, ascertain the cause of trouble; neither remove nor disassemble parts when it is unneccessary.

1. Remove the wiring from each part taking note of its color coding.
2. Remove the alternator.
3. Remove the bracket.
4. Remove the starter.

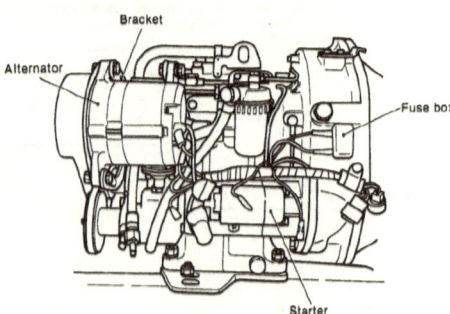

8. Remove the mixing elbow. Stainless steel bolt.

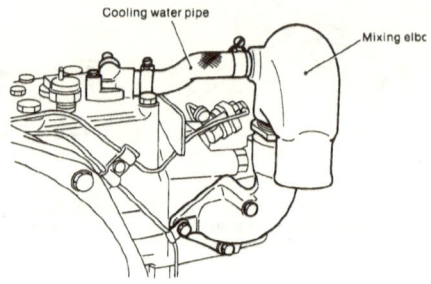

9. Remove the fuel injection pipe.
10. Remove the fuel return pipe.
11. By removing the fuel injection valve clamp remove the fuel injection valve.
    • Note the face and back side of the clamp.
12. Remove the rocker chamber.

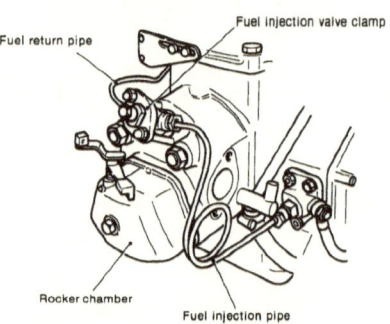

5. Remove the blow-by pipe from the intake silencer side only.
6. Remove the intake silencer paying close attention to the packing.

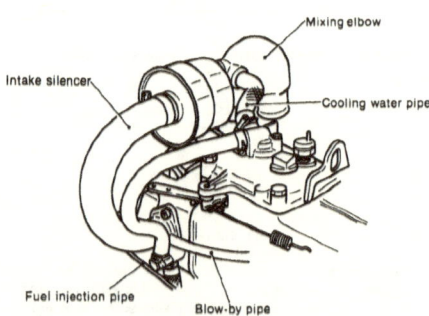

7. Remove the cooling water pipe which is installed between the mixing elbow and the block.

13. Remove the support for the intake and exhaust valve arm.
14. Remove the cap for the intake and exhaust valve. Be careful not to lose it.
15. Remove the push rod.
16. Remove the coupling bolt of the lubricating oil pipe for the cylinder head.
17. Remove the cooling water pipe from the head side only.

Chapter 14 Disassembly and Reassembly
4. Disassembly

18. Remove the cylinder head.

26. Remove the governor spindle support.

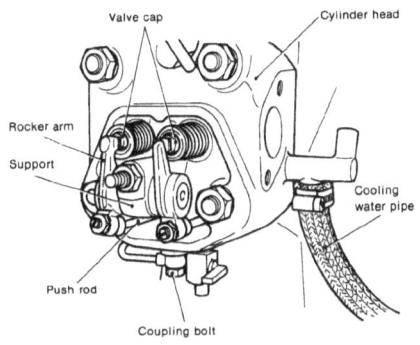

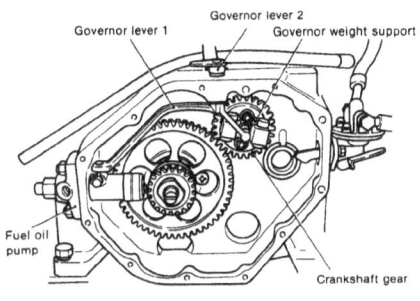

19. Remove the gasket packing.
    - Note the face and back side of the packing.
20. Remove the cooling water pump along with the cooling water pipe.
21. Remove the fuel oil pipe from the pump side only.
22. Extract the engine oil.
23. Remove the side cover along with the oil gauge rod.

27. Remove fuel oil pipe (B), (which is installed between the filter and the feed pump).
28. Remove the feed pump. Be careful not to damage the packing.
29. Remove the fuel filter bracket.
30. Remove the cylinder rear cover along with the blow-by pipe.
31. Remove the lubricating oil pipe.

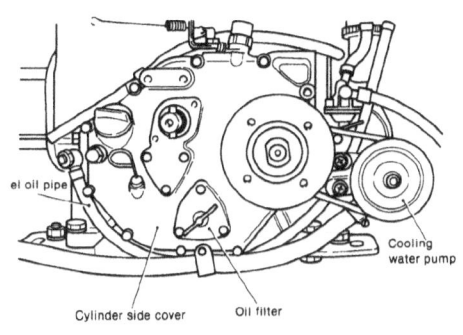

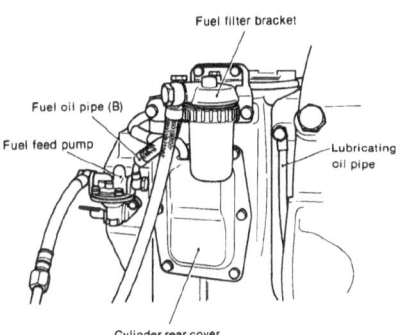

24. Remove the fuel oil pump. Be careful not to injure the regulator plate.
25. Remove the No.1 and No.2 levers for the governor.
    - They can be removed by extracting the taper pin.
    - Also remove the regulator spring.
    - Be careful not to lose the dust-proof cap.

32. Remove the neutral adjusting screw.
33. Remove the forward shaft rear box lid.
34. Remove the engine leg.

Chapter 14 Disassembly and Reassembly
4. Disassembly

SM/YSM

35. Remove the clutch case.

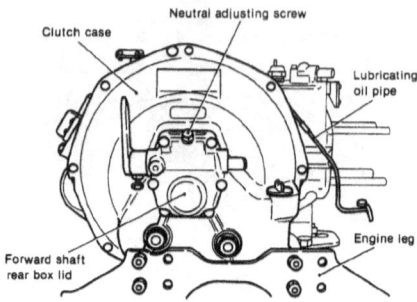

36. Remove the clutch.

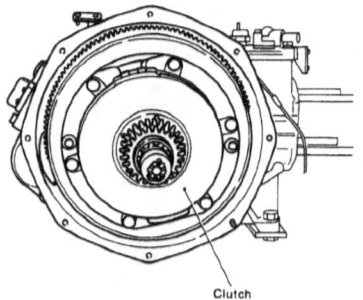

37. Remove the piston.
   1. Remove the connecting rod bolt.
   2. Align the TD mark on the flywheel with the flywheel housing mark.

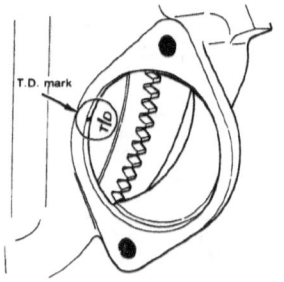

3. Extract the piston.
   • Remove the carbon sticking to the upper part of the cylinder liner. The piston can be pulled out without difficulty.
38. Remove the end nut.
39. Remove the flywheel.

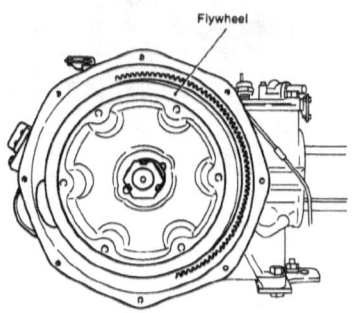

40. Remove the flywheel key.
41. Remove the flywheel housing. Be careful not to lose the clutch breather.

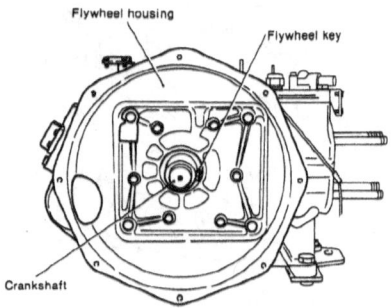

42. Remove the crankshaft.
   • Place the balancing weight at the cylinder block extracting position.
   • Be careful not to damage the thrust bearing metal.
   • Along with the crankshaft gear.
43. Extract the camshaft bearing retaining bolt.
44. Extract the camshaft.

Printed in Japan
A0A1001 8311

14-14

Chapter 14 Disassembly and Reassembly
4. Disassembly

45. Extract the tappet.

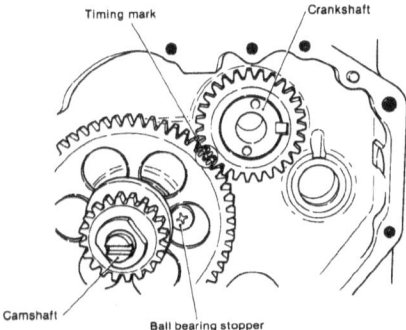

5. Reassembly

1. Insert the tappet.
2. Attach the camshaft.
3. Attach the clamp bolt for camshaft bearings.
4. Attach the thrust bearing for camshaft (the oil groove of the bearing is directed toward the camshaft side).

8. Mount the flywheel key. Don't forget the clutch breather.
9. Attach the flywheel.
10. Tighten the end nut.

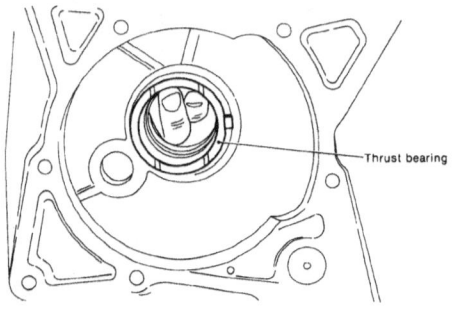

Thrust bearing

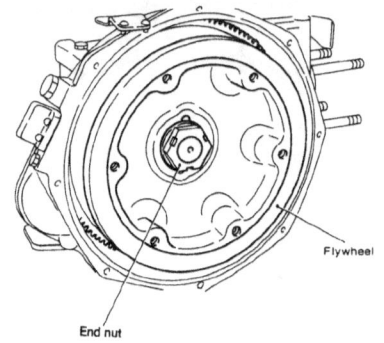

Flywheel

End nut

5. Attach the crankshaft. Be careful not to drop or damage the bearing.
6. Attach the flywheel housing.

	YSM8	YSM12
Tightening torque	27	35

kg-m

11. Secure the piston in place:

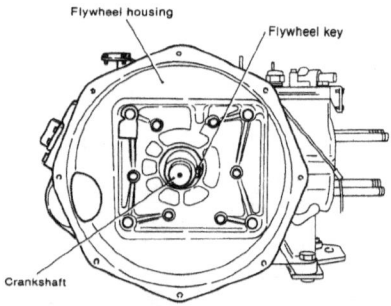

Flywheel housing
Flywheel key
Crankshaft

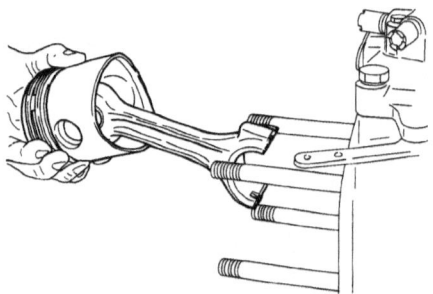

Tightening torque	Spanner 13	Spanner 17
	2.5	4.7

kg-m

7. Check the crankshaft side gap.
   Be sure that the bearing barrel packing is of standard type and brand new.

1. Position → the piston ring end.

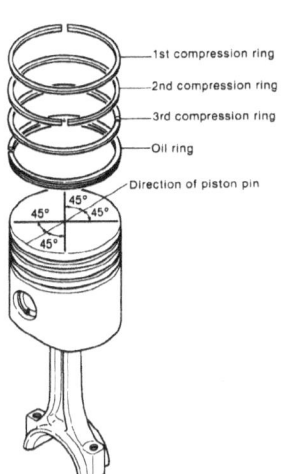

- 1st compression ring
- 2nd compression ring
- 3rd compression ring
- Oil ring
- Direction of piston pin

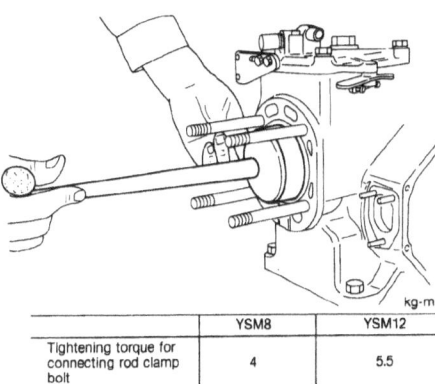

	YSM8	YSM12
Tightening torque for connecting rod clamp bolt	4	5.5

kg·m

12. Attach the clutch.

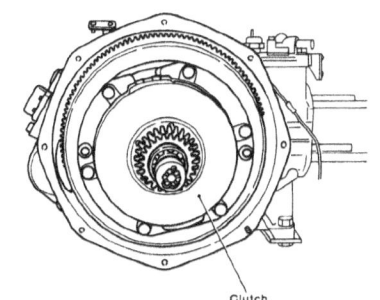

Clutch

	YSM8, 12
Tightening torque	4.4 to 5.0

kg·m

2. Align the TD mark of the flywheel.

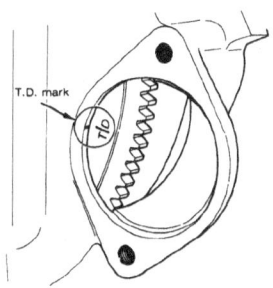

T.D. mark

13. Attach the clutch case.

	YSM8, 12
Tightening torque	2.3 to 2.7

kg·m

14. Attach the engine leg.
15. Attach the lid of the forward shaft rear box.

3. Insert the piston and secure it in place.
   - Lubricate the outer surface of the piston and the crank pin bearing metal.
   - Turn up the No. on the big end of the connecting rod assemble No. together.
   - Apply turve paste to the threads of the connecting rod clamp bolt and tighten the clamp bolt uniformly.

Chapter 14 Disassembly and Reassembly
5. Reassembly

SM/YSM

16. Attach the neutral adjusting screw.
    - Do not tighten the screw.
    - Lock the adjusting screw in the position where the propeller shaft will not rotate when the handle is set in the neutral position during operation.

21. Attach the fuel oil pipe (B).

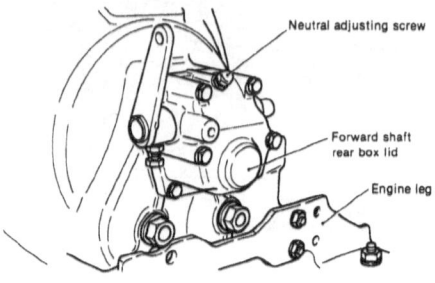

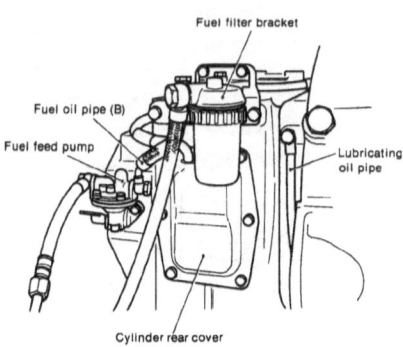

17. Attach the lubricating oil pipe.

22. Fit the crank gear in position.
    Align the matching mark of the camshaft gear.
23. Attach the governor support spindle.
24. Attach the No.1 and No.2 levers for governor.
    - Don't forget the dustproof cap.
    - Install the shorter hook of the regulator spring on the right side.

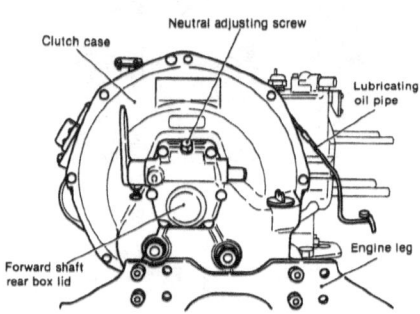

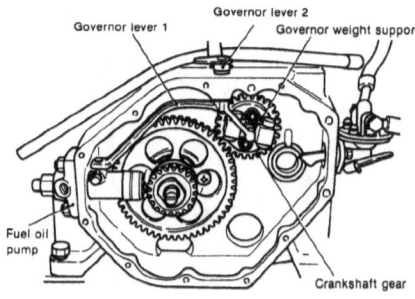

18. Attach the rear lid of the cylinder.
19. Attach the fuel oil filter bracket.
20. Attach the feed pump.
    - Note how the packing is placed.

Chapter 14 Disassembly and Reassembly
5. Reassembly

25. Attach the fuel oil pump.
    - Be careful not to injure the regulator plate.
    - Align the rack with the No.2 lever for the governor.

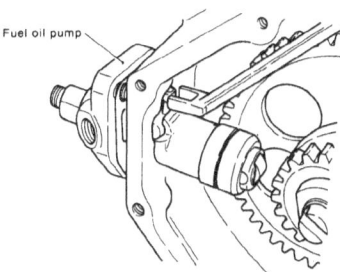
Fuel oil pump

26. Attach the side cover.
    - Along with the oil gauge rod.
27. Attach the fuel oil pipe.
    - On the pump side only.
28. Attach the cooling water pump.
    - Drive-belt deflection: 5 to 7 mm
    - The brand name indicated on the belt should rotate in the direction of pulley rotation.
29. Attach the gasket packing.
    - Note the face and back side of the packing.
30. Attach the cylinder head.

kg-m

	YSM8	YSM12
Tightening torque	9.7	13.6

31. Attach the cooling water pipe.
    - On the head side only.
32. Attach the coupling bolt of the lubricating oil pipe for the cylinder head.
33. Attach the push rod.
34. Attach the intake and exhaust valve cap.
35. Attach the rocker arm and support for the intake and exhaust valve.
    - Be careful not to drop the cap and push rod.
    - Be sure that the rocker arm is in proper contact with the valve head.

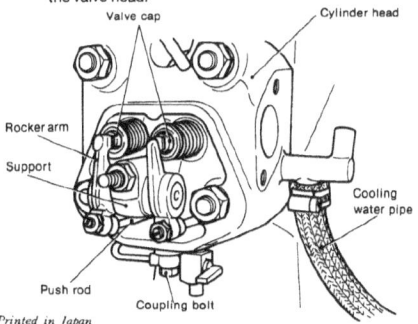
Valve cap, Cylinder head, Rocker arm, Support, Push rod, Coupling bolt, Cooling water pipe

36. Adjust the top clearance of the intake and exhaust valve.

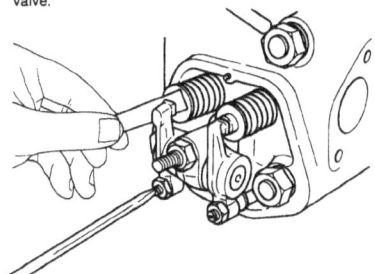

- Top clearance when intake and exhaust valve head is cold: 0.2 mm
- Adjust the clearance by means of compression TD.

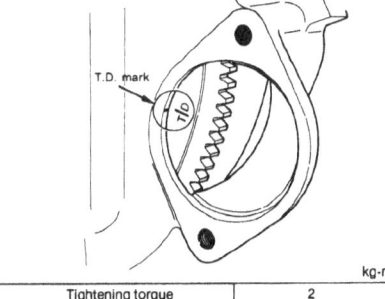
T.D. mark

kg-m

Tightening torque	2

37. Attach the bonnet
38. Attach the fuel injection valve.
    - Note the face and back side of the valve holder.
39. Attach the fuel return pipe.
40. Attach the fuel injection pipe.

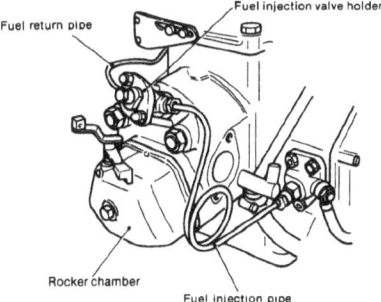
Fuel injection valve holder, Fuel return pipe, Rocker chamber, Fuel injection pipe

41. Attach the silencer.
    • Use specially treated SCM bolts.
42. Attach the cooling water pipe.
    • For the section between the silencer and the block.
43. Attach the intake silencer.
    • Pay attention to the packing.
44. Attach the blow-by pipe.

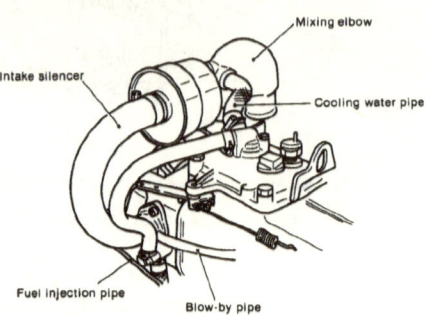

• On the silencer side.
45. Attach the starter.
46. Attach the bracket.
47 Attach the alternator.
    • Deflection of the drive-belt
48. Install the wiring for each section.

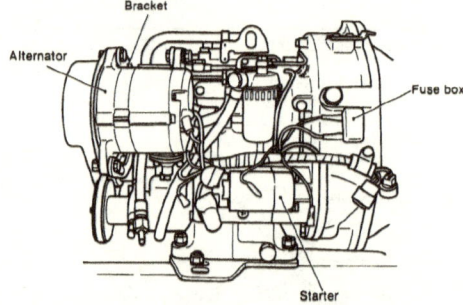

6. Tightening Torque

The bolts and nuts used in this engine employ ISO general metric threads stipulated in JIS (Japanese Industrial Standards). Pay careful attention to the thread dimensions when replacing bolts and nuts.
Tighten the bolts and nuts to the tightening torque given in the table below.

6·1 Main bolt and nut tightening torque.

Bolt/nut	Engine name YSM	Thread diameter	Width across flats	Tightening torque (kg·cm)
Flywheel housing mounting bolt.	8.12	M8	13	250
Flywheel housing mounting bolt.	8.12	M10	17	470
Connecting rod bolt.	8			400
Connecting rod bolt.	12			550
Cylinder head tightening nut.	8			970
Cylinder head tightening nut.	12			1,360
End nut.	8			2,700
End nut.	12			3,500
Case cover assembly mounting nut.	8.12	M6	10	80 ~ 100
Intake/exhaust valve rocker arm assembly mounting nut.	8.12	M10	17	360 ~ 380
Intake/exhaust valve clearance adjusting screw fixing nut.	8.12	M8	13	200
Cylinder rear cover mounting bolt.	8.12	M6	10	80 ~ 100
Reversing device assembly mounting bolt.	8.12	M10	17	440 ~ 500
Reversing device friction disk housing bolt.	8.12	M8	13	230 ~ 270
Clutch case mounting bolt and nut.	8.12	M8	13	230 ~ 270
Forwarding shaft rear box assembly mounting bolt.	8.12	M8	13	230 ~ 270
Valve rocker arm assembly mounting bolt.	8.12	M8	13	190 ~ 210

6·2 General bolt and nut tightening torque

(1) Hex bolts

Thread diameter	Width across flats	Tightening torque, kg·m	
		4T bolts	7T bolts
M5 × 0.2	9	0.2 ~ 0.3	0.3 ~ 0.5
M6 × 1.0	10	0.4 ~ 0.7	0.8 ~ 1.2
M8 × 1.25	13	1.0 ~ 1.6	2.0 ~ 3.0
M10 × 1.5	17	1.8 ~ 3.0	3.7 ~ 5.2
M12 × 1.25	19	3.5 ~ 5.5	7.5 ~ 10.0

(2) Pipe joint bolts

Thread diameter	Width across flats	Tightening torque, kg·m
M8 × 1.25	13	1.2 ~ 1.7
M12 × 1.25	17	2.5 ~ 3.0
M14 × 1.5	19	4.0 ~ 5.0
M16 × 1.5	22	5.0 ~ 6.0

7. Packing Supplement and Adhesive Application Points

The packing used in this engine is asbestos sheet sealed at both mating faces.
Be sure to use the correct supplement in accordance with the below table.

Be sure to remove the grease, and the adhesive, before applying new packing agents or adhesives.

Location applied	Name of packing agent and adhesive
The circumference of cylinder liner, inserted portion, O-ring portion	White oil paint
Cylinder head fixing bolt	Three Bond No.1
Feed pump bolt	Neji Lock Super 203M
Screw and washer for connecting rod bolt	Paste
Drain pipe	Neji Lock Super 203M
Cooling water pipe joint (head side)	Neji Lock Super 203M
Clutch case bolt (stud bolt)	Neji Lock Super 203M
Engine foot bolt	Neji Lock Super 203M

CHAPTER 15
INSPECTION AND SERVICING

1. Periodic inspection and servicing 15-1

Chapter 15 Inspection and Servicing
1. Periodic Inspection and Servicing

SM/YSM

1. Periodic Inspection and Servicing

Periodic inspection and servicing is necessary to keep the engine in top condition at all times.
The routine inspection period depends on engine application and usage conditions, fuel and lubricating oil quality, engine handling, etc., and cannot be definitely stated. However, a general guideline will be given here. The relationship between inspection and maintenance activities and operating time is given below.
Refer to pertinent inspection sections of this manual for details.
1. Perform inspection at the operating times given below, and quickly correct any defects found.
2. Before reusing disassembled parts, check that they are in good condition.

1-1 Routine inspection

○ Inspection ◎ Parts replacement

Item	Description	Operating time	Daily	Every 50 hours	Every 100 hours	Every 300 hours	Every 500 hours	Every 1,000 hours
Fuel system	Fuel tank level check and filling		○					
	Fuel filter cleaning			○				
	Fuel filter element replacement				◎			
	Injection valve	Injection timing check					○	
	Injection pump	Injection spray inspection					○	
		Main part disassembly and inspection						○
	Fuel feed pump	Disassembly and inspection					○	
Lubrication system	Engine side	Oil pan oil level check and replenishment	○					
		Oil change			○			
		Turn filter handle	○					
	Clutch side	Oil level check and replenishment	○					
		Oil change		○ (1st time)		○ (from 2nd time)		
	Lubrication (starting chain, etc.)		○					
Cooling system	Thermostat inspection					○		
	Cooling water discharge condition		○					
	Anticorrosion zinc inspection					○		
	Water pump	Water pump drive belt tension adjustment		○ (1st time)		○		
		Water pump disassembly and inspection					○	
Engine proper	Bolt retightening		After operation or 50 hours after restarting					
	Intake and exhaust valve head clearance adjustment					○		
	Combustion chamber cleaning					○		
	Intake and exhaust valve lapping							○
	Piston disassembly and piston ring inspection							○
	Bearing and rod bolt inspection							○
Remote control	Cable inspection and adjustment					○		
Intake and exhaust system	Intake silencer element cleaning					○ dirty condition	○ (normal condition)	
	Mixing elbow interior inspection					○		
Electrical system	Alarm lamps and alarm buzzer		○					
	Battery electrolyte level check and replenishment		○					
	Alternator drive belt tension adjustment			○ (1st time)		○		
	Main switch and starting button inspection					○		
Piping	Rubber pipe inspection and replacement		Should be replaced every 4 years					
Others	Flexible mount and flexible coupling		Should be replaced every 4 years					

15-1

Chapter 15 Inspection and Servicing
1. Periodic Inspection and Servicing

1·2 Routine maintenance and inspection procedures
Only the most common maintenance items will be described here. Refer to the pertinent chapters of this manual for details on various parts and workshop service.

1·2.1 Daily maintenance
(1) Oil level check
Check the engine and clutch oil levels with the dipsticks, and add oil up to the top mark. Oil level must not be allowed to fall below the bottom mark.

• Filler

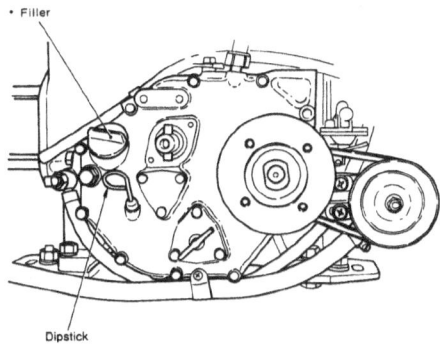

Dipstick

Distick (Filler)

(2) Draining the cooling water
The cooling water will freeze in cold weather, causing faulty operation and cracking of the cylinders, cylinder head, and exhaust manifold. Therefore, always drain the water from the engine after use if the engine must sit in freezing weather.

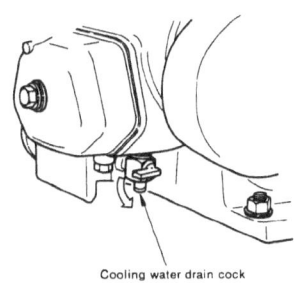

Cooling water drain cock

1·2.2 Maintenance every 50 engine hours
(1) Clean the fuel filter
Close the fuel tank cock and remove the bowl of the fuel filter, then clean the inside of the bowl and the filter element. After reinstalling the bowl and element, open the fuel tank cock and bleed the air from the fuel system.

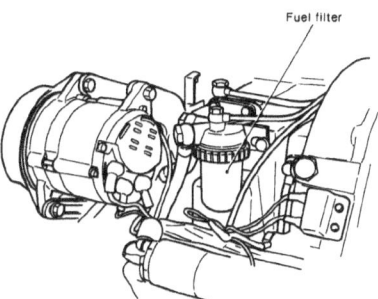

Fuel filter

CAUTION: Change the element every 100 hours.

	Crankcase	Clutch case
Dipstick	Cylinder side cover	Top of clutch case (filling plug with dipstick)
Filler		

CAUTION: Use same lubricating oils for the engine and clutch.

Chapter 15 Inspection and Servicing
1. Periodic Inspection and Servicing ————————————————————————————*SM/YSM*

(2) V-belt tension adjustment (every 300 hours after 2nd adjustment)
Check the tension of the water pump drive V-belt and alternator drive V-belt, and adjust as required.

1-2.3 Maintenance every 100 engine hours
(1) Fuel filter element replacement
Close the fuel tank cock, remove the fuel filter bowl and replace the element and clean the inside of the bowl. After reinstalling the element and bowl, open the fuel tank cock and bleed the air from the fuel system.

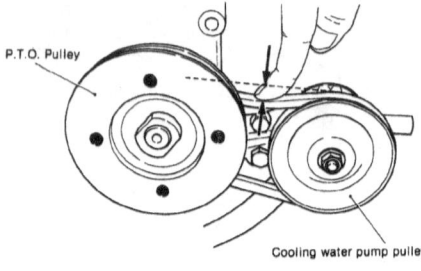

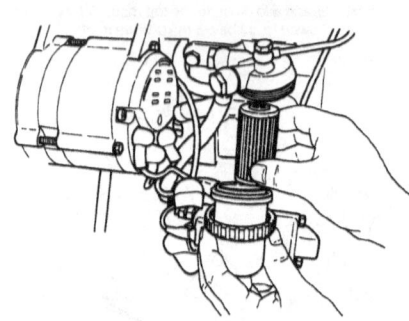

(2) Oil change
While the engine is still warm, pump the lubricating oil from the crank case and clutch case with a waste oil pump and refill both cases with new oil up to the top mark on the dipstick.
If the drain plug can be used, drain the oil by removing the drain plug.

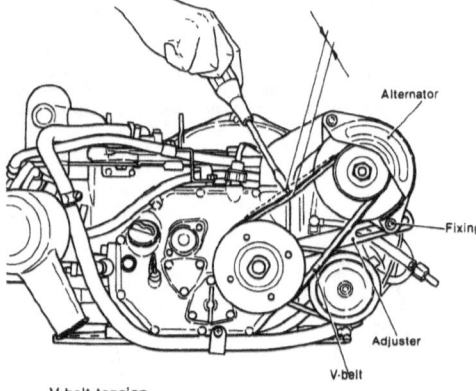

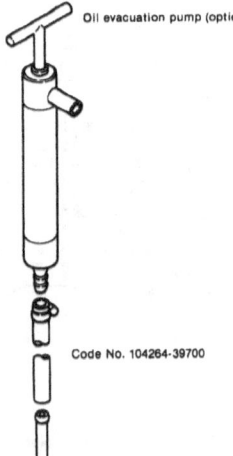

V-belt tension
(Pushed with a force of 10 kg (22 lb))   mm (in.)

Water pump	5 ~ 7 (0.197 ~ 0.275)
Alternator	5 ~ 10 (0.197 ~ 0.394)

(3) Tightening bolts
Check the engine mounting bolts, cylinder head bolts, gear case bolts, and the bolts of other main parts and tighten as required.
(Refer to the bolt tightening torque table.)

Chapter 15 Inspection and Servicing
1. Periodic Inspection and Servicing

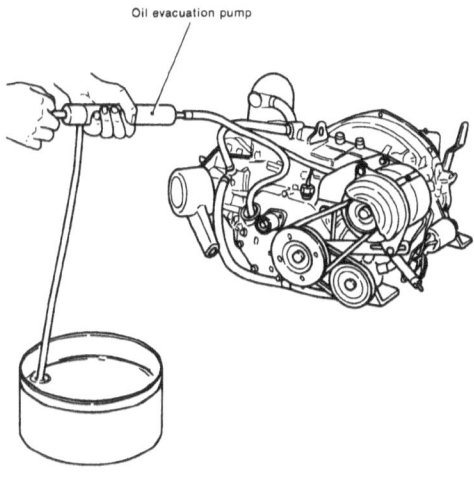

Oil evacuation pump

1-2.4 Maintenance every 300 engine hours
(1) Thermostat inspection
Remove the cooling water outlet flange on the top of the cylinder body and remove and inspect the thermostat.

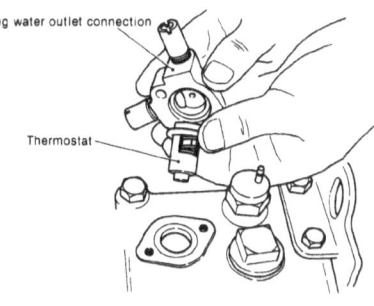

Cooling water outlet connection

Thermostat

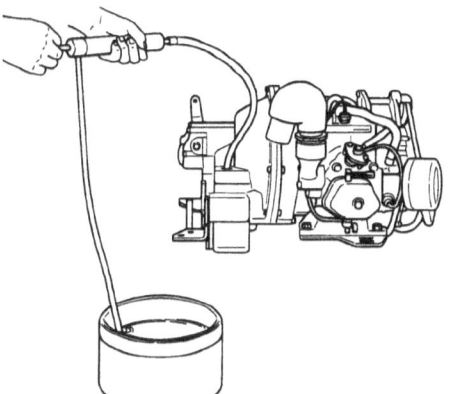

(2) Intake and exhaust valve adjustment
Remove the rocker arm chamber and check the intake and exhaust valve head clearance with a feeler gauge. Adjust if not within the prescribed limit.
(Refer to the cylinder head chapter of this manual for a description of the adjustment method.)

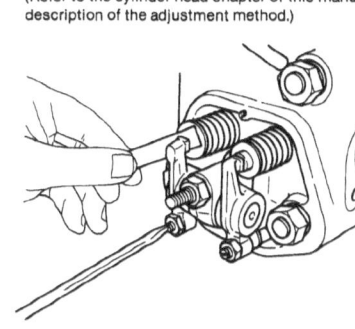

Chapter 15 Inspection and Servicing
1. Periodic Inspection and Servicing

1-2.5 Maintenance every 500 engine hours

(1) Anticorrosion zinc replacement
Replace the anticorrosion zinc at the top of cylinder head.

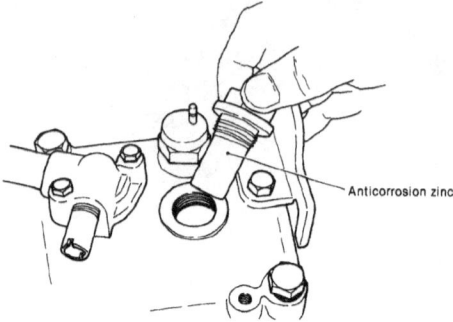

Anticorrosion zinc

(2) Inspect the fuel injection system
- Injection timing check and adjustment
- Delivery valve inspection
- Injection spray inspection
- Injection pressure check and adjustment
- Nozzle valve disassembly and cleaning

Refer to the FUEL SYSTEM chapter of this manual for a detailed description of inspection and adjustment methods.

(3) Inspect the rocker arm and valve guide.

www.ingramcontent.com/pod-product-compliance
Lightning Source LLC
Chambersburg PA
CBHW021943240426
43668CB00037B/710